CUIR DISSIDENCE

Cuir Dissidence

Tracing Restorative Criticism
and Breaking Bonds
with the Mexican Canon

FRANCESCA DENNSTEDT

VANDERBILT UNIVERSITY PRESS
Nashville, Tennessee

Copyright 2025 by Vanderbilt University Press.
First printing 2025.
All rights reserved.

Library of Congress Cataloging-in-Publication Data:

Names: Dennstedt, Francesca author
Title: Cuir dissidence : tracing restorative criticism and breaking bonds with the Mexican canon / Francesca Dennstedt.
Description: Nashville, Tennessee : Vanderbilt University Press, 2025. | Includes bibliographical references and index.
Identifiers: LCCN 2025003789 (print) | LCCN 2025003790 (ebook) | ISBN 9780826508027 paperback | ISBN 9780826508034 hardcover | ISBN 9780826508041 epub | ISBN 9780826508058 pdf
Subjects: LCSH: Mexican literature--Women authors--History and criticism | Mexican literature--20th century--History and criticism | Mexican literature--21st century--History and criticism | Feminism in literature | Gender identity in literature | Sexual minorities in literature | Canon (Literature) | LCGFT: Literary criticism
Classification: LCC PQ7133 .D46 2025 (print) | LCC PQ7133 (ebook)
LC record available at https://lccn.loc.gov/2025003789
LC ebook record available at https://lccn.loc.gov/2025003790

This book will be made open access within three years of publication to Path to Open, a program developed in partnership between JSTOR, the American Council of Learned Societies (ACLS), University of Michigan Press, and the University of North Carolina Press to bring about equitable access and impact for the entire scholarly community, including authors, researchers, libraries, and university presses around the world. Learn more at https://about.jstor.org/path-to-open/.

CONTENTS

Acknowledgments   vii

   INTRODUCTION. The Canon Deception   1

1. Fucking with Death and (Not) Yet Cuir: Choking Eroticism through the Work of Inés Arredondo in Complicity with Kati Horna, Leonora Carrington, and Xitlalitl Rodríguez Mendoza   23

2. The Restorative Possibilities of an Archive of Gender Playfulness: Women's Mustaches and the Third Gender   64

3. Snap, Snap, Snap!: Toward an Affective Cuir Method of Literary Critique   96

4. Communal Writings and the Canon Hoax: The Glu-Glu Fear and Other Elegant Emotions   121

   CODA. Acuerpar la lucha   149

Notes   155
References   183
Index   199

ACKNOWLEDGMENTS

I owe this book to a communality of countless friends, colleagues, and mentors. The list is not exhaustive, and I apologize if I manage to forget a name.

I am forever thankful to Emily Hind, Amanda Petersen, Ilana Luna, Laura J. Torres-Rodríguez, and Cheyla Samuelson for their unwavering support and love. You stood by me during the toughest four years of my career, which coincided with the creation of this book. The umbrella, the hours on zoom, and the numerous text messages kept me sane.

A special thanks to my *emisarixs* from across the border. For *el acuerpamiento* de Ave Barrera, Selma Rodal Linares—who read several parts of this book with her critical eye—and Lola Horner for *el chisme*. To my sister Leslie Michelle for always joining me on my scavenger hunts; to Minerva Reynosa and Xilo Guerra for the space to share my work and their friendship; to Ana Karenina for transforming my book ideas into ink and for inspiring the *talaveras* featured on the cover. Thank you to Gabriel Wolfson Reyes because he always pushes me to *repelar*; and, after almost twenty years, he continues to support my career through his friendship—por otros veinte años de querernos siempre igual.

I am also grateful to all the writers, artists, and cultural producers who shared their time with me, both formally and informally, during the making of this book. Xitlalitl Rodríguez Mendoza, Odette Alonso, Rosa María Roffiel, Ana Clavel, Amaranta Caballero Prado, Cristina Rivera Garza, Sara Uribe, Didí Gutiérrez, Maricela Guerrero, Adriana González Mateos, Mónica Mayer, Irasema Fernández, and Sayak Valencia.

To my mentors, who suffered through a very rough version of this manuscript—Stephanie Kirk and Ignacio Sánchez Prado—I have no words to describe your invaluable support over the last ten years. To Rebecca Wanzo and Elzbieta Sklodowska, thank you for your insights and time.

To my cohort of peers: JuanMa Ramírez Velázquez and Alejandra Márquez Guajardo, who, beyond reading parts of this manuscript, have always picked up the phone. To Mariel Martínez Álvarez, Emily Celeste Vázquez Enríquez, Osiris Aníbal Gómez, Natalia Guzmán Solano, Olivia Cosentino, Gaby Martín, Julia Brown, Madison Felman-Panagotacos, and Ivan E. Aguirre Darancou: without you, this would not be worth it.

Also, special thanks to Tamara Williams, Rebbecca Janzen, and Tammy Mitchel, because without their feminist killjoy winks, some scenarios would not have been the same. To Christina Baker, who was of tremendous support in the last stages of this manuscript. Extra appreciation for all the *cuirdos* that keep me insane. You know who you are.

In no particular order, I am also grateful for all the people who, in one way or another, have influenced the writing of this book and/or have supported the writing with moments charged by affect (and, of course, food and drinks): Rafa Acosta, Susan Antebi, Brian Price, Brian Gollnick, Laura G. Gutiérrez, Luis Felipe Lomelí, Paul Fallon, Jesús Nieto, Roberto Cruz Arzabal, Nuala Finnegan, Viviane Mahieux, Adriana Pacheco Roldán, Socorro Venegas, Michael K. Schuessler, Pavel Andrade, Akiko Tsuchiya, Carolyn Fornoff, Camila Torres Castro, Regina Pieck, Carmen Serrano, Olivia Lott, Ashley Wilson, Islandia (Carina Guzmán), Héctor Dominguez Ruvalcaba, Arcelia Paz, Sophie Esch, Jairo Antonio Hoyos, Amy E. Wright, Ever E. Osorio Ruiz, Adriana P. Limón, Bruno Ríos, Rebecca Ingram, Ale Vela Mar, Miguel Valerio, Marco Martínez, Sergio Gutiérrez Negrón, Britta Anderson, Ángel M. Díaz, Sara Potter, Diana Alderete, Ana Sabau, Bahia Munem, Laurel J. Fredrickson, Jennifer Smith, and Satoshi Toyosaki.

I am also thankful for the time and valuable insights from the anonymous peer reviewers. A special thanks to Zack Gresham and Steven P. Rodriguez for believing in this project, as well as the entire Vanderbilt University Press team. I am grateful for spaces like the Annual Bruce-Novoa Mexican Conference, the Mexican Studies Research Collective, and the various book clubs I have attended during the making of this book.

To my younger self: after all, you made it alive. To Tatiana, one of my best childhood friends, a victim of feminicidio—I am sorry I did not have the tools back then. And to Cecilia: today, we are not alone.

Tijuana, Baja California May 2025

INTRODUCTION

The Canon Deception

During my first years of college, I became acquainted with the Mexican literary canon, a list that largely dictates which books readers should read, especially within the university setting. The canon, as I would quickly discover, was predominantly composed of male authors, with only a scant inclusion of female "acquaintances." I deliberately use the term "acquaintances" here because it seemed to me that women writers were often categorized in one of three ways. They were either included merely to counterbalance male-dominated literature, celebrated as exceptions that reinforced the misconception of uncommon greatness among female authorship, or relegated to the status of "lesser" works. What I am recalling here is nothing new or surprising. In fact, since the mid-1980s with the Taller de Teoría y Crítica Diana Morán, a group whose main line of research is the study of Latin American literature from a cultural and gender studies perspective, women writers and intellectuals have taken on the task of revealing the heteropatriarchal practices that sustain the literary sphere in Mexico. The story is quite hackneyed and yet the unbelievable thing is that despite knowing about the historical bias in the formation of canons, the dismissal of women's writing—especially when it intersects with class, ethnicity, race, sexuality, ability, language, and education—is as common as it has ever been, regardless of what seems like a conscious appreciation of literature written by women with the rise of authors like Cristina Rivera Garza, Guadalupe Nettel, or Dahlia de la Cerda in the second decade of the twenty-first century.

The persistence of the tale of the male genius writer can be partly attributed to the operation of the canon. Functioning as a list of works esteemed by a cohort of intellectuals who manage the cultural sphere within a hierarchical structure (the "lettered city"), the canon often promotes certain works as having enduring value while concealing the supposedly defining characteristics of a literary masterpiece. In other words, the canon operates by deceiving and giving the false impression that literature written by women has a short-lived value or lacks the necessary aesthetic quality to become canonical. Today, women writers, literary critics, and scholars face the urgent challenge of elaborating a critique of canonicity that does not rest upon, and thereby reinforce the idea of a masterpiece for posterity derived itself from canonical ideals. Besides, this critique cannot reiterate the practice of building a counter-canon as the solution. The task requires an interrogation of the specificity of different works and moments in time at which traces of canonical erasure might be registered.

The present book endeavors to take up precisely this task. Rather than identifying a set of great works written by women, it tracks the operations of canonicity itself across various forms of cultural production throughout the twentieth and twenty-first century in Mexico. It interrogates how women writers have been rethinking the conceptual bases and theoretical assumptions that have governed the study and criticism of literature. In order to do so, the book pays attention to the junction between women's writing and *cuir* dissidence. Within Mexican literature, the work of women writers who identify themselves as nonheterosexual or whose work is primarily valued for its critique to heteropatriarchal structures has suffered a pervasive form of erasure, which has remained relatively stable throughout the twentieth and twenty-first centuries. This erasure includes blunt censorship, lack of publication opportunities, and the absence of dialogue around their works. The diverse chapters presented here explore the work of women writers and other artists who skillfully manipulate gender and sexuality to reinvent the literature sphere from a cuir standpoint. Specifically, these intellectuals invite us to consider the canon not solely in terms of aesthetic value, but as an affective encounter, as a matter of feelings.

The more I delve into their works, the more captivated I am by the mechanisms these women employ to elaborate their critiques. Some distance themselves from the canon and the conventions of the literary establishment, a practice I have come to identify as restorative criticism—a form of critique that aims to restore the damage left by the dismissal of literature written by women. In doing so, restorative criticism is both an interpretative methodology and something that is enacted by the text as a dissident strategy.

Others directly dispute the canon, the literary conventions, and their repercussions through various techniques that underscore affect as a potent force for the study of literature. Drawing inspiration from Sara Ahmed's notion of the snap, I identify these techniques as a form of breaking a bond with the establishment that potentially contains other configurations of canon formation. Most of these writers seem to share, either implicitly or explicitly, an opinion about the interplay between interpretation frameworks, the canon, and emotional responses to books. To put it plainly, most of them are either disappointed or angered by the processes behind determining which books deserve to be read and preserved for posterity, and which should be forgotten.

It is precisely for this reason that *Cuir Dissidence* takes upon the work of analyzing a diverse corpus that responds to canonicity in one way or another. It is not about restoring the presence of these writers or making efforts to circulate their work. The central argument is to propose their intellectual project as a premeditated act of rebellion, which I view as a strategic device of cuir dissidence. This dissidence, I believe, possesses the hope of deconstructing the heteropatriarchal structures deeply ingrained in Mexican literature written in Spanish, thereby creating space for these voices to flourish across time. All four chapters span a variety of historical and geopolitical configurations that shed light on the continual negotiation between gender and sexuality as analytical categories useful for the study of literature, their relationship with the canon and the cultural sphere, and affect as a main part of this negotiation. The chapters coalesce into a common understanding of the canon as a deceiving mechanism that needs to be challenged by acts of cuir dissidence. The result is a series of interventions that, taken together, evidence the production of cuir literature by women as an epistemic turn, centered on affect, which has been disturbing the idea of the canon or the cultural sphere itself since at least the 1920s.

Throughout this book the corpus is glued together by my own affect. Books serve as technologies of self-making and the pieces here studied have shape the way I read, my definitions of *lo cuir*, gender and sexual dissidence, their relationship with cultural histories and forms of canonical erasure. Above all, what unites this corpus is pleasure and a political-ethical standpoint. I could not bear to dedicate years of my life to studying books I did not enjoy reading or whose ideas I did not fully sympathize with because they reproduce, in one way or another, damaging ideas of gender and sexuality. If the coherence of this book ever falters, it could be attributed to my intention to weave together the works of these writers (and some artists) as examples of cuir dissidence, which I cherish both academically and personally, as I seek out pleasurable literature. And of course, this is totally subjective, risking the coherence of the book. But isn't there nothing more inherently cuir than embracing the feeling of disjointedness as a result of privileging enjoyment? I cannot help but think that some of the writers I study—as my reader will soon find out if they keep reading the book—were dismissed at some point in their careers as bad writers by literary critics, alleging a lack of coherence in their works just because they did not follow the masculine ways of writing. If cuir dissidence writing in Mexico involves a sense of disjointedness, then crafting a book on the topic that formally reflects this characteristic is a fruitful and delightful endeavor.

A Terminology for Cuir Dissidence

By the second decade of the twenty-first century, it has become evident to me that the term queer has penetrated the Latin American theoretical landscape from nearly every conceivable position that our twisted imagination is able to entertain, provoking both discomfort and profound pleasure. Latin American scholars have adopted the adjective queer from English, which, when translated, has been transformed into a noun (*lo cuir*), a verb (*encuirar*, *cuirizar*), a phonetic play (*kuir*), an equivalence (*teoría torcida*, *teoría bollera*), and even an exercise in sophisticated rhetoric (*cú-ir* as a wordplay with the Portuguese term for *ass*). These diverse transformations underscore a conscious and deliberate critical exercise that recognizes the importance of recontextualizing the term queer for the Latin American setting. It seems to me that what it is significant is not merely the word in itself, but rather the act of translating the term as a means of displacing it, which implies a political, cultural, and affective localization.

If queer theorists agree on something, it is that there is no singular genealogy that gives origin to *lo cuir* in Latin America. In the most recent publication discussing the translation of *cuir/queer*, the *GLQ: A Journal of Lesbian and Gay Studies* special issue "Cuir/Queer Américas," instead of a searching for origins, the editors propose *lo cuir* as "a staging of tensions, resonances, and contradictions."[1] This stance is easily traceable in the literature exploring the multiple translations of the term *queer*. For instance, Brad Epps and Bolívar Echeverría have highlighted sociocultural nuances specific to the English language context, such as the historical pejorative connotations of queer, which may not readily translate into the Spanish-speaking world. This discrepancy undermines the term's efficacy in that context.[2] For David Córdoba García, the English phonetics must be respected, proposing "lo queer" as a translation that "nos sitúa en una posición de extrañamiento, de una cierta exterioridad respecto de nuestra cultura nacional, en la cual somos/ estamos exiliados" (it places us in a position of estrangement, a certain exteriority with respect to our national culture, in which we are exiled).[3] This idea is also shared by Felipe Rivas San Martín who argues that the act of enunciation of the term *queer* in Spanish linguistic spaces implies a much-needed decontextualization.[4] Conversely, scholars like Norma Mogrovejo and Julieta Paredes reject queer, understood as a form of linguistic colonization.[5] More recent scholarship contends that sexuality and gender are inherently intertwined in Latin American thought, yet Latin America cannot fully disengage from global dialogues. Consequently, terms such as *lo* queer and its variations (*lo cuir, lo kuir, lo meco*) serve as tools for engaging in global debates about sexualities and gender from a localized perspective.[6] This issue exemplifies some of the tensions and resonances of cuir/queer studies in the Americas.

I am not interested in debating which term is the most appropriate, as all the proposals offer certain particularities that appear useful for cultural analysis and hold political significance to me. Instead, my aim is to align my work with more recent perspectives that encourage to resent queer theory and re-experience the possibilities of lo cuir/queer as proposed by Diego Falconí Trávez, Santiago Castellanos, and María Amelia Viteri in *Resentir lo queer en América Latina: Diálogos desde/con el sur* (Re-feeling queerness in Latin America: Dialogues from/with the South; 2014). Thus, I have opted for the term *cuir* for several reasons. First, I employ this term because it is one of the most used translations for *queer* in Spanish.[7] Second, *cuir* is the phonetic spelling of the English word *queer* in Spanish, visually signifying translation as an act of linguistic dissidence that situates us outside the English-speaking world while still enabling us to participate in the global dialogues of queer studies. Additionally, maintaining the Spanish phonetics in a book written in English might evoke some of the political incorrectness or dissonance that the word once had in English. Lastly, *cuir/queer* serves as a signifier that allows me to encompass a range of non-normative erotic, sexual, affective, and corporeal practices. *Cuir/queer* can refer to each and every combination of practices of gender and sexual dissidence that can be articulated or imagined. It is not limited to gender nonconformity or nonheterosexual erotic desire; it can also encompass non-normative ways of living, such as nonmonogamy, or even forms of organization that are not necessarily related to gender and sexuality but reject normative organizational structures. For example, the corpus studied in this book challenges canonicity as a cultural system of organization by using cuir tactics as exercises to reclaim spaces to produce women's culture. Another example could be certain forms of activism like the ones performed by feminist groups such as El bloque negro, who take on acts of political incorrectness, centered on the uses of the body, while also rearticulating traditional notions of gender and their relation to public spaces, thus embodying the essence of lo cuir.

My adoption of the term *cuir* is also a matter of affiliation and community. *Cuir/queer* has been a term mobilized within academic settings and is closely associated with cultural studies. For example, in Mexico, one of the first instances where the term emerges is to describe a multidisciplinary group fostering discussions around queer theory at the Universidad Autónoma de Querétaro. Therefore, in embracing cuir, I align myself with an intellectual tradition that utilizes cuir/queer as a category of cultural analysis. However, cuir/queer has been gradually displaced by the framework of transfeminism in some areas of Latin America, a discourse that combines elements of feminist thought and resistance with an emphasis on acknowledging and embracing gender diversity and fluidity.[8] While I politically align more with transfeminism, I see it less as a category of analysis and more as a movement driven by activism and street protests, rather than a utilitarian term shaped by the academia. Thus, I find cuir to be a more appropriate term to describe a methodology for analyzing women's literature, visual art, and their relation to the lettered city.

Despite its natural alliance with academia, cuir/queer also represents a mode of political inquiry aimed at exposing inherent normativities and fostering communities that actively pursue unconventional forms of relationality. In this sense, cuir indeed transcends the academic setting and has evolved into a descriptor for a form of political intervention, a way of living, and a word that delineates affective relations beyond societal norms. Throughout this book, in sum, cuir does not necessarily indicate an identity or signify non-normative erotic desire, but rather serves to embody an antinormative dissident positionality that can encompass sexuality and gender, but it is not limited by these categories.

Over the span of this book, my use of terms such as *cuir*, *cuir/queer*, *cuiridad*, *lo cuir*, and *gender* and *sexual dissidence* can appear sketchy, lacking detail, or clarity. Offering comprehensive definitions of these terms risks reproducing a monolithic idea, which contradicts the very essence of lo cuir as a form of knowledge production that seeks to escape such individual categorizations while actively denouncing the singular and hierarchical way of knowledge production imposed by colonial modernity as the sole route.[9] Nevertheless, I am aware that some guidelines are necessary to follow my arguments. To begin with the simple, I use *cuir* to refer to *queer* outside of the English world, and *cuir/queer* to denote a space where both worlds collide.

Now for the slightly more complicated part, which involves settling on a word that serves as a localized translation of queerness. The expression *lo cuir* is commonly used in Spanish to convey queerness, but I remain unconvinced by this translation. In Spanish, abstract nouns can be expressed in various ways but these different expressions are not necessarily equivalent. For instance, "crueldad" does not equate to "lo cruel," nor is "mexicanidad" synonymous with "lo mexicano," despite all referring to abstract concepts. In these instances, "lo" functions as a neutral pronoun preceding the adjective to turn it into a noun, while adding the suffix "-dad" also forms an abstract noun. The difference lies in the degree of abstraction, with "lo" signaling a higher level of abstraction. Returning to queerness, I propose that there are two ways of translating this term, which are not interchangeable but complementary. First, lo cuir "determina la imposibilidad de referirse a un particular en específico" (determines the impossibility of referring to a specific particular).[10] San Martín explains that the vagueness of the syntagma "lo" functions as a linguistic metaphor for the indeterminacy and analytical confusion of queerness.[11] This scholar does not mention what happens when this syntagma is replaced by the suffix "-dad," which reduces the degree of vagueness. I propose that *cuiridad* becomes a term that denotes the possibility to refer to something specific, without losing the quality of indeterminacy.

Cuiridad expresses a quality of something that may not necessarily be perceptible through our senses as such, but is still contained in gestures within books, archives, readers, situations, etc. On the other hand, the abstract nature of *lo cuir* creates a sense of distance, as if it cannot be grasped in the present moment. In this sense, *lo cuir*, as an expression implying a profound level of reverie, can be compared to the utopian function of queerness that José Esteban Muñoz theorizes in *Cruising Utopia: The Then and There of Queer Futurity* (2009). In a way, *lo cuir* embodies the political idealism of *cuiridad*. However, it is important to remember that Muñoz's ideas invoke a redefined notion of utopia in the service of subaltern politics, which conceives of futurity as a dialectical relationship with the present.[12] Therefore, in Spanish, both translations work in relation to each other, denoting different intensities and temporalities: *cuiridad* represents the everyday surplus of *lo cuir*.

Since, for me, *lo cuir* and *cuiridad* speak about different states of queerness and their dialectical relationship, I am not arguing for one translation over the other, but for using both words to denote different degrees of abstraction and proximity. Throughout this book, I use *cuiridad* as a translation of queerness when it appears to me that this characteristic is not merely on the horizon, but manifests itself anchored to tangible things, even when the word itself remains an abstract idea. For example, in Chapter 1, cuiridad emerges as a process of negotiating the limits and creative potentialities of sex and eroticism within various forms of *Dominant/submissive* relations depicted in literature written by women during the sixties, even though lo cuir, as in ideal, is not yet present. Cuiridad signals the nonnormative practices in existence in Mexican literature, and lo cuir, to paraphrase Muñoz's, is that thing that lets us feel that this is not enough.[13] The dialectical use of these terms introduces nuances without establishing a fixed meaning or absolute value for the word; instead, it functions as a relational method. In the first chapter, the palpable cuiridad in the literature of the sixties emerges through a complex interplay between gender, discourses of eroticism, "perverse" sexuality, the lettered city, and the positionality of the woman intellectual. Meanwhile, lo cuir remains as affect, an indescribable sensation that resonates within us physically, through our bodily reactions, yet eludes full articulation or transformation into recognizable emotions and actions.

Lastly, in *English*, queer serves as an umbrella term for individuals who identify as nonheterosexual and/or noncisgender. However, in Spanish, "disidencias sexogenéricas" is preferred. I use *gender and sexual dissidence* as a rough translation of this term to encompass those who diverge from binary norms and/or heterosexuality. Unlike the acronym LGBTQ+ (and its multiple variations), commonly used in identity politics, Latin America often employs the word *disidencias* to describe this spectrum. While cuir/queer theory is prevalent in academic and artistic circles, gender and sexual dissidence is a more appropriate umbrella term when discussing specific corporalities and individuals in the Mexican context. Using *dissidence* in this book is not only a matter of preference but an alliance with the political history of the term and its connotations.

The term *disidencias* holds a dual meaning, suggesting both disagreement (disentir) and a departure from established norms (disidir), as explained by Gabriela González Ortuño.[14] By embracing dissidence as both disagreement and movement, I distance myself from the identity politics framework that characterizes the LGBTQ+ acronym. Instead, I welcome the rejection of identity as a tool for mobilizing cuir politics, which has characterized the movement in Mexico. I interpret dissidence as a framework of affect, echoing Carlos Monsiváis's notion of a "geopolítica del relajo y el deseo" (geopolitics of leisure and desire), which highlights the role of feelings in cuir politics.[15] Monsiváis's words emphasize the political nature of dissidence's visibility, as it fractures the heteropatriarchal system from a localized standpoint of pleasurable messes. Additionally, the term dissidence also describes the relationship women writers have had with the literary establishment across the twentieth and twenty-first centuries—either distancing themselves from it or expressing disagreement as a form of political visibility centered on messy pleasures and other forms of cuir affect.

Ultimately, pairing the word dissidence with cuir reflects my own affective reaction to the negative assumptions about cuir/queer studies that have permeated Latin American thought, particularly in the past decade with the emergence of transexclusionary movements. Francesca Gargallo, in her essay "A propósito de lo queer en América Latina" (Regarding queerness in Latin America), asserts that there is no such thing as a queer Latin American movement, suggesting instead that the presence of lo cuir/queer in Latin America primarily manifests as a matter of affect, albeit without explicitly labeling it as such. Gargallo writes: "queer en América Latina se utiliza para hablar de sexos raritos en un clima de términos bonitos" (Queer in Latin America is used to talk about odd genders in a climate of pretty terms), evoking the discomfort that the term elicits.[16] While Gargallo's conceptualization differs significantly from mine, she acknowledges that the affect associated with cuir movements may be deemed necessary in specific political contexts. The current political landscape of Latin America and the world, particularly concerning cuir/queer and gender studies, is not promising. (I write this shortly after Javier Milei's election and the publication of Judith Butler's new book, *Who's Afraid of Gender*; I edit just months before the inauguration of what will probably become, judging by the current landscape, the disappointing six-year term of Mexico's first elected female president, and just months before the treat of another four years of Donald Trump). In this context, cuir has become a buzzword aligning oneself with the trenches of trans-inclusive movements, recognizing sex work as legitimate labor, understanding sadomasochism as a sexual practice separate from one's feminist credentials; and echoing Gargallo's sentiments, who claims her dislike of dildos as proof of her lack of queerness, cuir signifies a love for vibrators and other sex toys. In other words, *cuir* is a word imbued with uncomfortable affects; a political standpoint, a necessary form of dissidence in our present circumstances.

Tracing Restorative Criticism

In this book, restoration describes the processes of overwriting the canon in works where traces of canonical erasure are registered. I borrow the language of restoration as a feminist critical exercise of two seemingly disconnected events that occurred in Mexico in 2019. The month of March saw the publication of Ave Barrera's fiction *Restauración* (Restoration; 2019), and later the *colectiva* Restauradoras con Glitter was formed after protests erupted due to the authorities' lack of interest, sensitivity, and inefficient response to reports of the rape and sexual assault of a minor and a homeless woman by police officers.[17] These protests included *pintas*—a form of graffiti denouncing gender violence—on the monument known as Ángel(a) de la Independencia. Despite their political significance, the media, government officials, and large segments of society perceived *las pintas* merely as vandalism. In response to this wave of rejection, Restauradoras con Glitter, a *colectiva* of women specialists from various disciplines actively dedicated to the conservation and study of cultural heritage, was created to offer a professional opinion on *las pintas* found on cultural assets. These restorers advocate for meticulously documenting *las pintas* to preserve collective memory, raise awareness, and find solutions to the problem of gender violence. However, they argue that cultural heritage restoration should not proceed until the federal government ensures the safety of women and other affected so-called gender minorities, and until the state punishes gender violence in all its forms.[18] Thus, *las pintas* can be seen as a tactic of overwriting and repurposing powerful symbols for political claims rather than erasing them.[19] As I see it, restoration is the method of overwriting powerful objects or ideas, such as cultural heritage or the canon, without obscuring either the process itself or the surface where it happens—*las pintas* adhere to monuments and transform them into something else without destroying or removing the pieces. By not demolishing the monument but intervening on it, *las pintas* highlight the restoration process itself as central to the preservation of historical memory, with its erasures and dissents.

On the other hand, I contend that Ave Barrera's fiction is an example of restoration as a reading and writing practice. In *Restauración*, Barrera overwrites the canonical fiction *Farabeuf o la crónica de un instante* (*Farabeuf, or, The Chronicle of an Instant*; 1965) by Salvador Elizondo as means of critique and leveraging Elizondo's book to support her feminist arguments. By emphasizing the significance of the body and emotions in the act of reading, Barrera

FIGURE 1.1. The Monumento Hipsográfico covered with *pintas*.

FIGURE 1.2. A riot fence covered with feminist *pintas*.

FIGURE 1.3. The Glorieta a las Mujeres que Luchan (formerly the Glorieta de Colón).

ALL IMAGES COURTESY OF THE AUTHOR EXCEPT AS NOTED.

prompts readers to pause and reflect on how they engage with and process the unfathomable aspects of Elizondo's narrative, particularly the violence endured by his female characters and partners, as we know the violence depicted in *Farabeuf* did not stay confined to the realm of fiction.[20] Thus, I read Barrera's fiction as a form of translating her complex emotions—horror, disgust, and perhaps even a "perverse" sense of pleasure—into a form of restoration within the effects of the violence of gender and Mexico's crisis of *feminicidio*.[21]

What I glean from Barrera's fiction is her transformative treatment of the unassimilable—the gender violence depicted in *Farabeuf*—into something meaningful: "No puedo revivirlas, el daño ya está hecho, pero creo que si hay una restauración más allá de la narrativa de esos dos personajes. Quizá queda fuera, es extratextual, pero está" (I cannot bring them back to life; the damage is already done. However, I believe there is a restoration beyond the narrative of those two characters. Perhaps it lies outside, it is extratextual, but it is there).[22] Through her intricate engagement with a canonical piece of Mexican literature, Barrera manages to transmute her affective bond with *Farabeuf* into a process of rectifying the harm inflicted by the pedagogies of cruelty, which are central to the plot development in Elizondo's fiction. These pedagogies, as described by Rita Segato, entail a series of rituals or systemic processes of socialization and education aimed at reinforcing the dominant position of masculinity, forcibly imposed upon feminized bodies.[23] I argue that the restorative force, emerging as an overflow from the text, constitutes an affective impulse that navigates between the present-day realities of gender violence and the enduring echoes of the past. This highlights how texts can circulate in the present without reproducing the damage or forgetting it.

The language in Barrera's fiction and the *colectiva* Restauradoras con Glitter made me think about restoration in relation to the reparative modes of reading that emerged in the mid-1990s in queer and gender studies in the US. The valorization of this type of reading was integral to the epistemological affirmation of affect as a "vehicle for knowledge," now recognized as the reparative turn.[24] One of the earliest essays exploring this turn, "Paranoid Reading and Reparative Reading" by Eve Kosofsky Sedgwick, contends that paranoia tends to be historically specific, emerging during devastating moments in queer life, such as the years of the AIDS crisis.[25] Rather than consistently anticipating trouble or fixating on the violence inherent in queer life, Sedgwick proposes a shift toward embracing more experimental and pleasurable forms of reading. This call suggests moving away from mere critique toward repair as an invitation to embrace more positive feelings. However, a turn to reparation does not necessitate complete abandonment of negative feelings or critique, as "reparative and paranoid are bound together by the glue of shared affect," but rather offers the possibility of envisioning critique beyond damage.[26] Yet, several scholars have criticized the reparative turn as a liberal approach to justice, deeply implicated in imperialist, colonial, and settler colonial histories.[27]

In *The Ruse of Repair*, Patricia Stuelke offers a genealogy of the reparative turn, demonstrating reparation as "historically implicated in short-circuiting rather than successfully realizing attempts to break with the world as it is in order to create equality."[28] Stuelke turns to Latin America to explain how this region has served as a "laboratory" for the reparative turn, where the practice has provided relief from US imperialist violence instead of actively challenging it.[29] While reparative criticism emerges as a more ethical and humane reading method, Stuelke demonstrates how it falls short in countering US empire and neoliberal capitalism. Thus, reparations as a method can also perpetuate a "closed circuit of injury and repair."[30] In my view, the restoration approach proposed in this book has the capacity to disrupt this cycle, reshaping the reparative process into a communal endeavor focused on memory preservation, documentation, and affect, all while preserving rather than obliterating the past as a political surface of resignification.

In literature, the most common way of reparation has been recovery work. Since the mid-1980s, with El Taller de Teoría y Crítica Literaria Diana Morán and the interest of international scholars such as Jean Franco and Claudia Schaefer, significant efforts have been made to re(un)cover the works of Latin American women writers. The inclusion of women writers, artists, and intellectuals in Mexican cultural histories is also considered the foundational moment for gender as a category of analysis for literary and cultural studies. The ongoing recovery project aimed at rediscovering and recognizing the contributions of these women has probably had the most impact on scholarly and critical practices in the mainstream of the field. Thanks to these recovery efforts, Nellie Campobello, Inés Arredondo, Josefina Vicens, Guadalupe Dueñas, Amparo Dávila, among others, joined the names of Elena Garro and Rosario Castellanos to form a representative core of Mexican women writers of the twentieth century.

While recovery work has been, and continues to be, indispensable, it runs the risk of framing women writers in ways that can limit our understanding of their historical, intellectual, social activism, and artistic contributions. Therefore, it reproduces the injury and repair cycle previously denounced.

An example of this cycle can be seen in the signifier "Mexican woman writer," which, at its best, is understood as an institutional construction; at its worst, as a category that essentializes women writers.[31] In a previous scholarly text, Laura Torres-Rodríguez and I discussed why the debates surrounding the category of "woman writer" are insufficient today.[32] The insistence on the label as a useful category of analysis directly reflects the sexism that permeates Mexican literature and reinforces the idea that literature written by women is a product of a minority, an odd exception. It also promotes the homogenization of women's writing and reduces the problem to a question of identification—either women writers choose to be identified as such, or they reject the label. Thus, the types of questions this debate prompts in the present tend to reinforce conventionally gendered narratives and overlook their full significance.

Is there a way then to recover from recovery work itself?[33] I consider whether the timing to transition away from recovery is opportune, especially considering that women writers have progressed from marginalization to, at best, representation, but not yet to indispensability. To illustrate this point, I observe the significant visibility that women writers have gained in recent years through various means such as prizes, translations, and multiple globally circulated editions. Notable examples included the work of Cristina Rivera Garza, Mariana Enríquez, Brenda Navarro, Fernanda Trías, Mónica Ojeda, María Fernanda Ampuero, and Fernanda Melchor, among others. However, this editorial phenomenon has been wrongfully named as the "nuevo boom femenino." In response, women writers argue that this label: "promueve la homogenización de sus obras, perdiendo las características que las diferencian, el ser catalogadas y encasilladas dentro de una subcategoría y que sus éxitos sean visto como un fenómeno efímero y transitorio. María Fernanda Ampuero (Ecuador) ha dicho sobre esto que ser categorizada por su género 'pone el foco en algo equivocado'" (It promotes the homogenization of their works, losing the characteristics that set them apart, being categorized and boxed into a subcategory, and their successes being seen as an ephemeral and transitory phenomenon. María Fernanda Ampuero [Ecuador] has said about this that being categorized by her gender "puts the focus on the wrong thing").[34] It is still too early to fully assess the consequences of this newfound visibility of women writers. Nonetheless, the tendency to homogenize their works under the "nuevo boom" label undoubtedly obscures the distinctions in their literary projects and aesthetic practices. This tendency is to the point that what seems to unite writers like Cristina Rivera Garza,

Fernanda Trías, and Jazmina Barrera is their perceived gender, reinforcing the old conventionally gendered narrative.

Besides, other problems arise when we view recovery work through the lens of cuir/queer studies. First, the gender disparity that characterizes the construction of value of Mexican literature is often approached from a binary perspective, which obscures the presence and contributions of gender and sexual dissident writers. Consequently, the debate surrounding the category of "Mexican woman writer" clashes with the performative nature of gender that has been central to cuir/queer studies since the beginning. Another problem of recovery work and cuiridad/queerness is that identifying cuir/queer identities, positionalities, attitudes, politics, and aesthetics can be challenging due to the historical persecution and censorship that has affected their production until well into the twenty-first century. This repression also affects the ways in which we approach the archive, as our colleagues in colonial studies insist on reminding us. Lastly, the elusiveness of lo cuir/queerness, which resides "in the haunting gap between here and there," a moment that is not yet here but can be felt in the quotidian adds to the complexity of recovery work.[35]

This book argues that one vital approach to recovering from the work of recovery is through restorative criticism. This form of critique dares to engage less on the mere rescue of forgotten texts and instead urges a profound focus on understanding how these texts demand to be reintegrated into circulation taking into account the present and the horizon. Drawing inspiration from Barrera's concept of overwriting the canon, the idea of restoration put forward by Restauradoras con Glitter, and the reparative modes of reading proposed by queer studies, I offer restoration as a process aimed at returning, renewing, or preserving the qualities of cuir dissidence found in various works of women writers from the twentieth and twenty-first centuries in Mexico. This is achieved by adopting a mode of reading that considers affective encounters as a mode of literary critique. In other words, I propose involving our gut reactions and enhancing the emotional aspect of reading and writing as keys to uncovering restorative forces and tracing canonical forms of erasure in cultural production by women. In consequence, this process seeks to restore not the critical essence of so-called women's writing, but the strategies used by women writers to distance themselves from the types of *pigeonholing* discourses that first brand them as women writers, only to later discard them for the same reason. By examining these strategies, I provide a genealogy of cuir dissidence that had been long lost. As demonstrated by the work of these women writers and artists, cuir dissidence is not an anomaly, exception, or fluke in Mexican cultural history but an intellectual project that needs to be renewed and preserved as such.

Snap! Breaking Bonds with the Canon

In the initial two chapters of this book, I trace cuir dissidence through a series of works by women writers and artists as a process of distancing oneself from normative ideas, resulting in a restorative effect. However, in the last two chapters, cuir dissidence emerges as a breaking point. I argue that affective encounters serve not only as a means of restoration but also as moments when emotional intensity reaches a breaking point, leading to an irreparable rupture and a change in direction. In *Living a Feminist Life*, Sara Ahmed conceptualizes the "snap" as a praxis for creatively and positively thinking about the breaking points of feminist practice: the snap is a moment when one bursts to evoke a crisis; it contains an opening or moment of change.[36] Ahmed illustrates the role of the feminist killjoy—the one who snaps at a family dinner over sexist and racist comments, or the one who dampens the party by denouncing sexual harassment—as an example that points to the theoretical implications of the snap and the everyday experiences of feminists as political interventions. In the second half of this book, I am interested in exploring the concept of snap within literary analysis, particularly how it sheds light on the relationship between cuiridad and the establishment of literary canons. When I refer to the canon, I am thinking the concept in its simplest meaning: a body of works that are seen as outstanding or authoritative within a specific literary tradition, time period, or genre. These works are typically deemed to possess enduring value and are often studied, analyzed, and taught as representative or foundational texts.

In Mexico, the question of affect has not been absent in debates about the canon. Ignacio Sánchez Prado, in examining Harold Bloom's influence in the Latin American context, highlights that "reading Bloom's canon in English or Spanish, in Mexico or the United States, can yield very different affects and ideas."[37] According to Sánchez Prado, when exploring the history of Mexican literature, there is something compelling about Bloom's enthusiasm for the sublime, a prevailing consequence of *The Western Canon's* popularity in Mexico.[38] From my perspective, this enthusiasm commonly translates into the idea that great literature is defined by the inherent qualities of the text—"el arte por el arte" (art for art's sake), as commonly explained. However, the sublime is a sense of ecstasy that readers experience when encountering a writing style that elevates itself above the ordinary—an affective encounter that does not necessarily manifest as inherent qualities within the text or a set of characteristics to measure greatness. As far as I am concerned, the enthusiasm for the sublime can also suggest that the canon can be built up through the evocative affect of a literary piece.

Rather than considering affect solely as a psychological state, Sara Ahmed's conceptualization portrays it as a social and cultural practice, illustrating how affect is generated through "effects of circulation."[39] In the context of literature, this means that our emotional responses can be understood as outcomes of specific affects circulating within a cultural milieu, rather than inherent qualities of the literary works themselves. Ahmed's framework enables us to perceive how the canon, typically seen as a fixed category of cultural representation, actually evolves into a discourse of cultural value shaped by the circulation of affect. Thus, I propose to see cuir literature as "objects of feeling," where affects are imprinted onto bodies—whether material or symbolic—and then circulated.[40] I am particularly interested in texts where an intensification of the body becomes apparent through a transformative snap that reshapes the canon itself. In essence, this snap operates as an economy of affect, influencing individuals, communities, and objects. For instance, the cultural value attributed to a book can be understood as a result of the circulation of this affective economy. By recognizing that cultural value is tied to how affect circulates at a given moment, we can better understand the relationship between affect and the formation of literary and cultural canons, especially as explored within women's cuir cultural production.

In the case of Mexico, canon formations are influenced by two seemingly contradictory ideas: the criteria of representation for Mexican culture—Octavio Paz's *El laberinto de la soledad* (*The Labyrinth of Solitude*)—and the historical struggle to assert Mexican culture's universal citizenship through cosmopolitanism—the work of Salvador Elizondo.[41] According to Sánchez Prado, the best writers would be those who "develop a canonized formal style" and "whose style can be understood as a formalization of some kind of political truth regarding Latin America."[42] On the other hand, Emily Hind proposes an interesting hypothesis: canonical literature is created through a performance of power and a network of complicit peers: "The 'best' or canonical texts, not as residing at the top of the pyramid of aesthetic quality, but as the most connected nodes in a network in which all works exists in a horizontal plane."[43] The horizontal plane signifies that "the most interconnected texts do not just happen to be written by men. They reflect friendships among potential equals built on shared assumptions and prejudices, and these commonly held beliefs come to stand for 'quality' among the members of the mutual admiration society."[44] Both scholars primarily focus on a corpus from the twentieth century and provide limited insights into more recent cultural production. In fact, little research has been conducted on how the concept of the canon operates in the twenty-first century, which is less about canonized formal styles, a formal exploration of Latin American thought, or connected nodes, and more about rethinking our relationship with the canon at large.

In the twenty-first century, Mexican women writers are reorganizing aesthetic practices, places of enunciation, and the constructions of the public and communal spheres in response to their feelings of *hartazgo*, anger, and disappointment due to the processes of erasure from the lettered city that have kept women's writing in the margins. This rearrangement is a productive challenge to ideas about the canon, the functionality of national literature, and the role of intellectuals and writers in the twenty-first century. Therefore, in the second part of this book, I examine what the concept of the canon looks like in women's cuir literature by exploring it first as a series of snaps that register what cannot be easily assimilated by previous configurations of canon formations such as global citizenship, performing authorship, or national identity. Secondly, I analyze how women's cuir literature utilizes feelings to both break with and restore the canonical fracture, indicating a redefinition of the canon as a communal and everyday bodily communication system. This results in a collaborative process of writing and reading that shifts focus away from the idea of authorial "genius" and the enduring value of a work as the essential characteristics for a canonical text. Alternatively, this restructuring may also imply that the canon itself is inherently deceiving without entirely dismantling its structure. Similar to the *pintas* on monuments, the aim is to highlight how the canon operates as a violent form of erasure while preserving the memory of this act to eventually overwrite it.

Cuir/queer affect teaches us that feelings do not originate from identity but rather "from the mundane and repetitive labor in which queer subjects are forced to comply and sustain heteronormative spaces as their bodies encounter them in everyday interaction."[45] Thus, the form of cuir dissidence embraced by women writers may or may not be related to their sexual and gender dissidence. It is also not necessarily about topics, politics, or characters related to gender and sexual dissident communities. What makes this corpus cuir is the search for messy relationalities, aiming to create alternative discourses of value centered on the body and its affective iterations as a form of writing, reading, and researching literature.

The Compulsory Chapter Outline

The first chapter centers on the reconfiguration of eroticism and literature during the sixties with the work of Inés Arredondo, Kati Horna, and Leonora Carrington. I pay attention to how alternative sexual intimacies play a role in women's writing and how writing "messy" texts—those that test our sanity or make us uncomfortable—can affect their relationship with the lettered city. By recognizing BDSM as a pleasurable erotic practice through my own affective reaction to the work of these women, I interpreted this sexual practice as a form of restoration. These women were producing literature and art during a time of gender and sexual reconfiguration in Mexico, which had an impact on literary and visual aesthetics. In the sixties, a generation of writers, predominantly male writers, became obsessed with French discourses of eroticism that were plagued with normative and misogynistic assumptions about female pleasure. Instead of breaking with these discourses, these women chose to engage with eroticism as a practice of restoration, privileging their own pleasures. However, time has rendered their contributions as feminine versions—perfect imitations—of the masculine trend, in part, because literary criticism failed to recognize in their writing cuir dissidence as a conspicuous act of rebellion to overwrite normative discourses.

Pairing the work of Arredondo, Horna, and Carrington with Xitlalitl Rodríguez Mendoza's recent publication recalling her BDSM experience as a form of literary critique, I renew these women ideas to propose their work as pioneering in the conceptualization between the relation of women's cuir pleasure and the figure of the woman intellectual. Thus, in this chapter, the process of restoration is twofold: Arredondo, Horna, and Carrington overwrite eroticism to develop their theories of jouissance, vulnerability, and transgression, while I undertake the critical task of restoring their intellectual projects as exercises of cuir dissidence. This serves to counteract the erasure and dismissal of their novel contributions.

In the second chapter, "The Restorative Possibilities of an Archive of Gender Playfulness: Women's Mustaches and the Third Gender," I delve into the restoration of an archive of gender dissidence primarily through the study of fiction and *acciones*. My restorative critique emerges as a gut reaction to the rise of essentialist ideas of gender and transphobia that we are witnessing throughout the second decade of the twenty-first century. Instead of breaking with these discourses, the recovery of this archive helps restore a genealogy of cuir cultural production that continually occupies the category of "woman" to draw political actions without mobilizing the signifier "woman" as a biological entity or as a monolithic term. This archive restores gender dissidence as a cuir-feminist practice with a profound history in Mexico. Together, these chapters illustrate the different forms of overwriting the literary establishment, either by proposing to investigate discourses that have affected the Mexican canon from a cuir perspective, or by preserving an archive with the means of re-evaluating the presence of gender dissidence in Mexico.

Utilizing Ahmed's feminist snap theory as a cornerstone for feminist praxis, Chapter 3 traces snaps in lesbian literature as instances of breaking with the canon. It takes up two case studies: *Amora* (Beloved; 1989) by Rosa María Roffiel and *La reinita pop no ha muerto* (*The Little Queen of Pop Is Not Dead*; 2013) by Criseida Santos Guevara. In my view, *Amora* is the materialization of Roffiel's own snap against the negative portrayal of lesbians in Mexican literature. *Amora* was perceived by literary critics of the time as a failed narrative, with little value attributed to it beyond being the first lesbian novel published in Mexico. Through my own emotional response to the book, particularly upon discovering that *Amora* features a bisexual protagonist who adopts lesbianism as a political strategy, led me to view the novel as a complex work that breaks with the Mexican literary tradition. *Amora* is not only a text that incorporates fiction, autobiography, theory, and a pamphlet-like tone but also disrupts heteronormative conceptions of gender and sexuality, all through the perspective of a bisexual woman who adopts lesbianism as a form of militance. The combination of formal elements and content results into a novel form of writing.

Roffiel's snap, coupled with my own snap toward the effacement of bisexuality, highlights the systematic erasure of female sexual dissidence in Mexican literature, which persistently fails to portray complex lesbian or bisexual characters. This perceived failure of lesbian literature is addressed by Criseida Santos Guevara in *La reinita pop no ha muerto*, where the protagonist effectively snaps at the canon, ridiculing the simplistic exclusion of cuir women writers. Together, these fictions demonstrate how the snap can serve as a cuir method of literary critique, redirecting attention to affect as a means of dismantling literary norms.

In Chapter 4, I delve into how Cristina Rivera Garza's *La cresta de Ilión* (*The Iliac Crest*; 2002) and Didí Gutiérrez's *Las elegantes* (The elegant ones;

2021) incorporate writings by others within women's writing itself. By playfully integrating the work of others in their fictions and emphasizing the production of affect with their mischievous nature—eliciting a bodily response in the reader—they actively engage readers in the writing process. This approach serves as means to challenge the established canon. In *La cresta de Ilión*, Rivera Garza compels the reader to become part of the narrator's nightmare, prompting them to take a stance against the disappearance of the *Emisarias*, which, I argue, represents the erasure of women from the canon of Mexican literature. Rivera Garza's work highlights the communal nature of writing to reevaluate the value not only of contemporary literature but also of literature that has been overlooked in the past. Taking communal writing to its ultimate consequences, *Las Elegantes* creates a collective force that accumulates and circulates affect as an economy to maintain the potency of *Las Elegantes* in an effort to defy the common outcome of women's writing—if the book keeps circulating, *Las Elegantes* cannot be forgotten. The trick is that to continue their circulation, *Las Elegantes* needs readers who are oblivious to the history of women's writing in Mexico, as well as a more informed audience. The former circulates the text as an exercise in recovery work, while the latter circulates the book as a hoax that reinforces the canon as a deceiving mechanism. It is my contention that *Las Elegantes* as a literary hoax breaks with the status, function, and credibility of the canon from a cuir dissidence standpoint.

La cresta de Ilión and *Las Elegantes* are literary works that incorporate the writings of others within their pages, either by directly citing figures such as Amparo Dávila or Guadalupe Dueñas, or through a metanarrative that not only comments on the story itself but also involves the reader and their emotions in the production of the story. Rivera Garza imagines an Amparo Dávila that diverges from the real writer, yet this imaginative exercise has had an impact on the revival and study of her narrative. Similarly, Gutiérrez creates a generation of women writers as a cuir-feminist hoax that sparks debates about the relation between the "empirical" work of academic research and the affective relation scholars have with their chosen objects of study. Because of this, in my opinion, these books also engage in a debate about the boundaries between imagination, creative writing, and academic research, a debate that I explore not only as a topic but rather through the form of my writing in Chapter 4. Consequently, not everything is as it initially appears since some parts of my chapter adhere to the imaginative proposals of Rivera Garza and Gutiérrez as breaking mechanisms. The reader's task is to pay attention to their bodily reactions and decide whether they want to continue participating in the game or not. After all, *Cuir Dissidence* is a pleasurable way of playing with the canon as a mechanism of deception that can be restored only to be broken again, and again.

CHAPTER 1

Fucking with Death and (Not) Yet Cuir

*Choking Eroticism through the Work of Inés Arredondo
in Complicity with Kati Horna, Leonora Carrington,
and Xitlalitl Rodríguez Mendoza*

Whether they provoke arousal, disgust, or a feeling that is difficult to disentangle into a recognizable emotion, messy books, for me, are the ones that push my own limits, test my sanity, and force me to rethink what I thought I knew or believed. Put another way, messy books are those that I feel in my body in an uncomfortable way. Yet there is a great deal of pleasure in experiencing this uneasiness. I had the delight of discovering the messy side of literature in my early years as an undergraduate student when I read works such as *La condesa sangrienta* (The bloody countess; 1966) by Alejandra Pizarnik and "El niño proletario" (The proletarian boy; 1973) by Osvaldo Lamborghini. For example, I was fascinated by the double-edge sword meticulously created by Lamborghini—a tangled web of a messy narrative, where the reader grapples with the seductive allure of a twisted societal fantasy of domination and submission. At the same time, the narrative unfurls a vivid confrontation with the palpable brutality inherent in the repressive model of the Argentine dictatorship. Because this short story is crafted to evoke a perverse curiosity in the reader, simultaneously inducing nausea and repulsion, it can be described as messy. I must confess that I have always felt a strong fondness for these types of books, especially those that prove difficult to handle due to their tortuous prose, their filthy content, or because they entangle the reader in disturbing ethical conundrums, such as experiencing arousal from violence. Their messiness sticks with me, lingering for a long time.

I was fortunate enough to have a professor during my undergraduate years who knew how to nourish my interest in this type of literature without imposing their judgment, taste, or ideas. One way in which this professor supported my curiosity was by offering me a research assistant position to investigate topics such as sadomasochism, the pornographic industry, and sex dolls. I found these topics to be messy, as I was not sure how I felt about them. The goal was to provide context for a scholarly piece on perversion and naturalism in the Mexican short novel. I tend to get oddly obsessed with the things I am researching, but these topics consumed me in ways I had never experienced before. Suddenly, I wanted to take classes on S/M, unexpectedly available near the Museo del Chopo, and find a way to read Gayle Rubin (surprisingly unavailable at my undergraduate university library). I craved to understand weird things such as why sex dolls with fixed vaginas are more popular than those with replaceable ones, especially when the former is considered more hygienic (yes, it is the tightness of the fixed ones). Above all, I wanted to connect all this with Mexican literature. In consequence, I hope for the possibility of outlining an undergraduate project filled with messy books, the common thread among them being their ability to trouble my naive perception of the world, in particular, what I thought I knew about sexuality. And because I like to complicate things, it also had to be literature written by women. Needless to say, I failed and ended up writing a thesis about baroque aesthetics in *La sodomía en la Nueva España* (Sodomy in New Spain; 2010) by Luis Felipe Fabre.

During that time, I was under the false impression that literature written by women was preoccupied with depicting sex as dangerous, destructive, and negative—highlighting almost exclusively topics such as sexual abuse and rape. I was a teenager trying to use literature to break free from the constraints imposed by my Catholic family, not revive them. Thus, I had zero interest in literature that always seemed to punish transgression without much room for anything other than accepting the punishment as a normal consequence of deviant sexuality. Alternatively, I thought this literature focused solely on traditional forms of relationality, such as romantic and monogamous couples, providing a limited representation of positionalities that ultimately privileged the experiences of heterosexual women. Because I was interested in the pleasurable aspects of messy relations, I found myself frustrated by the lack of a corpus to work with and eventually decided to let go of the project.

Obsessions are a funny thing; they tend to flourish during times of stress. So, of course, my obsession with perverted literature resurfaced during graduate school when, once again, I was looking to build a corpus of cuir women's texts that I could see myself working with in the next decade of my life. My focus was on cuir women, but I struggled to find books beyond those about lesbian representation, and I wasn't sure if I could force myself to appreciate the *cursilería* of the Mexican lesbian novel enough to write a whole book about it. However, I knew I didn't want to do yet another research project on *El vampiro de la colonia Roma* (The vampire of the Colonia Roma) or cuir Octavio Paz. I also knew I didn't want to create a project where Carlos Monsiváis finally and indisputably comes out of the closet.[1] Jokes aside, what I mean is that I was sure that this time I did not want to succumb to the pressure of the archive and end up writing about the experiences of male writers, as I did with my undergraduate thesis. Thus, subconsciously, I found myself wishing for a cuir version of Inés Arredondo, one of my favorite Mexican writers. I wondered how a woman with such a perverted imagination could be so mainstream and "straight"?

Before succumbing to frustration, I decided to procrastinate by re-reading Arredondo's short stories. To my surprise, my traditional literary education had hindered me from recognizing some of her works as feminist-cuir interventions into eroticism. As I delved into her perverse world, I noticed nuances I had previously overlooked. In her stories, BDSM practices sometimes function as devices of cuir-feminist agency, while at other times, they reinforce heteropatriarchal structures. This realization led me to reflect on my reading methods; perhaps my frustration with the lack of a messy corpus had more to do with how I approached the cuir work of women writers and less with the work itself.

However, it would not be until the publication of a series of *crónicas* in which the poet Xtlalitl Rodríguez Mendoza narrates her first experience with BDSM, supported by photographic evidence, that I would seriously consider writing about how alternative sexual intimacies play a role in women's writing and how writing messy texts can greatly affect their relationship with the lettered city and the canon. By alternative sexual intimacies, I refer to practices that reject reason, safety, usefulness, and instead celebrate risk, excess, perversity, danger, and torture as forms of pleasure and play—practices usually simplified with the acronym BDSM. This acronym stands for Bondage/Discipline, Dominance/submission, and Sadism/Masochism.[2] In BDSM communities, "play" is a term that describes the activities taking place within a "scene," a pre-planned space and time where BDSM activities occur after a negotiation process. During this negotiation process, the Top/bottom or the Dominant/submissive (terms used to describe the assigned roles for the duration of the play) establish their limits, safe words, desires, and plan the scene that will take place at an agreed-upon time and location. Participants temporarily set aside their desire to play to establish safe and consensual conditions for the play.

Consent is a core concept for BDSM practitioners, but it is also a deeply problematic notion. A liberal approach to consent assumes "that it is an easily agreed-upon contact entered into by autonomous subjects with free will ... the individual is the one who knows best what is good for her/him."[3] In contrast, critical consent is viewed as a mutually beneficial agreement that does not feed the illusion of freedom or privilege rational processes of individual choice, emphasizing that decisions are not made in a vacuum by autonomous individuals who are fully free and rational. From a critical perspective, consent is not just a matter of one person agreeing or disagreeing but rather a collective, relational process. It considers how consent is shaped by external factors such as power imbalances, structural inequalities, and social norms, which may limit an individual's true freedom to choose. Therefore, critical consent is an affective making-process and "includes a degree of equality that ensures that each partner has the power to decide to engage in sex without fear of consequences ... a position of empowerment that enables one to deal with the material, social, and emotional consequences of saying no to sex."[4] Establishing critical consent is particularly crucial in new relationships where trust has not yet been established or when there are hierarchical issues between the players, such as gender, race, age, or ability status. Critical consent is also essential when engaging in any type of edgeplay and experimenting with new risky practices. Edgeplay is a subjective term for any sexual or mental activity that challenges safe, sane, and consensual schemas. If the people involved are aware of the risks and consequences of this type of play—which might include the possibility of death or long-term harm—and are willing to accept this possibility, the activity is considered Risk-Aware Consensual Kink. Types of edgeplay include but are not limited to breath play and consensual nonconsent.

Talking about BDSM negotiation and critical consent is not without purpose. As the title of the chapter suggests, I analyze how women writers and artists negotiate their fascination with "perverse" sex inside the constraints of a heteropatriarchal society and a male-dominated intellectual sphere. Echoing Gayle Rubin's ideas, I define "perverse" sex as any type of sexual practice that deviates from what is considered "good," "normal," and "natural." "Perverse" sex includes a wide range of sexual practices and intimacies that go from nonheterosexual encounters to practicing nontraditional relations such as nonmonogamy and commercial sex. It can involve pornography, fetish objects, sex toys, and roles beyond the gender binary.[5] In the case of the writers and artists here analyzed, this "perverse" sexuality often manifests itself through practices, such as choking, necrophilia, S/M dynamics, consensual nonconsent fantasies, voyeurism, and fetishism.

In this chapter, I begin with Xitlalitl Rodríguez Mendoza's *crónicas* to later delve into the sixties, a period of gender and sexual reconfiguration in Mexico. During this period, I identify two cases of underappreciated examples of BDSM in women's writing as attempts to negotiate a space for themselves in the lettered city. Inés Arredondo's short stories, in complicity with the collaborative photo-essay by Kati Horna and Leonora Carrington, envision an alternative sexual ethics linked to their intellectual projects. The depictions of troubled sexual practices carried out by Arredondo, Horna, and Carrington produce feelings of discomfort, disgust, and even anxiety. But that reader/viewer can also choose to experience these practices as pleasurable. Paying attention to the pleasurable side of their messy relations is a form of restorative criticism that highlights the urgency of thinking about the work of these women as exercises that rehearse a cuir dissidence, especially in relation to sexuality, to reconfigure the literary scene. Although many women writers were challenging heteropatriarchal constructions from a cuir and feminist perspective before the 1960s, I am interested specifically in BDSM and its relation to the figure of the woman writer as a process of restoration. Momentarily stepping away from their relatively privileged positions in heterosexual relationships with stable economic standings, the flirtatious encounters with danger and the celebration of perverted sex by Horna, Carrington, and Arredondo need to be seen as cuir gestures. Their work demonstrates how they "choked" eroticism, suppressing its vitality, to reveal the limits, risks, and possibilities of a creative sexual discourse.

In addition to Alberto Chimal's *Los esclavos* (The slaves; 2009), Liliana Blum's *Pandora* (2017), Carlos Velázquez's *La marrana negra de la literatura rosa* (The black sow of pink literature; 2010), and Artemisa Téllez's *Crema de vainilla* (Vanilla cream; 2015), BDSM is seldom depicted in Mexican literature. While I can argue that certain elements of BDSM are present in Mexican culture, ranging from lucha libre to the influence of the *postporno* movement in performance artists like Lechedevirgen Trimegisto and La Congelada de Uva, my specific interest lies in exploring non-normative sexual practices in literary projects as a negotiation process between women intellectuals and the male-centered lettered sphere, which is also a process that restores female pleasure and agency. Consequently, in this chapter, I delve into cuiridad as a process of negotiating the limits and rehearsing the creative potentialities of sex and eroticism in various forms of Dominant/submissive relations (D/s) while also grappling with the messiness of what it means to be a woman writer who writes about and enjoys kink in heteropatriarchal times.

The Messy Pleasures of Mr. Magic Wand (or Why Hire a Pro Dom in Times of #RopaSucia)

In November 2015, the poet Xitlalitl Rodríguez Mendoza published a series of *crónicas* in which she narrated her first personal experience with BDSM, accompanied by a series of photos of the session along with a detailed list of the sex toys used, serving as evidence of her intimate sexual experience. These *crónicas* were commissioned for the digital medium *Vice*, where Rodríguez Mendoza mainly worked as a proofreader at the time. The *crónicas* represent a singular moment in Mexican literature, as they are the first texts published by a woman writer to openly address their BDSM experience. While Rodríguez Mendoza explores novel sexual practices, authors such as Salvador Novo and Carlos Monsiváis have previously employed the *crónica* to position themselves as writers troubling the sexual norms of their time. As a genre that is challenging to define and offers great formal flexibility, the *crónica* is ideal for delving into cuiridad, as highlighted by scholars such as Viviane Mahieux and Alejandra Márquez. Thus, this genre can help establish an intellectual position within the lettered city, where the exploration of sexuality is regarded as a site of critical resistance and a tool for generating productive noise that aids the writers in positioning themselves.

Similarly to Novo and Monsiváis, Rodríguez Mendoza also elaborates on an intellectual position where sex appears as a political and epistemological practice to rethink the concept of vulnerability in relation to the figure of the Mexican woman writer. In recent years, increasing importance has been given to vulnerability as a concept that can redefine power structures and the relationship between ethics and politics in neoliberal times.[6] The question of how to think about feminist politics from vulnerability has been generating different lines of thought focused on violence and precarity but also on resistance and coalitions, suggesting that vulnerability can be reclaimed as "a condition of intersubjective freedom, action, and political engagement."[7] Rodríguez Mendoza's *crónicas* appear at a time of change when the pedagogies of cruelty often used in the literary world—sexual harassment, exclusion, aggression—are publicly and loudly denounced, exposing matters that the masculine intellectual sphere would prefer not to be made public. With this exposure, women writers are using their vulnerability as form of political action and engagement.

A few months before the publication of the *crónicas*, Paula Abramo, Maricela Guerrero, and Xitlalitl Rodríguez Mendoza launched a discussion forum on Twitter addressing cases of sexism and misogyny in the Mexican cultural sphere. This forum, compiled under the hashtag #RopaSucia (dirty laundry), brought together more than 15,000 tweets. Some examples of the content include quotes like "A la verdadera literatura solo la escriben los hombres" (true literature is only written by men), attributed to someone from FONCA (the National Endowment for Culture and Arts), or "Ella no escribe mal, pero acá entre nos, la poesía es cosa solo de hombres" (she doesn't write badly, but just between us, poetry is something only for men), as said by a literary historian.[8] Abramo, Guerrero, and Rodríguez Mendoza transformed this Twitter forum into an art exhibition. The exhibition featured a clothesline displaying underwear and garments soiled with wine, coffee, and ink, embroidered with the phrases collected on Twitter. Zote soap bars accompanied the clothesline, representing gender inequality statistics about some of the main national recognitions for writers and artists. The concept aimed to bring to light and wash away gender bias in the Mexican intellectual environment: "[E]n una comunidad que trabaja con la palabra es grave que se sigan reproduciendo prejuicios y negando otras visiones del mundo, otros lugares desde dónde ponerse a ver las cosas. Porque las otras violencias, las que llegan a los feminicidios, parten de considerar a las mujeres como seres inferiores o utilizables" ([I]n a community that works with words, it is serious that prejudices continue to be reproduced and other worldviews, other perspectives from which to see things, are denied. Because other forms of violence, those that lead to femicides, stem from viewing women as inferior or disposable beings)—the women intellectuals behind the project explained.[9] This project exposed the normalized pedagogies of cruelty within the Mexican cultural sphere, preceding the rise of the Primavera Violeta in 2016 and the movement MeTooEscritoresMexicanos in 2019, which, in a massive and organized way, continued this unraveling.[10]

Fueled by the momentum of these feminist movements in the 2010s, I believe we are witnessing a reordering of the lettered city driven by women writers who are tired of hegemonic literary practices that tend to marginalize their experiences. This reordering is evident in thematic changes, such as the rise of the topic of motherhood in literary aesthetics, exemplified by books such as *Casas vacías* (*Empty Houses*; 2019) by Brenda Navarro and *Linea nigra* (2020) by Jazmina Barrera. However, this shift is not limited to themes alone; it extends to material changes involving shifts in the modes of production, emphasizing elements such as the collective nature of writing. Furthermore, it represents a political and epistemological change, aiming to modify the role of women writers in their sociopolitical context.

To me, this reordering seems akin to an affective turn, as women writers are increasingly concerned with the role of materiality and emotions as sites of knowledge production. This approach enables them to reinterpret literature's place in relation to political activity and prompts a reconsideration of their vulnerable status as a form of political action in response to the pedagogies of cruelty within the literary sphere. In the specific case of Rodríguez Mendoza, BDSM emerges as a provocative form of intimacy that, when exposed, highlights the prevailing heteropatriarchal structures aired through the dirty laundry of the art exhibition, adopting a playful and pleasurable standpoint. In the *crónicas*, BDSM is not merely a sexual curiosity meant to stir controversy or a vaguely defined identity. Instead, it is a political proposition that prompts us to think about the materiality of bodies and the role of literature written by women in the public sphere. This is particularly crucial within a heteronormative nation.

Divided into three parts, the *crónica* appears to be a text without clear aesthetic concerns. By this I mean that it seems that the intention is none other than to generate controversy and curiosity with the goal of winning readers, which aligns perfectly with the editorial line of a medium like *Vice*. In a conversation, Rodríguez Mendoza clarified to me that she did not suggest the topic. Instead, it was the magazine's editor, who had a friend supposedly dedicated professionally to the world of BDSM, that proposed it. The editor believed that a topic like this could generate attention and controversy, which are productive for a digital medium of this kind. So, the editor asked one of the journalists to write the story, but they declined, and that's when Rodríguez Mendoza decided to take on the project.

In the first part of her *crónica*, Rodríguez Mendoza interviews a psychologist who practices BDSM. The purpose of this discussion is to situate BDSM within the context of gender violence, specifically in Mexico. Throughout the interview, the psychologist suggests that within the realm of BDSM, the exploration of vulnerability can function as a space for feminist sociability and political engagement. Vulnerability and subversion are presented by the psychologist as useful tools to question established hierarchies. I believe the interview sets up the groundwork for the type of intellectual figure that interests Rodríguez Mendoza—one who playfully and messily explores the vulnerability of situated bodies as a writing device to disentangle and air out the biases inside the male-centered lettered city.

In the second part of the *crónica*, the author discusses the preparation involved in one's first sadomasochistic scene. This includes considerations such as waxing for protection and hygienic reasons, anal douching, safety measures such as safe words, and the rules set by her Dom Héctor (a fictitious name used to identify the professional involved). Moving to the final part of the *crónica*, the session is openly described, accompanied by photos, and a brief overview of the selected sex toys such as a gag ball, anal hook, mitts, Wartenberg wheel, and a magic wand. In these pieces, sadomasochism becomes a device that rearticulates power through bodily vulnerability and becomes an epistemic moment that ultimately shapes Rodríguez Mendoza's writing.

Allow me to inspect the following quote (pun intended):

> Después de inspeccionarme el culo puso un pie sobre mi nuca y me dijo: "Ah, la curiosidad periodística. Tú dices que es de trabajo pero en realidad esto te gusta." Sentí una profunda vergüenza porque era cierto, pero de alguna forma extraña el hecho de que estuviera pisándome la cabeza me reconfortaba. *Esas son honestas búsquedas literarias y no chingaderas*, pensé, y antes de reírme recibí el primer azote con un látigo. *Así se hace la buena crítica lit*. Otro. Rompí en llanto.[11]

> After inspecting my ass, he placed a foot on my neck and said, "Ah, journalistic curiosity. You say it's for work, but in reality, you enjoy this." I felt a deep shame because it was true, but in some strange way, the fact that he was stepping on my head comforted me. *These are honest literary pursuits and not nonsense*, I thought, and just as I was about to laugh, I received the first lash of a whip. *That's how good literary criticism is done*. Another. I broke down in tears.

After being inspected by the Dom—a common form of playful and consensual degradation—he warns Rodríguez Mendoza that the BDSM session is not mere journalistic curiosity but something she really enjoys doing. Rodríguez Mendoza confesses to the reader that she feels ashamed, and at the same time, her vulnerability comforts her. After each flogging, she situates her kink experience as a method to think about literature, quoting writers like Santa Teresa de Jesús, Susan Sontag, and Anne Carson, but also commenting on her own experience as an editor and a writer: "Entró como mantequilla [the anal hook]. Soy editora: me pagan por ser una anal retentiva. Así que cuando esto entró, con dos o tres indicaciones de mi amo pero sin mayores complicaciones, sentí que había logrado algo en la vida" (It went in like butter [the anal hook]. I'm an editor: I get paid for being anal-retentive. So, when this went in, with two or three instructions from my master but without major complications, I felt like I had achieved something in life).[12] Throughout the text and in her later poems, the author constantly refers to BDSM as a particularly useful form of literary exploration for understating women's writing in the context of heteropatriarchy: "Las mujeres somos buenas en el sector cultura. Es lo que dicen. Funcionales, presentables, ordenadas. Cuando me echaron no me dijeron que era por mis mentiras; culparon a mis poemas, mis nudos, dijeron, palabras personales para estirar" (Women are good in the cultural sector. That's what they say. Functional, presentable, organized. When they fired me, they didn't say it was because of my lies; they blamed my poems, my knots, they said—personal words stretched too far).[13] As the quote suggests, a few months after publishing the *crónicas*, she got fired from *Vice*. In addition to facing job insecurity due to her "nudos"—a word that references the practice of *shibari* or rope play—Rodríguez Mendoza was criticized for documenting and publishing her sexual exploration, which is seen as the opposite of functional, presentable, and tidy, as the poem implies.

Emily Hind reminds us that the appeal of sex sells, depending on the gender of the author.[14] In this case, Rodríguez Mendoza's *crónicas* did not generate the "right" type of attention, as the notion that a woman writer should not delve into "perverted" subjects still prevails in our very conservative Mexican cultural scene. Instead of creating a buzz, her dismissal from *Vice* resulted in an awkward silence and Rodríguez Mendoza struggled for a while to secure stable employment. Interestingly enough, and despite the projects being only a few months apart, no one linked the *crónicas* with the RopaSucia exhibition, even though both explore vulnerability as a zone of political action within the constraints of heteropatriarchy. It is very difficult for me to imagine a greater degree of self-explored vulnerability than having your ass inspected and then writing about it, especially when you are a poet with a certain visibility and cultural capital who has denounced the misogyny of the Mexican literary system. Yet, there is also a great amount of pleasure in reading Rodríguez Mendoza's bold *crónicas* and how she situates herself as a woman writer, finding in the messiness of the topic the necessary affect to keep fighting.

Though it may seem strange, the publication of the *crónicas* led Rodríguez Mendoza to write more. During our conversation, she clarifies, laughing, "si escribo mucho, el buscador de Google no arrojará las crónicas en la primera página" (If I write too much, Google's search engine won't show the chronicles on the first page).[15] I apologize for potentially placing her back in the spotlight with my interest in BDSM. However, she quickly answers, "no importa, de todas formas, ni nos leen" (It doesn't matter; they don't read us anyway).[16] We both burst into laughter right in the middle of the café inside the Rosario Castellano's bookstore. The plural form "ni nos leen" has a double meaning, suggesting that the works of women writers are not being read and the research produced on them tends to be ignored, regardless of how many bookstores are named after women writers to honor their legacy. Rodríguez Mendoza's comment is a way of highlighting that no matter what, women's writing is always brushed aside. So, we may as well have a little fun while we write and do research about it.

Cuir/queer studies often suggests that sexual practices offer the potential to unravel the predetermined meanings attached to bodies and actions. Thus, eroticization and pleasure provide an opportunity to transform the pain and social rejection experienced by Mexican women writers. At the same time, BDSM manifests itself as a practice charge with the necessary affect to trouble the literary system from the standpoint of pleasure. The pain of the whip, the humiliation games, and the erotization of rope play are scenarios in which Rodríguez Mendoza explores her role as a woman writer. She concludes that her "caligrafía shibari" (*shibari* calligraphy), as she calls it, creates a space to redefine the figure of the Mexican writer not solely as a monolithic category of identification, but rather as a product of multiple affects, encompassing context, imagination, actions, bodily pleasures, and the material conditions under which one writes. It seems to me that Rodríguez Mendoza complicates what a woman writer can do, especially when she knows it can get messy. Her *crónicas* demonstrate that the Mexican intellectual sphere continues to be terrified of female cuir pleasure, and the affective vulnerability that this fear mobilizes is useful to position herself amid the lettered city.

There is a lingering question suggested by the title of this section that points to the complexity of hiring a pro Dom in times of #RopaSucia. Writing about BDSM in a sociopolitical context where the eroticization of violence is prevalent is not without challenges, and it requires an ethics of writing that is aware of the context from which it emerges. This is not unfamiliar to Rodríguez Mendoza. In fact, her *crónicas* begin straightforwardly with this issue. The first question that the author asked the psychologist Omar Feliciano, who also studies and practices BDSM, was how pertinent it is to talk about the topic in the context of gender violence: "¿Qué tan pertinente es hablar de BDSM en México en un momento en el que pasan cosas horribles como el asno de Ciudad Juárez que abusó de la conductora y luego Televisa hizo lo propio?" (How relevant is it to talk about BDSM in Mexico at a time when horrible things happen, like the jerk from Ciudad Juárez who abused the host and then Televisa did the same?)[17] The example refers to a case of sexual harassment that occurred during the live Mexican TV show *A toda máquina*, where the host Enrique Tovar inappropriately touched the host Tania Reza, who left the set clearly upset. Despite the public's reactions to the video, which also identified the incident as sexual harassment without any kind of nuance—something surprising in a country where opinions on these issues are usually sharply divided—Televisa broadcasted a video where both hosts explained that it was a planned joke. However, Televisa's painful attempt at damage control did not change the public opinion.

In response to Rodríguez Mendoza's query, Feliciano affirmatively addresses the issue by highlighting the feminist perspective on this sexual practice:

> La visión feminista de estos actos tiene que ver con la vulnerabilidad, la elección, con el daño y con la explotación. Son cuatro ejes en los que el feminismo puede arrojar luz sobre este tipo de prácticas, en un contexto donde las mujeres son explotadas, violadas y asesinadas. El contexto es muy pertinente. Aquí la palabra clave es *agencia*: la posibilidad que un sujeto tiene de incidir en el mundo; el tema de la agencia de las mujeres, la posibilidad de elegir actuar y de actuar con intención.[18]

> The feminist perspective on these acts is related to vulnerability, choice, harm, and exploitation. These are four axes through which feminism can shed light on these types of practices, in a context where women are exploited, raped, and murdered. The context is highly relevant. Here, the key word is *agency*: the capacity a subject has to affect the world; the issue of women's agency, the ability to choose to act and to act with intention.

Similar to Feliciano's decision to explore BDSM as a form of agency, Rodríguez Mendoza *chooses* to write with *intention* on a taboo topic, recognizing its potential to explore the different types of agency that women writers have in a heteropatriarchal environment that eroticizes violence, allowing them to carve out a space for themselves in the public sphere. This simultaneously exposes the hypocrisy and the sex negativity prevalent in the literary system concerning women's sexuality. Despite the messiness, hiring a professional

Dom and documenting the experience, amid a constant stream of reports on harassment and violence against women and other "minoritized" bodies, is a productive cuir-feminist endeavor that unravels the layers upon layers of the damage left by the pedagogies of cruelty in Mexican society.

In a manner akin to the re-victimizing discourse faced by survivors of gender violence, Rodríguez Mendoza concludes the *crónicas* by recalling her friends' reactions: "Muchos amigos hombres, muy queridos todos, me dijeron que no escribiera esto, pero ¿no es una nueva forma de decir: 'No te pongas minifalda porque te van a violar'? Hubo muchos que me alentaron y cuidaron en el proceso: a todos ellos, muchas gracias. ¡Sí me gustó!" (Many male friends, all very dear to me, told me not to write this, but isn't that just a new way of saying, "Don't wear a miniskirt because you'll get raped"? There were many who encouraged and supported me throughout the process: to all of them, thank you so much. And yes, I enjoyed it!)[19] This quote highlights why hiring a Dom can be an act of feminist agency within the context of the erotization of violence. It also clarifies that despite the negativity and discouragement, Rodríguez Mendoza was not left alone in the process, and she had friends who cared for her and encouraged her writing. Besides, Rodríguez Mendoza is not the only one using BDSM as a messy tactic to position herself in the literary environment. There is also the work of writers and artists who preceded her, engaging in irreverent attempts to take control of their "perverted" sexuality and writings while troubling the walls of the lettered sphere in the Mexico of the sixties.

Perverting the Canon: Turning to Masochism in Heteropatriarchal Times

During the 1950s and 1960s, Mexico underwent a significant cultural transformation that brought about changes in gender and sexuality. One notable change was the professionalization of women writers, led by authors such as Josefina Vicens, Rosario Castellanos, and Elena Garro in the 1950s. Until that period, women had been systematically excluded from national culture, making it extremely challenging for them to earn a living through writing. However, with the gradual incorporation of women into the public sphere, the conditions of production started to change, and women writers began to engage in professional writing. An illustrative example is Rosario Castellanos, who not only studied at the Facultad de Filosofía y Letras at UNAM and wrote for the most important newspapers of the period but also, through her writing, was able to teach and eventually became Mexico's ambassador in Israel. Another significant example highlighting changes in the conditions of production is the establishment of the Miguel Lanz Duret literary award in 1941 by the news journal *El Universal*. This award recognized the work of many women writers, thereby altering the landscape by granting them visibility and symbolic cultural capital.

A second change had to do with the reconfiguration of the relationship between eroticism and aesthetics. Sexual moralism prevailed in Mexican literature until a group of mostly male writers decided to challenge sexual taboos shortly before the sexual liberation movement began in the late 1960s in response to the cultural climate of disappointment that permeated the country. By the end of the 1950s, the promises of the Mexican Revolution had not been fulfilled, and socialism was no longer seen as a viable solution to national politics. Therefore, in 1956, a small group of writers interrupted the scene in Mexico City to break away from the nationalist and pamphleteering trend that sought to expose the failures of the revolution, escape provincialism, and find venues to express themselves freely.[20] The group proposed a re-conceptualization of art and a new way of understanding Mexico, and its global relations, through eroticism. As a result, there was a simultaneous reorganization of gender and sexuality in Mexican literature and the intellectual sphere, enabling cuir dissident attitudes as a way of doing politics and thinking about aesthetics.

There is no agreed-upon way to name this group of writers and artists. They are known by various names such as the "generación de medio siglo," "generación de la Casa del Lago," "de la *Revista de literatura mexicana*," or "la generación de la insolencia," as suggested by member Huberto Batis. There is no tacit agreement on the members of this generation, either. Besides Batis, the frequently associated members include Carlos Valdés, Juan Vicente Melo, Sergio Pitol, Tomás Segovia, Jorge Ibargüengoitia, Juan García Ponce, Salvador Elizondo, and Inés Arredondo. Some of these writers collaborated in journals like the *Revista de literatura mexicana* or *S.Nob*. They shared a cosmopolitan vision, an avid intellectual and critical awareness, a contrary stance to nationalist tendencies, and an interest in the relationship between literature and the sacred.[21] What interests me is the fascination some of these writers held toward George Bataille's and Pierre Klossowski's ideas on eroticism.

Broadly speaking, these philosophers viewed eroticism as counternarrative to rational modernity, religious tradition, and the bourgeois economy of accumulation and social productivity. In Mexico, in accordance with their ideas, eroticism was seen as a means of breaking free from the constraints of national discourses, promoting an aesthetic that disavowed any coherent political discourse. Writers such as Salvador Elizondo and Juan García Ponce perceived eroticism as a form of transgression beneficial for advocating the collapse of singular meanings and absolutist discourses. Consequently, this transgression serves as a refreshing way to understand the world after the political disappointment of socialism. During this period of cultural reorganization, the prevailing notion was that art should take a political stance, and eroticism emerged as a potential means of escaping the alleged limitations of political compromise.[22]

According to Bataille and Klossowski, eroticism is not merely about sexual pleasure; rather, it is a potent force that transcends everyday experience, leading to a profound transformation of the individual.[23] Viewed as an aesthetic practice, eroticism has the ability to captivate the reader, diverting attention from the meaning of discourse and encouraging an embrace of the rupture or rapture of *jouissance*. For the French philosophers, this experience is unattainable without engaging in transgressive practices linked to taboos, such as voyeurism and D/s dynamics: "What Bataille enables is focus on how taboo structures of morality can be *transgressed* in a complimentary erotic process that *returns*... as *jouissance*—and how pre-Platonic cultures develop sacred rituals for its structured affirmation."[24] Since eroticism involves a transgressive breaking of boundaries and taboos, *jouissance* is perceived as an instant of pure pleasure that arises from surrendering the self to the unknown and the irrational.

Bataille's conception of eroticism, specifically his idea that eroticism is a violent transgression perpetuating the objectification of women, reinforces patriarchal power structures. According to Bataille, eroticism involves a ritualized exchange between a victimizer (masculine) and a victim (feminine), reducing femininity to passivity, to mere objects of male desire: "[women] put themselves forward as objects for the aggressive desire of men."[25] In his view, women's sexuality is portrayed as something to be consumed and controlled, with their lack of subjectivity serving as a marker of difference and a site of transgression. Klossowski adds to this by asserting that the presumed perverted condition of femininity cannot be dissociated from the masculine gaze.[26] The masculine gaze operates as an imaginary frame for feminine transgression, suggesting that women exist primarily to be looked at and desired by men. This perspective defines women's sexuality in relation to men's desires. These ideas about eroticism rooted in essentialist notions about gender and sexuality perpetuate heteropatriarchal structures in Mexican fiction of the time. This formulation is evident in the works of Juan García Ponce, such as his numerous short stories like "El gato" (the cat), novels like *La cabaña* (The cabin; 1969) or *Inmaculada o los placeres de la inocencia* (Immaculate, or the pleasures of innocence; 1989), and in his theoretical pieces such as *Teología y pornografía* (Theology and pornography; 1975). Additionally, it serves as the theoretical basis for Salvador Elizondo's *Farabeuf o la crónica de un instante*, which, as mentioned in the introduction, constitutes Ave Barrera's project of feminist restoration in her novel *Restauración*.

As the only woman writer often associated with the "generación de la insolencia," Inés Arredondo's short stories bring to the fore a complex link between the group's aesthetics and gender dynamics. Most of Arredondo's work is complicit with what I call the masculine view of eroticism, exemplified by these ideas. Nonetheless, her short stories also reveal spaces of agency and moments when her female characters possess an embodied subjectivity. At the same time, Arredondo proposes a re-articulation of eroticism itself by suggesting that masochism, and the vulnerable state experienced during play, can be practiced in a way that reconfigures gender roles. My proposal is reading Arredondo's work through the lens of masochism to illuminate how a woman negotiated being a "pervert" in a heteropatriarchal time.

Sadomasochism is an extremely marginalized sexual practice that focuses on the ritualized exchange of power between two or more people. As a sexual practice, it is a type of role-play that enacts a pre-written scene where the masochist is willing to give up control to the sadist, to renounce their agency with the purpose of pleasure. Since it is a practice in which subjects reconfigure their own relationship to power by manipulating bodies and pleasures, s/m dynamics can be liberating. Michel Foucault emphasizes sadomasochism as a creative enterprise to explore new possibilities of pleasure not necessarily attached to sexuality, gender, or genital practices of pleasure.[27] Thus, BDSM can operate to destabilize gender roles. Additionally, masochism implies an extreme self-degradation that pushes the subject to embrace radical vulnerability as a space of multiplicity. For Bataille, this multiplicity emerges from the violent rupture provoked by the rapture of *jouissance* that annihilates the self and erases differences. Instead of violence, the focus on vulnerability produces a moment of empathy "as way of feeling through another" that transforms rather than unmakes the self, leaving a "lacuna of sensations and feelings" that binds things together.[28] This vulnerability in combination with the creativity of BDSM produces a momentary critical freedom to experiment and redraw traditional power relations.

The theoretical shift that I propose from eroticism to masochism, more than a novel approach, suggests an affective cuir move that avoids the trap of projecting contemporary understandings of sexuality back in time because the relationship between eroticism and literary language as theorized by Bataille in *Inner Experience* leaves room for messy interpretations. For this philosopher, language and eroticism are two similar types of perversion that function as "a support for ripping" and disrupt meaning.[29] In literature, language is deployed in a manner that is "different from its 'normal' purpose, such as the smooth communication of messages," perverting the function of ordinary language.[30] Like the erotic encounter, poetry is also an act of sacrifice where words are liberated from their utilitarian function to lead the way from the known to the unknown.[31] To decipher literary language, one requires a particular mode of reading that emphasizes the affects produced by the erotic encounter—that is, a mode of reading that is attentive to the sensations aroused in the reader.[32]

Since the interpretation of the literary work depends on the sensations felt by the reader and language is a perverted discourse that leads to the unknown, any reading that privileges perversion and *jouissance* is a fair interpretation for Bataillean texts. While one could argue that rejecting Bataille and Klossowski as the primary lens through which to understand Arredondo's work is a case of infidelity to the author's work itself (pun intended), turning to masochism as a mode of messy reading can help navigate the complicated aftermath of being a "perverted" woman in a patriarchal time. This mode of reading resembles queer theories of embodied reading that underscore the importance of the corporeal and the affective links between reader, text, and the writer.[33] Moreover, this type of cuir/queer reading implies an ethics of undoing the material and immaterial harm done by structures of oppression. Turning to masochism can be seen as a form of restorative criticism because it unravels the theoretical interventions done by Arredondo.

BDSM and Female Pleasure as Restorative Criticism in "Mariana"

A restorative reading of Inés Arredondo's work through a masochistic theoretical lens proposes that the influence of eroticism in her writing is not as straightforward as it first appears. Throughout her life, Arredondo published three collections of short stories: *La señal* (The sign; 1965), *Río subterráneo*

(Underground river; 1979), and *Los espejos* (The mirrors; 1988). Although eroticism plays an important role in all her books, there is a subtle change between *La señal* and the following books that, despite having been noticed by literary critics who have studied eroticism in Arredondo's short stories, is simply explained as the result of reaching her maturity as a writer. This change, however, has more to do with the influence of Bataillean thought than maturity. When Arredondo published *La señal*, the presence of both Bataille's and Klossowski's thought was still new and developing.

The influence of Bataille in Latin America began in the mid-1960s with Julio Cortázar's *Rayuela* (*Hopscotch*; 1963) and in Mexico with *Figura de paja* (Straw figure; 1964) by Juan García Ponce and *Farabeuf* (1965) by Salvador Elizondo. As Juan Carlos Ubilluz explains, the first Spanish translation of *L'érotisme* appeared in the Argentine magazine *Sur* in 1969.[34] In the case of Klossowski's work, its translations to Spanish began to circulate in the seventies along with *Teología y pornografía* (1975) and *La errancia sin fin* (The endless wandering; 1981), Juan García Ponce's books about this philosopher. Although most of the writers of la "generación de la insolencia" read these French philosophers in their original language, this genealogy shows that the spread of their ideas in Latin America occurs with more force at the end of the sixties. Thus, the publication of *La señal* precedes the widespread dissemination of this discourse. Besides, after divorcing Tomás Segovia in 1965, Inés Arredondo strengthened her relationship with Juan García Ponce and Huberto Batis, which most likely nourished the exchange of ideas to the point where the treatment of eroticism in García Ponce and Arredondo became very similar. I propose to read *La señal* as a collection of short stories where Arredondo theorizes eroticism from the positionality of a "perverted" woman and expresses doubts about this sexual discourse because it formulates power in terms of possession and reproduces this notion as a gendered binary, one where the woman is always portrayed in terms of lack. Ultimately, I imply that Arredondo finds transgression in embracing sadomasochism as a cuir-feminist practice.

Three short stories—one from each book—have been identified by literary critics as pivotal to the development of Arredondo's aesthetics. Víctor Hugo Vásquez Rentería explains that these texts are different, differences that the scholar suggests account for the development of Arredondo's writing. Thus, as an earlier work, the short story "Mariana" is viewed as experimenting with "el sentimiento primitivo, el instinto básico: la necesidad de adueñamiento y de ser poseída" (the primitive feeling, the basic instinct: the need to dominate and to be possessed) without transforming this primitive physical impulse into something "más original" (more original) like she later does in "Las mariposas nocturnas" (The nocturnal butterflies).[35] However, it is not until "Sombra entre sombras" (shadow among shadows) when Arredondo supposedly achieves "[la] suma total de toda una concepción del mundo ... la realización de un proyecto de vida, en el cual la salvación no es otra cosa sino la entrega definitiva y definitoria, a lo que se quiere" ([the] total sum of an entire worldview ... the realization of a life project, in which salvation is nothing other than the ultimate and defining surrender to what one desires).[36] What is astonishing to me is that several critics share more or less this reading (Fabienne Bradu, Berenice Romano Hurtado, and Huberto Batis to mention a few). These short stories represent different ways of relating to Bataille and Klossowski's ideas with "Sombra entre sombras" being the one that adheres more closely to their vision of eroticism—this is why the reading proposed by Vásquez Rentería is pervasive among Arredondo's scholarship. The issue that I have with this reading is that it assumes that the erotic discourse of Arredondo reaches its full potential once she manages to perfectly imitate the in vogue masculine philosophical claims about eroticism. As I will elaborate in the following pages, Arredondo's originality and transgression lies in "Mariana" as a short story that outlines a theory of sexual desire that proposes a sadomasochistic cuir turn, one in which the political value of eroticism lies in paying attention to the vulnerability at play of the bodies engaging in a consensual D/s dynamic instead of the very masculine idea of *jouissance*, violence, and the *petite mort*. In other words, "Mariana" offers a restorative critique of Bataille's ideals.

It is important to note that it is time to review the work of Arredondo to incorporate newer reading methodologies like the one I propose here to exert a criticism that seeks to restore the damage done by heteropatriarchal discourses. In this vein, much of the work done so far revolves around the task of uncovering the work of this writer that has been excluded from the canon far too long. This recovery has been done by members of the Taller de Teoría y Crítica Literaria Diana Morán (1984), a group focused on the study of literature with a gender perspective. Moreover, literary criticism has followed four traditional lines when approaching Arredondo's work: a biographical approach (Claudia Albarrán and Graciela Martínez-Zalce); an effort to insert the work of Inés Arredondo in the history of Mexican literature (Aline Pettersson and Fabienne Bradu); formal analysis centered in the identification of style, literary trends, and topics (Luz Elena Gutiérrez de Velasco, Erica Frouman-Smith, and Brianda Domecq); and finally, a comparative approach (Aralia López González, Luz Elena Zamudio Rodríguez, and

Ana Rosa Domenella). A cuir approach gives Arredondo's work a new vitality, which adds to the feminist efforts of some of these scholars by expanding how gender and sexuality operate in her short stories as an epistemological turn to theorize eroticism in a novel way in Mexican literature—that is, the sadomasochistic cuir turn.

Before delving into the analysis of "Mariana," it is important to demonstrate how "Sombra entre sombras" and "Las mariposas nocturnas" more closely adhere to the precepts proposed by the French philosophers. As previously mentioned, this adherence is regarded as a positive trait and a sign of Arredondo's maturity as a writer, as recognized by scholars. However, I believe the issue lies not so much in how Arredondo writes these short stories but in why criticism insists on labeling them as masterpieces above "Mariana." In other words, the problem is not inherent to the work of the writer but in the reading methods that privilege certain aesthetics and traits while obscuring women writers' original contributions and disruptions.

Both short stories take place in small rural towns, in times of feudalism, and involve three people with power imbalances—the cacique, a servant, and an innocent girl. Even though the reader witnesses a D/s dynamic where the female characters verbally agree to play, BDSM practices are not represented here since there is no informed consent, and the dominant does not take responsibility for the physical and emotional damage inflicted on the submissive. There is also no consideration about female pleasure to the point of even denying female subjectivity and their agency. In these short stories, the female characters engage in different types of *edgeplay* without risk awareness nor critical consent. BDSM communities identify two types of practitioners—those who perform practices that are considered safe, sane, and consensual; and those who practice risk awareness and critical consent. While the first ones avoid *edgeplay*, the latter engage in more risky practices such as choking and blood play. What the reader is witnessing is emotional and sexual abuse disguised as an erotic practice tied to heteropatriarchal understandings of sexuality, gender, and power.

Narrated in the first person by a nameless protagonist that only regains her name after the death of her husband, "Sombra entre sombras" tells the story of a fifteen-year-old girl whose mother convinces her to marry Ermilo—the town's forty-seven-year-old cacique—to avoid a life of poverty "llena de hijos, de platos sucios y de ropa que lavar" (Full of children, dirty dishes, and clothes to wash).[37] The protagonist is not aware of the rumors surrounding Ermilo's sex life, which lead Doña Asunción (the bride's mother) to question Ermilo's intentions without telling her daughter, Laura. But Ermilo assures the mother that he would never corrupt the purity and morality of her daughter. As the reader anticipates, after the wedding, Ermilo includes the protagonist in his sexual games.

Ermilo is a sadist who likes to inflict pain to later play the role of the caretaker. His sexual encounters involve the use of fetish objects such as masks, and practices such as humiliation, physical and emotional torture, and even rape. Sexual assault is insinuated by Laura's feelings of fear and hate that leave her petrified to the point of wishing her own death. During sexual encounters, the physical torture is so intense that Laura requires stitches and remains isolated until the bruises disappear. The story only gets more twisted as time goes by, ending with a decrepit seventy-two-year-old woman performing sexual acts in a house covered with semen and vomit.

Despite being the only short story of those analyzed here narrated from the point of view of the victim, Laura's voice is mediated by her traumatic experiences. One can even argue that she suffers from Stockholm syndrome, a condition that causes hostages to develop psychological alliances with their captors. This reading is supported by how Laura describes her situation as a prisoner where "todo está cerrado y enrejado" (Everything is closed and barred), which forces her to live in isolation while grasping for the little moments of pleasure and peace—such as eating ice cream or attending her wounds—given by her own captors.[38] By the end of the story, Laura has been stripped out of almost her entire subjectivity. I say almost because this is the moment when the reader finally learns the name of the protagonist, regaining some humanity back. At this point, the protagonist is described as a toothless old body that is only worth something because she is a sexual object still capable of "chupar" (lick) and to "cumplen conmigo sus más abyectas y feroces fantasías" (they fulfill with me their most abject and fierce fantasies).[39] This attempt to restore her humanity fails and ultimately Laura will never be free.

By forcibly erasing her subjectivity, Laura becomes the empty vessel necessary to experience Bataille's *jouissance*. "Sombra entre sombras," which critics consider the masterpiece of Arredondo's work, follows the masculine recipe of eroticism without deviating too far from it. However, Arredondo still demonstrates the damaging implications of this discourse, showcasing, for example, the material consequences of eroticism on women's bodies. Additionally, Arredondo continues to manifest discomfort with the idea of eliminating any trace of subjectivity from her female characters. This is exemplified by what appears to be a last-minute decision in naming her character, though I believe it is a carefully calculated move. Lastly, the title "Sombra entre sombras" could be seen as a direct critique of Batailleah thought. It suggests that all characters are shadows in a diffuse narrative where no one seems to explore their sexual desires in a pleasurable and sustainable way.

In "Las mariposas nocturnas," Arredondo more openly resists and redraws the damaging aspects of theorizing eroticism from the standpoint of masculinity. Narrated by the servant Lótar, the plot of this short story revolves around a complicated D/s relation between Don Hernán, Lótar, and Lía. A difference between Lía and Laura is that the first is willing to submit to Hernán in exchange of knowledge. As the story develops, Lía becomes more knowledgeable to the point of taking care of the *hacienda* and learning new languages while also performing the ideal model of patriarchal femininity—an immaculate and beautiful possession to display. At this point, Lía has replaced Lótar, who is not even included in the sexual acts anymore. Feeling wounded, Lótar expresses doubts about Lía to Don Hernán who ultimately dismisses his concerns. According to Lótar, Lía is not the innocent young woman that she once was but a dangerous being capable of agency: "Solamente faltaba un paso . . . para que ella fuera soberana absoluta" (Only one step was missing . . . for her to become the absolute sovereign), says Lótar.[40] This last step occurs during the final ritual performed by the characters:

> Esta vez, como las otras, Lía, desnuda, parecía una estatua. Él le abrochó al cuello un collar de esmeraldas de las compradas en el viaje. Comenzaba el rito acostumbrado. Pero cuando, con otro collar en las manos, se acercó a ella de frente, para colocárselo, la estatua se movió intempestivamente y sus brazos rodearon a don Hernán atrayéndolo hacia sí. Hubo un momento infinito en el que no se movieron, luego él la rechazó con violencia haciéndola caer hacia atrás. Ya firme sobre sus pies, ella lo miró con una mirada seca, despreciativa, se arrancó el collar y se lo arrojó a la cara.[41]

> This time, like the others, Lía, naked, seemed like a statue. He fastened a necklace of emeralds, bought on the trip, around her neck. The usual ritual began. But when, with another necklace in hand, he approached her from the front to put it on her, the statue suddenly moved, and her arms wrapped around Don Hernán, pulling him toward her. There was an infinite moment in which they didn't move, then he violently rejected her, making her fall backward. Once steady on her feet, she looked at him with a dry, disdainful gaze, tore off the necklace, and threw it at his face.

As the passage suggest, Lía breaks her role as a statue and regains her subjectivity. The story ends with Lía leaving the hacienda empty-handed but with the possibility of a new life.

In this short story, Arredondo fictionalizes her epistemological doubts about eroticism as a cruel optimistic discourse for women and other feminized bodies. As Lauren Berlant explains, "a relation of cruel optimism exists when something you desire is actually an obstacle to your flourishing."[42] Even when Lía manifests her desire toward Don Hernán and their sexual practices, she also recognizes her precarious positionality as a poor woman without a network of support, situation that puts her at risk. Like Laura, what makes Lía a good candidate for Don Hernán's rituals is that she is a young poor woman that does not have any authority figure in her life and poses an uncontrollable eagerness for knowledge—Lía is presented as an empty vessel that only Hernán has the means to fill. However, the short story ends differently than "Sombra entre sombras." Instead of remaining a statue, an object like Laura, Lía acquires a life of her own through knowledge, which ultimately grants her what Lótar sees as absolute sovereignty. Here lies Arredondo's gendered disruption—Lía never loses her subjectivity. On the contrary, one could argue that she only gains more power as she gains more knowledge, ultimately breaking free from the victim-victimizer ritual.

In a way, Lía is a character who faces a crossroads, that of being simultaneously complicit and rebellious to Don Hernán's erotic rituals. Before moving on to "Mariana," it is necessary to clarify that even when Lía voluntarily remains in the relationship, the question of whether consent is exercised or not is messy. Lía verbally agrees to Don Hernán's proposition but Lótar deliberately conceals the most sinister details and manipulates her economic precarity in favor of his master. Both male characters isolate Lía and make her dependent of their games. Thus, critical consent is not exercised, and once more the reader faces a story of sexual abuse. Of course, this does not take away Lía's agency who at the end decides that the price is too high to pay and abandons the abusive D/s dynamic.

In my view, the short story "Mariana" is the first in which Arredondo explores power relations and D/s dynamics from a feminist and cuir standpoint. The fact that the protagonist's name is also the title of the short story suggests that the plot differs from the other short stories I have analyzed. The name Mariana has two possible origins; according to Hebrew etymology, it means a beautiful woman chosen by God, while the Greek origin refers to a rebellious woman. In Arredondo's story, Mariana is a beautiful and rebellious woman who enjoys consensual non-normative sexual practices, involving masochism, erotic asphyxiation, and impact play. Erotic asphyxiation and impact play are common BDSM practices. The first one refers to the intentional restriction of oxygen to the brain for sexual gratification and it is considered a high-risk practice. The latter involves striking a person for sexual gratification, using a variety of instruments such as whips, floggers, paddles, or even bare hands. Done correctly, it is not considered a high-risk practice.

The plot summary is simple: Mariana falls in love with one of her classmates, Fernando, but her father opposes their relationship. The father is depicted as an antiquated man who still thinks women are mere objects at his disposition. Thus, Mariana and Fernando decide to run away. After some time, the couple returns to seek the family's forgiveness and get married. Years pass by, they have four kids, and everything seems normal until Mariana's husband is imprisoned in an insane asylum awaiting castration. The reader then learns that the couple liked to practice choking and water breath play (drowning), types of activities known as breath control that are considered *edgeplay* due to their high death-risk factor. Choking involves the restriction of breath and blood supply to the brain by applying pressure to the blood-rich carotid arteries, while water breath play restricts breathing. Both activities may or may not include loss of consciousness and, if done improperly, can cause death. Fernando is inexperienced and accidentally loses control, and chokes and immerses Mariana in water until she passes out. Not realizing what is happening, Fernando thinks he has killed Mariana. The family finds out and decides to intervene, sending Fernando to an asylum while leaving Mariana devastated and attempting futilely to explain that it was a consensual act for the purpose of erotic pleasure.

However, the story of Mariana begins with her funeral. At the end of the story, the reader discovers that Mariana was killed by a stranger. The story is narrated in the first person by one of Mariana's female friends, who is attempting to uncover the truth about what happened. As the plot unfolds, the reader is challenged to piece together the events through the narrator's investigations and the testimonies of Fernando, Concha Zazueta (a childhood friend), and Mariana's killer. By the end, the reader can organize the facts and gain clarity on the plot. Following her forced separation from Fernando, Mariana desperately searches for some form of relief and continues to engage in breath play with strangers until she eventually dies of erotic suffocation at the hands of an inexperienced stranger in a hotel room.

In "Mariana," Arredondo delves into sadomasochism to explore pleasure from a gendered standpoint. The first thing that the reader notices is that the relationship between Fernando and Mariana is equal, which is unlike the other two stories. Both characters are close in age, economic status, education, and have families. They met at school, where they had friends and their own lives. Over time, Mariana and Fernando built a trusting relationship. Although we as readers do not have access to their negotiation process, the way they relate to each other suggests that there is mutual consent. There is no manipulation, social isolation, or power imbalances such as economic precarity. With these characteristics, "Mariana" is already quite different from "Sombra entre sombras" and "Las mariposas nocturnas." However, Arredondo's breakthrough lies in crafting a complex female character whose subjectivity and sexual pleasure are central to the development of the plot.

Mariana is depicted as a strong, intelligent woman who continually challenges the authority figures in her life. She is never presented as a powerless victim or empty object, but as someone that enjoys relinquishing control—momentarily suspending her agency—in exchange for sexual gratification and pleasure. When contextualizing the history of masochism, Amber Musser explains that the naturalization of women's submission "made it difficult for psychiatrists to imagine a separate category of female masochists," thus women were not usually considered as such.[43] This patriarchal naturalization is at play in the discourses of eroticism as well as in part of Arredondo's work. However, instead of reproducing transgression as something obtained through the naturalization of the negation of women's autonomy to gain pleasure, Arredondo presents female masochism as a practice that can manipulate bodies and power relations to illuminate forms of organization outside the heteropatriarchal norm. This is in line with Deleuze's ideas on masochism as a discourse of disavowal and suspense, aiming to dialectically imagine a counterpart to the world capable of containing its violence and excess.[44] Thus, Arredondo uses masochism as a critical act to restore women's pleasure and agency, suggesting vulnerability as the key to transgress the meaning of language.

In "Mariana," there is an admiration for perverted sex practices but also a desire to think about power differently. Arredondo plays with the eroticization of power—not the power of eroticism—in connection to gender and heteropatriarchal structures, connections that other scholars such as Foucault have ignored. Thus, my restorative criticism of "Mariana" entails recognizing this short story as an epistemological turn where Arredondo proposes a novel theoretical approach using masochism to highlight the blind spots of Bataille and Klossowski's proposals. To support this argument, I pay attention to a series of elements that show how Arredondo proposes new ways of understanding eroticism. These elements are the gaze, Mariana's ending, and the messy structure of the short story.

The gaze of the characters is a recurring motif in "Mariana," serving as a structural unit that holds theoretical significance as the pivotal moment of pleasure. Mariana's eyes or gaze is mentioned in every scene, emphasizing the significance of looking as a vital component of her subjectivity. For instance, consider the following passage:

>—¿Por qué viniste pintada?
>—Era peor que vieran esto. Fíjense.
>>Y metió el labio inferior entre los dientes para que pudiéramos ver el borde de abajo: estaba partido en pequeñísimas estrías y la piel completamente escoriada, aunque cubierta de pintura.
>—¿Qué te pasó?
>—Fernando
>—¿Qué te hizo Fernando?
>>Ella sonrió y se encogió de hombros, mirándonos con lástima.[45]

>—Why did you come painted?
>—It was worse for them to see this. Look.
>>And she pressed her lower lip between her teeth so that we could see the bottom edge: it was split into tiny ridges and the skin completely raw, although covered in paint.
>—What happened to you?
>—Fernando.
>—What did Fernando do to you?
>>She smiled and shrugged, looking at us with pity.

Mariana's refusal to answer the question verbally, coupled with her expression of pity, suggests that her bruises might not be the result of sexual abuse, but rather that something else is going on. This becomes even clearer when, on other occasions, Mariana's gaze operates in the opposite way, emphasizing the authoritarian violence exerted on female bodies that has been normalized to the point of passing unnoticed. As an example, when Mariana's father slaps her multiple times for dating Fernando, the scene is described as follows: "Estaba tan furioso que todos sentimos miedo, pero Mariana no. Se quedó quieta, mirándolo. Entonces la soltó y se fue" (He was so angry that we all felt fear, but Mariana did not. She stayed still, looking at him. Then he let go of her and left).⁴⁶ The next day, her friends asked Mariana what had happened to her face, and she lied, saying that she had fallen. In this case, there is no room for interpretation: Mariana is suffering abuse from her father. In these examples, the gaze emphasizes Mariana as a woman who is not afraid to fight back against the heteropatriarchal and normative structures that oppress her persona and sexuality. At the same time, the gaze makes us—the readers—accomplices in the normalization of violence and the reproduction of sexual morality.

The sophistication of Arredondo's theoretical approach to eroticism and the gaze reaches its peak with Fernando's testimony: "Fue ella la que me mostró sus ojos en un acto inocente. Impúdico. Otra vez sin mirada, sin fondo, incapaces de ser espejos, totalmente vacíos de mí. Luego los volvió hacia los médanos y se quedó inmóvil" (It was she who showed me her eyes in an innocent act. Shameless. Once again without gaze, without depth, incapable of being mirrors, completely empty of me. Then she turned them toward the dunes and remained motionless).⁴⁷ If Klossowski argues that women's perverted condition cannot be dissociated from the masculine gaze, which in turn operates as a mirror, Mariana's eyes are incapable of functioning this way.⁴⁸ Thus, Mariana's perversion is not associated to Fernando. Instead of mimicking the violent power relations of the real world, Arredondo proposes masochism as a political practice capable of staging these relations to explore new conceptualizations of power, specifically one that exposes the natural assumptions surrounding gender, feminized bodies, vulnerability, and submission.

In *Dominatrix*, Danielle J. Lindemann shows how sadomasochism has implications beyond the sexual sphere. Drawing from Judith Butler's work on the practice of drag, Lindemann argues that by caricaturing the practices of sadomasochism that are naturalized in everyday life, such as the father slapping her daughter as punishment for defiance, they are recontextualized. This recontextualization contributes to our understanding of their naturalization: "Sadomasochistic interactions are stylized representations of dominance and submission, but they are able to both lay bare and destabilize the taken-for-granted assumptions underlying such practices . . . in their putative reversal of gendered erotic roles, they actually provide an amplification of those roles as they exist in the 'real world.'"⁴⁹ What Lindemann lays out in this quote is what Arredondo is suggesting with her sadomasochistic turn. Arredondo recognizes S/M relations as performative acts and as a practice that tries out different routes for denaturalizing heteropatriarchal constraints, while the writer also considers how the material conditions of the bodies, such as financial stability, affect the disruptive potential of the performative component. Thus, masochism is presented as messy.

Fernando's testimony continues as follows,

> El furor que sentí el día de la boda, los celos terribles de que algo, alguien, pudiera hacer surgir aquella mirada helada en los ojos de Mariana, mi Mariana carnal, tonta; ... Furor y celos inmensos que me hicieron golpearla, meterla al agua, estrangularla, ahogarla, buscando siempre para mí la mirada que no era mía. Pero los ojos de Mariana, abiertos, siempre abiertos, sólo me reflejaban: con sorpresa, con miedo, con amor, con piedad. Recuerdo eso sobre todo, sus ojos bajo el agua, desorbitados, mirándome con una piedad intensa.[50]

> The fury I felt on the day of the wedding, the terrible jealousy that something, someone, could make that cold look appear in Mariana's eyes, my carnal Mariana, foolish; ... Fury and immense jealousy made me hit her, put her in the water, strangle her, drown her, always looking for the look that wasn't mine. But Mariana's eyes, open, always open, only reflected me: with surprise, with fear, with love, with pity. I remember that above all, her eyes under the water, wide open, looking at me with intense pity.

This passage provides clarity regarding the events that unfolded on the night Mariana lost consciousness. Fernando's words imply that his loss of control stemmed from jealousy and frustration, as he realized he could never possess Mariana. This loss of control disrupts the performative sadomasochistic scene, returning the characters to the realm of heteropatriarchal violence in the real world. It also symbolizes the rupture of critical consent. Once again, Mariana's gaze reveals the consequences of Fernando's actions. She pities him because he fails to fully comprehend the theatrical possibilities of sadomasochism and is unable to recontextualize them beyond heteropatriarchal frameworks. Considering this, the impeding chemical castration for Fernando holds a dual interpretation: it serves as a punishment for engaging in non-normative sexual practices, but it also signifies the danger of normalizing heteropatriarchal violence. Ultimately, Arredondo suggests that the elusive erotic piercing moment, which obsessed both Bataille as much as the rest of Arredondo's generation, cannot be achieved until gender roles are deconstructed.

As we are aware, Mariana dies at the end of the story, and this can be interpreted as a punishment for her sexual behavior. This interpretation implies that sadomasochism reinforces heteropatriarchal ideologies instead of challenging them, as the feminist panic of the 1980s in the US tried to demonstrate.⁵¹ However, this perspective hides a double-edged sword: it denies Mariana's agency while promoting a moralistic view of sexuality that ultimately portrays her as a victim. To avoid these detrimental interpretations, it is crucial to embrace a restorative criticism and a reparative mode of reading that acknowledges subtle nuances. This can be achieved by examining the various roles of the gaze in this short story or by shifting the interpretative lens from eroticism to masochism, thereby offering a more nuanced reading. As the master writer she is, Arredondo complicates the various elements that shape the story, including the fluctuating focus and the nonlinear organization of the plot. This method of storytelling encourages readers to pause and reflect on the unfolding events, discouraging simplistic interpretations by prompting deeper consideration of the plot. The structure of "Mariana" is messy and not a straightforward story like "Sombra entre sombras," but rather a narrative puzzle that prompts us to question everything—including Mariana's death.

Despite the risks highlighted by what happened with Fernando, Mariana is still actively seeking random encounters in hotel rooms to engage in sadomasochistic dynamics, even at the expense of her own life. To Mariana, sadomasochism serves as an embodied method for amplifying gender roles and sexual practices, as a method to restore herself after all the damage. It also becomes a coping mechanism for the physical and emotional abuse inflicted by her father and, most importantly, a ritualized power exchange that generates pleasure. Whether masochism implies complicity or ends up perpetuating the same power dynamics Mariana wants to escape is inconsequential because complicity can be a mode of self-fashioning and a source for agency that provides access to power and pleasure.

Mariana's decision to defy heteropatriarchal morality and embrace her non-normative life represents a courageous act of resistance. This act is even braver and more radical than merely dismissing masochism based on its potential dangers. While Mariana may find her individual freedom and pleasure sufficient for pursuing a life of perversion, these motivations alone do not suffice for a discourse that seeks to develop a literary language blended with eroticism as a theoretical statement. Deleuze argues that the purpose of pornographic literature is to challenge language by pushing it to its limits. According to Deleuze, this challenge can only be achieved by internally dividing language itself: "the imperative and descriptive function must transcend itself toward a higher function, the personal element turning by reflection upon itself into the impersonal."⁵² Arredondo employs various narrative techniques to surpass mere storytelling to politicize the reader's affective experience. By doing so, Arredondo shifts the focus of the narrative from the individual to the collective and the political, rather than the impersonal, as suggested by Deleuze.

Rogelio Arenas Montreal has already paid attention to the point of view of the story, as well as the different narrative techniques used by Arredondo to highlight the significant moments of Mariana's story. The story is narrated from the perspective of a nameless female friend who skillfully weaves together various narrative threads, supported by the testimonies of Concha Zazueta and Fernando. This narrator addresses an unspecified person who could very well be the reader. Arenas Montreal also suggests that Mariana is not a typical main character but rather "un gran objeto de referencias" (a great object of references)—references that only hold meaning under the scrutiny of others.[53] If in the first instance the protagonist of the story appears to be Mariana, the focalization suggests otherwise—the protagonists are the narrator and her interlocutor.

On several occasions, the narrator questions her own motivations for telling Mariana's story. The narrator claims that Mariana and Fernando "no necesitan testigos: lo son el uno del otro" (They don't need witnesses: they are witnesses to each other) yet she persists with her scrutiny: "Sé que te parece que hago mal, que es antinatural este encarnizamiento impúdico con una historia ajena. Pero no es ajena. También ha sucedido por ti y por mi.... La locura y el crimen.... ¿Pensaste alguna vez en que las historias que terminan como debe de ser quedan aparte, existen en un modo absoluto? En un tiempo que no transcurre?" (I know it seems to you that I'm doing wrong, that this shameless obsession with someone else's story is unnatural. But it's not someone else's. It has also happened because of you and me.... Madness and crime... Did you ever think that the stories that end as they should remain separate, exist in an absolute way? In a time that does not pass?)[54] As the quote shows, the story stops being solely about Mariana's sexual choices and becomes a story about sexuality in heteropatriarchal times. It is interesting that the nameless narrator is engaging in an act of cuir voyeurism, as she derives pleasure from observing Mariana on several occasions. Furthermore, the reader becomes entangled in this voyeuristic scene, where the act of reading symbolizes our consensual participation. Suddenly, the story is not about Mariana's individual erotic choices, but also about her friend's and even our own. With this perspective, Arredondo forces us to acknowledge that the issue at hand goes beyond Mariana's personal decisions. Instead, it revolves around the larger societal narratives and discourses that shape and define sexuality.

Lastly, the female voyeur-narrator interrupts the patriarchal objectification of the female body proposed by Bataille and Klossowski in two significant ways. First, the voyeur is a woman, breaking once more with the traditional male gaze. Second, the narrator's jouissance is linked to Mariana's masochism, a practice that involves consciously renouncing subjectivity to become an object in exchange for pleasure. By making Mariana an object of her gaze, the narrator restores Mariana's momentarily denied subjectivity, which had reduced her to the role of the victim, by revealing the layers upon layers of her story. By framing Mariana's story as an act of voyeurism, the narrator places female pleasure as the leitmotif of the plot. It is through pleasure that an act of cuir-feminist solidarity is performed among the participants. The story does not conclude with Mariana's death, but rather the realization that her life exemplifies the pursuit of absolute sovereignty, a pleasurable life, and a willingness to embrace vulnerability toward others as a modern way of thinking—ideas that remain seductive and productive for women writers in the twenty-first century as demonstrated by Rodríguez Mendoza's *crónicas*. The role of the female voyeur in "Mariana" is to transcend language to reveal what remains unspoken, such as violence but also the possibilities of vulnerability, female pleasure, and cuir dissidence.

Reading "Mariana" implicates readers in an act of voyeurism, where our interpretation holds the power to either reinforce heteropatriarchal views or embrace our complicity. Recognizing my own complicity, I choose to utilize S/M relations as means to delve into the intricate history of gender relations "in an idiom of pleasure," as Elizabeth Freeman suggests and as the voyeur-narrator implies.[55] Drawing on Freeman's words, the scandalous and transformative potential of BDSM lies in its capacity to employ bodily sensations in the deconstruction of traditional gender roles and sexual norms.[56] Engaging in a restorative critique of Arredondo's work becomes crucial, as it represents an epistemological shift that examines BDSM as a practice of cuir dissidence, challenging the harmful discourse of eroticism perpetuated by the men of her generation.

Kati Horna and Leonora Carrington's Complicity: Necrophilia and Other Fetish Gestures

S.Nob magazine disrupted the cultural scene of the 1960s with its informal and irreverent tone. Although the magazine lasted only a few months due to lack of funding (from June 20 to October 15, 1962), the seven issues published are considered one of the most ambitious undertakings of the "generación de la insolencia." *S.Nob* was sponsored by Gustavo Alatriste and created by Juan García Ponce, Emilio García Riera, and Salvador Elizondo. The magazine boldly combined traditional literary genres such as fiction, translations, and book reviews with a wide range of other texts, including cooking recipes, collages, gossip, and magic. This blend of content was further enhanced by the inclusion of scandalous topics such as drugs, sex, and violence, as announced in the first issue: "La nueva Revista abrirá a sus lectores las puertas de lo 'insólito'; en sus páginas los más destacados escritores y artistas darán libre curso a sus obsesiones, manías persecutorias, complejos de inferioridad, frustraciones, vicios secretos, fantasías 'eróticas,' y revelarán a través de ellas la verdadera imagen de nuestro mundo" (The new magazine will open to its readers the doors to the "insolent"; in its pages, the most prominent writers and artists will give free rein to their obsessions, persecutory delusions, inferiority complexes, frustrations, secret vices, "erotic" fantasies, and through them, will reveal the true image of our world).[57] The magazine became a space to openly explore the most controversial obsessions of this generation of writers and intellectuals.

The experimentation was such that Claudia Albarrán refers to *S.Nob* as a pilot laboratory where inexpert writers, tired of censorship and institutions, found space for new forms of expression.[58] Similarly, Jonathan P. Eburne suggests that the magazine was a "cultural upstart circulating *sine nobilitat* among the leading lights of the modernist nobility."[59] Eburne views *S.Nob* as a "regular digest of the contemporary arts" focused in contributing to emergent experimental literature in Mexico and tracing a new cosmopolitan genealogy away from literary nationalism.[60] The artists and writers that collaborated regularly in *S.Nob* were Jorge Ibargüengoitia, Juan Vicente Melo, Juan García Ponce, José de la Colina, Salvador Elizondo, and Tomás Segovia. Only four women participated in this magazine: the photographer Kati Horna with "Fetiches," the artist Leonora Carrington with the section "Children's Corner," Teresa Salazar with an essay about jazz, and the journalist Ana Cecilia Treviño, who, under the pen name Cecilia Gironella and Dalia Amadís de Gaula, published a section on geomancy.

Although the editors of *S.Nob* refused to adhere to a specific editorial line, one notable aspect of the magazine is its framing by Batailleans ideas. David A. J. Murrieta Flores has analyzed the influence of Bataille in this magazine in detail, specifically highlighting eroticism and Bataille's conception of inner experience as means to "undermine the entire apparatus not only of Mexican culture but culture at large."[61] As we have seen in the previous sections of this chapter, women's bodies are central to eroticism as objects of desire and transgression. Rumors say that Gustavo Alatriste suggested to Elizondo that the magazine could follow the *Playboy* style by including a section with naked women. Allegedly, this is the reason behind Horna's section.[62] However, and as Elizondo complained, the result of this section was different: "lo malo es que salían muy oscuras y en lugar de mostrar mujeres desnudas, mostraba puras sombras y parecían más artísticas de lo que eran" (The problem was that they came out too dark, and instead of showing naked women, they only showed shadows, and they seemed more artistic than they actually were).[63] Despite not adhering to a specific editorial line, one could argue that, for *S.Nob* magazine, women's bodies function as a political and aesthetic unit.

Beyond Horna's section, women are depicted as inanimate objects of worship, evil criminals who seduce men, or foolish and ill creatures. The fetishization of women's bodies was so prominent that the editors even claimed that *S.Nob* would transition from a weekly magazine to a "menstrual" one—a reference to women's "disruptive" periods. It is worth mentioning that the most notable examples of this fetishization can be found in the sections about medicine and criminology. As an example, Ibargüengoitia writes a humorous entry about the perils of marriage as a criminal institution that sacrifices men for women's satisfaction. This example, among others, reveals a willingness to challenge certain taboos and critique heteronormative institutions, but from a patriarchal standpoint.[64] As I mentioned before, during this period, women intellectuals began to be recognized as such, and men sensed their possible loss of power as gatekeepers of the literary sphere. Thus, the criticism of certain moralities and institutions in *S.Nob* reveals more about an anxious masculinity trying to preserve itself than a "genuine" sexual revolution.

"Fetiches," which appeared in four of the seven issues of *S.Nob*, stands out for its presentation of women's bodies in a different manner. Curated by Kati Horna, this section featured various female models and objects of worship, aiming to redefine the notion of fetishism beyond the objectification of women for male pleasure. The first series in this section, titled "Oda a la necrofilia" (Ode to necrophilia), explores alternative sexualities often associated with BDSM practices, such as voyeurism and necrophilia, and features artist Leonora Carrington as the model. The other series showcases Kitzia Poniatowska in "Impromptu con arpa" (Impromptu with harp), Luz del Amo in "Paraísos artificiales" (Artificial paradises), and Lucero in "Sacramentalia." Although the last photo-essay, "Sacramentalia," is credited to an unidentified artist named Berna. This indicates that it might not be the work of Horna. What unifies these photo essays is their redefinition of fetishism and women's bodies.

Exploring this body of work reveals that Arredondo was not the only one challenging the patriarchal gaze of eroticism. While Arredondo's "Mariana" presents a female masochist, Horna herself becomes a female fetishist, proposing a kind of fetishism that does not revolve around masculinity, the death drive, or violence. The epistemic turn enacted by Horna's collaborative project with Carrington differs from Arredondo's approach because these artists not only rearticulate eroticism to restore women's agency but also mock the masculine anxieties caused by the fear of castration and the perverted female body implied in such discourses.[65] In doing so, Horna's work gestures toward affect as an important tool for the practice of restorative criticism in heteropatriarchal times.

Borrowing Juana María Rodríguez's and José Esteban Muñoz's ideas on the gesture as something that "cannot or should not be expressed in words" and that sometimes can signal "what one wishes to keep outside of sound's reach," I identify a series of cuir gestures in "Oda a la necrofilia."[66] These gestures shed light on how these women navigated their non-normative sexual imaginaries withing a magazine that was aesthetically designed based on ideas about the annihilation of women's subjectivity. I interpret these gestures as meaningful actions because Horna's interest lay not in the aesthetic aspect of the photograph itself, but rather in the potential evocations through complicity and context.[67] To fully grasp the significance of Horna's photos, viewers must be willing to interpret these gestures and their affective residues beyond the confines of each individual photo. Otherwise, as Rodríguez suggests in her perspective on gestures, their impact may go unnoticed. The cuir gestures I identify in "Oda a la necrofilia" include the mask/corpse as a synecdoche of masculinity, the presence of the female fetishist and Leonora Carrington as disruptive devices, and the circulation of the photographs as an affective assemblage. These gestures form the structural foundation of the photo-essay, which aims to challenge the heteropatriarchal viewpoints of the "generación de la insolencia."

In "Oda a la necrofilia," the story of a woman grieving the loss of a loved one is depicted through seven photos.[68] The title itself suggests a connection between death and erotic pleasure. The model is portrayed in two contrasting ways: either dressed in a black outfit with a veil covering her face or completely naked, with her body contorted on the bed. This juxtaposition serves to emphasize the eroticism associated with death. Acting as a lifeless figure, a white mask without any identifying features represents the corpse.

The mourning process is accentuated by the chiaroscuro tones, with a single candle illuminating a private room, reminding the viewer of our role as witnesses to a personal moment of grief. As published by *S.Nob*, the identity of the model remains undisclosed. However, an unpublished photo in the series reveals Carrington's face through a mirror. In this image, Carrington is seen smoking a cigar while holding an umbrella in front of a window. Daylight subtly filters through the window, hinting at the conclusion of the grieving process. At the foot of the bed, a pair of men's shoes is the sole object that alludes to the identity hidden behind the white mask. This photo serves as the culmination of the narrative: an unnamed woman mourns the death of her lover, concluding her grieving journey with an erotic encounter that restores her identity and brings forth the possibility of a new and vibrant beginning.

Given Horna's complete creative freedom, it can be assumed that the decision not to publish this particular photo was intentional. However, the question remains: why withhold the key to what could be the climax in "Oda a la necrofilia"? I argue that concealing Carrington's identity prevents her fetishization and instead forces the viewer to pay attention to nuance: who is the fetishist and who is the object of fetishism in this photo-essay? By withholding the climax, Horna also redirects our attention from the death drive to the affect of the erotic encounter, suggesting a different relationship to the erotic moment, one that does not rely on violence but perhaps on collaboration and complicity.

David A. J. Murrieta Flores has already identified Horna's "Fetiches" as a challenge to *S.Nob*'s approach to women, and as photographs that depict an unconventional viewpoint to Bataille's eroticism.[69] I take his argument further to suggest that Horna opposes the classical definition of fetishism, proposing that the political power of eroticism lies in the vulnerability experienced through the complicit encounter with the other. The classical definitions of fetishism at play here are, on the one hand, the Freudian version, which fails to account for female fetishists as it associates fetishism with the fear of castration and the phallus. On the other hand, the Bataillean version which associates fetishism less with the subconscious world and more with the experience of real desires that can evoke a religious-like fervor centered on the death drive. Murrieta Flores explains how these different versions are present in Horna's photos:[70]

> Her lens exploits the Freudian suggestion that the fetish is a psychological substitute that compensates for the realization of the lack of a female phallus,

in the sense that the repression involved is invariably entangled with a contradiction.... The themes that guide Horla's [sic] series metaphorically assimilate the opposition of death and life into the opposition of subject and objects carving the Bataillean path that centers such relationship as an erotic one.[71]

Amanda Fernback explains that, in classical fetishism, the fetishist is drawn to the artificiality of women and their open wound to conceal the fetishist's own anxieties. According to Fernback, the fetish object serves to repair the imagined mutilations inflicted upon the mother and to act as a defense mechanism against the fetishist's castration anxieties.[72] Considering Fernback's feminist perspective, I believe Murrieta's interpretation fails to acknowledge the impossibility of a female fetishist within the classical understanding of fetishism.

Throughout the four "Fetiches," the models assume dual roles as objects and subjects of desire. Horna views them as fetish objects, while the models themselves worship their own desired objects. Carrington seeks sexual gratification through a corpse, Poniatowska through a Chiapaneca harp once owned by Rosario Castellanos, and Luz del Amo through dolls, masks, and even herself. The dynamic of who plays the fetish for whom sets the stage for a series of actions by Horna that manipulate the meaning of fetishism. Simultaneously, these actions celebrate women's bodies, accomplishments, and their intellectual emancipation from male-centered discourses surrounding sexuality and art.

Though the photo essays with Kitzia Poniatowska and Luz del Amo also defy the classic notion of fetishism, I pay attention exclusively to "Oda a la necrofilia" because it is by far the boldest essay and is an unflinching approach to the masculine obsession with women's bodies, probably encouraged by Carrington's complicity. Additionally, something similar to the case of Arredondo's "Mariana" occurs with the analysis of Horna's "Fetiches." Elva Peniche Montfort argues that "Paraísos artificiales" is the most experimental photo-essay of the series.[73] Horna intervenes directly in the negative by scratching it to create the illusion of rain and employs a photomontage technique. Peniche Montfort further defends this series as the most interesting because it is the only one that focuses on the female naked body as a fetish: "'Artificial Paradises' is different from the preceding series, since here the fetish is the body itself.... Instead of alluding to objects that are symbolically related to the model, the body itself becomes, through photographical manipulation, the central fetish on the image. The woman's body is that vision which, through a semiconscious drug induced state, is concluded, reveled, distorted, fragmented, and duplicated."[74] I allow myself the long quote because, once again, it demonstrates how critics choose to praise the pieces that emulate the masculine discourses of eroticism. Selecting "Oda a la necrofilia" as my focus of analysis is another way of turning to sadomasochism as a method of restorative criticism. I argue that the decision to not publish Carrington's face is a gesture that implies a rupture with these patriarchal views, as it prevents the fetishization of Carrington herself and presents a clear departure from the *Playboy* style that Elizondo so eagerly desired.

Horna's camera compels the viewer to focus their attention on the possible identity of the white mask, which serves as a synecdoche for masculinity as suggested by the men's shoes. Apart from Carrington's face, there are other significant elements in the unpublished photo. She holds an umbrella in her right hand, the mask in her left as an accessory, and a cigarette in her mouth as a symbol of the modern woman. Standing upright, Carrington gazes at herself in the mirror, no longer in mourning but sporting a radiant smile that I perceive as the aftermath of pleasure. This photo conveys everything explicitly, leaving no room for the viewer's imagination: it is a new beginning, liberated from the constraints of a phallocentric discourse. The artists employ gestures that guide the viewer, particularly those willing to engage in their feminist endeavor, to discern what cannot be directly expressed—the happiness Carrington experiences stems from the demise of the phallus.

As I mentioned earlier, the first disruption of classical fetishism occurs by presenting women as fetishists. A person becomes a fetishist when they experience "recurrent, intense sexually arousing fantasies, sexual urges or behaviors involving the use of nonliving objects."[75] In this case, Carrington's sexual urges toward a corpse/mask and Horna's gaze are the behaviors that define them as fetishists. Horna's gaze is particularly intriguing because, through her eyes, Carrington's body momentarily undergoes a temporary transformation into an object of worship. By inserting herself into one of the photos—there is a shadow in one of the photos that corresponds to Horna's persona—the photographer explicitly engages as a voyeur in one of the most erotic scenes of the series. On the left, we see Carrington's naked back, holding a candle to illuminate the mask/corpse. Atop the bed's frame, a bra lies carelessly discarded, nearby is a book with an unidentified object resting on its open pages. The photo suggests an erotic moment: Carrington is on the verge of engaging in the act necrophilia.

Before delving into this sexual act, let me return to Horna's gaze. By positioning herself in this pivotal moment of the series, she ensures that she will be perceived as a fetishist, worshipping Carrington's body, while simultaneously alerting the viewer to the objectification taking place in the scene. It is a form of objectification that consistently involves the subject—that is, a mode of subject-object-subject relations, rather than the traditional subject-object dynamic proposed by classical fetishism—because ultimately, Carrington's pleasure is at the core of the photo-essay. By presenting female pleasure as an intimate act of collaboration, Horna and Carrington remind us that fetishism is not solely about sexuality but also about perception and power. The perspective of the photo suggests a cuir dissident approach to fetishism, one that celebrates non-hierarchical differences and thereby generates a new concept of fetishism.

Unlike classical fetishism, cuir fetishism is concerned with embodied re-articulations of gender relations and sexuality. It primarily focuses on anti-normative moves.[76] The mask represents a bodily transformation without a proper gender. Simultaneously, the men's shoes in the unpublished photo suggest that the corpse belongs to a man. However, following the earlier classical argument—what is a man without a phallus?—Horna and Carrington playfully engage with the performative and surreal nature of gender. They mock the masculine economy of desire that is centered around the absence of a phallus. They also reclaim femininity and feminization as potential tools for transforming the future of gender and sexuality. To illustrate this point, let me refer to "Mariana," short story in which the character dies because BDSM, as a practice showcasing gender as drag, proves insufficient in subverting the concrete hierarchical binary roles within Mexican society. Conversely, Horna and Carrington propose that due to the systemic nature of hierarchical gender roles, gender as drag is a possibility yet to come. This cuir gesture highlights the enigma encapsulated in the chapter's title: cuir, as it holds the potential for a better future, and not yet cuir, as this moment is still pending.

Horna and Carrington complete their collaborative joke with a reference to necrophilia. The extreme repulsion associated with this sexual practice is what turns it into a fetish and an anti-normative move. For most people, it is difficult to grasp why someone would be sexually excited by a corpse. The obscurity of necrophilia makes this fetish an ideal one to explore the epistemic moment that these photos capture. As I mentioned before, within eroticism, there is a concern with the death drive and its relation to the instant of pure pleasure. By utilizing necrophilia, these women artists satirize this connection. Rather than linking pleasure to self-annihilation, Horna and

Carrington associate pleasure with their flourishing subjectivity and a relational vision of erotic intimacy. An anecdote serves to illustrate this point:

> Not long before Horna and Carrington worked together on the series, José had suffered a near fatal heart attack which left him in a frail condition. According to Horna's daughter, it was this traumatic experience that motivated the theme of the series--a creative collaboration between Horna and Carrington, photographed with great spontaneity as means to make sense of their complicated emotions over their shared fear of José's imminent passing, which indeed took place the following year.[77]

Instead of relinquishing pleasure after José's predicted death, who was Horna's husband, "Oda a la necrofilia" suggests a new erotic beginning between the two friends. Whether this erotic beginning is real or merely an artistic gesture is inconsequential. What matters is that erotic desire is not tied to self-annihilation but to the possibilities that emerge with the dismantling of traditional gender roles. By replacing women's subjection, the mask as an inanimate object signifies the demise of masculinity while simultaneously symbolizing novel avenues of pleasure not attached to gender or sexual organs.

I want to conclude by exploring Carrington's (and Horna's) provocative engagement with the concept of 'fucking with death.' In addition to the previously discussed psychoanalytic mockery, I argue that necrophilia embodies the crisis of gender and sexuality examined throughout this chapter.[78] Rather than presenting a pathological understanding of this sexual practice, my focus is on the pleasurable aspects of fucking with death, aiming to dismantle the prejudices that associate necrophilia with male power and female subjugation, as well as mere perversion. By replacing an actual corpse with a mask, these artists aim to question the common understanding of necrophilia as an action driven by hierarchical power dynamics or perversion. Instead, they propose that it is primarily about one's affective perspective. As exemplified in the photographs of "Oda a la necrofilia," Carrington portrays her erotic desire for a deceased loved one as a pleasurable form of mourning. Simultaneously, necrophilia holds appeal as it places the focus solely on the pleasure of the individual engaging in the act. The distinction between, for instance, using a dildo for masturbation and engaging in sexual activity with a lifeless body lies in the perception that the latter still possesses some degree of subjectivity. In Carrington's case, the lifeless body is replaced with a mask to suggests this subjectivity while also protecting it. Besides,

Carrington's climax is evident through Horna's gaze and not through the rapture of the death drive, suggesting a utopian piercing moment, one when gender and genitalia become irrelevant in erotic encounters. Thus, necrophilia is employed for its transgressive potential as a means to envision alternative forms of relationality and to embrace cuir perspectives through female complicity and vulnerability.

Nothing More Beautiful than Unsettling the *Nudos*

As I bring this chapter to a close, I recall a moment from my conversation with Xitlalitl Rodríguez Mendoza that afternoon at the Rosario Castellanos's bookstore, which, in a certain way, accompanied me all the way in the writing of this chapter. Being face-to-face with a writer whose literary works I enjoy discussing and analyzing has never appealed to me. As a reader, I have no desire to disturb the tacit understanding between writer and reader, where the narrative voice remains distinct from the tangible presence of the author. In other words, I felt no inclination to exchange the Sisi Rodríguez I had envisioned in my mind while reading the *crónicas* for the real person made of flesh and bones. On top of that, interviewing a writer about their sexual intimacies, even if they are public, is a bit messy. All this to say that I must confess that preparing for this interview was not an easy process. I aimed to address the topic with the utmost respect while posing the necessary questions without sugarcoating them. Although I am unsure to what extent one can sugarcoat a topic like BDSM. I decided to write down my questions along with the corresponding text excerpt, as well as the reasons behind my inquiries, in the hope of maintaining coherence and professionalism.

As I attempted to wrap up our conversation, however, an unspoken question lingered in my mind. I struggled to find a straightforward justification for incorporating this inquiry into my research, and as a result, I refrained from including it in my outline. The question felt deeply personal, and I hesitated to impose it on our interaction. Despite my reservations, the words "¿te arrepientes?" ("Do you regret it?") unexpectedly escaped my lips, carrying a mixture of regret and curiosity in my body language. Rodríguez Mendoza responded with a smile, countering my question with another: "¿de hacerlo o de publicarlo?" ("doing it or publishing it?") Uncertain, I replied, "No estoy segura" ("I am not sure"). She looked directly into my eyes with a mischievous smile, and without any doubt, she proceeded to explain that it was complicated, again, a bit messy.

Despite the very real consequences, such as losing her job and facing judgment from her friends, it is difficult for her to harbor regrets when the initial motivation persists—the satisfaction of unsettling the reader with her "nudos" ("knots"). Perhaps she regrets her mother reading the *crónicas*—she tells me, laughing, mortified—but the pleasure of making the reader uncomfortable with a topic as unconventional as BDSM and disruptive as female pleasure can sometimes be inside the conversative walls of the lettered city, continues to captivate Rodríguez Mendoza in a seductive manner. She concludes that she does not think she regrets it. We never clarified whether we are discussing regretting playing or publishing about the scene; we both know that this distinction is tricky, a bit messy.

Perhaps we share a deep affection for messy writings, or maybe our mutual interest in this subject transcends mere intellectual curiosity, as mentioned by her Dom. Regardless of whether this is true or not, her response made me smile in complicity. After all, I too enjoy unsettling readers, and I too was warned by some friends and colleagues not to publish about my kinks and desires because it was not proper, presentable, nor a "real" intellectual pursuit. Would I come to regret writing about BDSM? Yet, her response was not only resolute but it also framed affect, our joy and pleasure, as the crux of everything.

So, it seems fair to end up with the pleasurable affect that makes us accomplices. Concluding her *crónicas* with a beautiful appraisal of the magic wand, possible the finest vibrator in the realm of sex toys, Rodríguez Mendoza writes: "Nada más hermoso que esto. Chicas: por favor, por favor, por favor no mueran sin antes haberlo probado" (Nothing more beautiful than this. Girls: please, please, please don't die without having tried it first).[79] I interpret her plea both literally and metaphorically—to test the waters of the scandal of BDSM as a sexual practice, but more importantly, as a messy political stance to "choke" the literary system. "Fucking" the system might be complex, but it is always a pursuit worth undertaking. So, *chicas*: please, please, please, let's not die without giving it a try.

CHAPTER 2

The Restorative Possibilities of an Archive of Gender Playfulness

Women's Mustaches and the Third Gender

During the summer of 2017, I persuaded my dear academic spouse to spend one of the few remaining mornings of our research trip grave hunting at the largest cemetery in Mexico City. A couple of nights before I had learned about the existence of an individual who, dressed as a man, mocked Mexican society at the beginning of the twentieth century and was buried at the Panteón Civil de Dolores.[1] The grave was described to me as a monument that recognizes the gender nonconformity of this character. As I would find later, the grave is also an embodied archive that documents their life and pranks in *talavera* tiles displayed as a storytelling mosaic. Contrary to what one might think, a colorful *talavera* monument is very hard to find in a cemetery full of grey tombstones and mausoleums. To get the location of any grave one needs to visit the cemetery's office and provide a full name and death date, which of course I did not have. A bit frustrated by what it is obviously the most proper way of organizing this type of records, I was about to leave the office aimlessly when an eager person came out of nowhere asserting—with a playful authority—that I was looking for Conchita and that they would draw me a map. This map marks the beginning of my scavenger hunt for the material remnants of a strange and forgotten episode in Mexico's cuir history.

Known as the "Balmoreadas," these elaborate pranks were orchestrated by a group of friends and accomplices of Concepción Jurado (1865–1931), who dressed as a rich Spaniard named Carlos Balmori, deceived the elites, and

The Restorative Possibilities [65]

FIGURE 2.1. *Talavera* tiles on Concepción Jurado's grave, featuring Carlos Balmori in formal attire. The plaque above reads, "Construido y decorado por Casa Cervantes, Av. Juarez 18, México, D.F., Pintó JL. Greenham."

FIGURE 2.2. Detail of *talavera* tiles on Jurado's grave, depicting Carlos Balmori and a woman in early twentieth-century attire. Balmori wears a hat, glasses, and a suit, gesturing with one hand, while the woman, dressed in a coat and cloche hat, stands beside him.

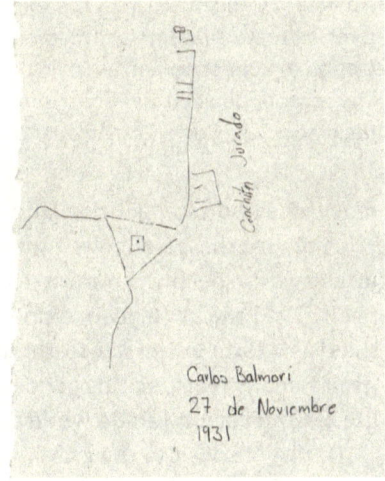

FIGURE 2.3. A map, hand-drawn on textured paper by a cemetery employee; I added the name, "Carlos Balmori," and the date, "November 27, 1931."

mocked their false morality during the years that followed the Mexican Revolution. Insisting on their desire to do business and share their fortune in Mexico, Balmori seduced their victims with promises of large sums of money,

FIGURE 2.4. Concepción Jurado's tomb, located in the Panteón Civil de Dolores. The tomb's structure resembles a chimney, with inscriptions on the slanted surface. Some tiles on the upper portion are missing or damaged, exposing the underlying cement. The artwork depicts a library scene. At the bottom, a plaque reads: "Construido y decorado Casa Cervantes, Av. Juárez 18, Mexico, D.F. Pintó JL. Greenham."

fancy jobs and cars, political and economic alliances, and even marriages.[2] The *talavera* tiles, along with the texts documenting their life, suggest that Jurado was so deeply committed to their mischievous *acciones* that they practically lived their last years embodying Balmori, in what today can be identified as a form of *travesti* aesthetics.[3] It is astonishing to see how the grave itself visually registers this gender dissidence, with one side celebrating the life of Concepción Jurado while the other honors the life of Carlos Balmori.

During the visit to the grave, however, what caught my attention was an irony of fate: the side dedicated to Jurado's life had been vandalized, and the *talaveras* forming the upper part of their body had disappeared—leaving behind a large square of grey cement—while the other side shows the erect and untouched image of Carlos Balmori. Most of my feminist readers will be familiar with the bodily reaction I am about to describe. I remember looking right at the grey square, laughing, and shaking my head while mumbling something about the unsophisticated patriarchal tools used to erase—systemically and systematically—the production of women's cuir culture and history. Of course, it is impossible to find out who, when, and why the monument was damaged—believe me, I tried. The point is that I decided to interpret the decapitated Conchita as symbolic proof of the need to materialize my desire to work with their story as a metaphorical ensemble that captures the affective energy that is at the core of my ideas about restorative criticism.

Yet, at the same time, the grave was another kind of metaphor since their embodied archive was teasing me with a surface of failed hope. Their story kept slipping away with seductive evasion; almost suggesting that any attempt to reconstruct it would be an unfruitful and frivolous task. Attesting to the type of affects often produced by embodied cuir/queer archives, Julieta Singh suggests that the elusive characteristic of the archive is also an enabling fiction: "it is the thing you say you are doing well before you are actually doing it, and well before you understand what the stakes are for gathering and interpreting."[4] It is something that "catches us in our becoming."[5] There is something deeply compelling about thinking of the embodied archive as an enabling fiction for my own becoming: what kind of "doing" will allow this grave and my desire to fix it?

I attempted to envision Conchita's restoration but quickly dismissed the idea of reconstructing their head, as filling the gap left by the destruction of the tiles felt off. The restorative turn I suggest throughout the book is precisely one beyond the process of fixing something just to be put back into circulation. It is about paying attention to how the object wants to be restored in our present. With this archive, restoring the headless Conchita becomes messier when we think about their gender dissidence—was there an "original" Conchita in the first place? Thus, what at first seemed like a mischievous way of erasing Conchita's life now presents itself to me as a productive opening of the signifier "woman" that enables my own research. The restorative criticism that I propose here is to use the information of these forgotten episodes as an affective way to move beyond the current impasse between feminism and cuiridad (and transfeminism) that I address at the end of this chapter. As such, it is not about recuperating voices nor incorporating them into/within a (cuir) canon but enabling an embodied practice of cultural criticism as a political response to our present, with the hope of reshaping our horizon.

In what follows, I analyze three instances of gender dissidence within both *acciones* and print literature to explore the potential of the restorative move. As illustrated by my description of the grave, Conchita's evasion of gender norms opens the signifier "woman" to a multiplicity that remains elusive. Through their gender playfulness, the case of Jurado/Balmori reveals the intricate challenge of acknowledging that a feminist praxis cannot rely on the signifier "woman" as neither a biological entity nor an ontological foundation. Simultaneously, it must navigate the necessity of strategically occupying the category of "woman" for political mobilization. While Jurado/Balmori's gender dissidence disrupts any semblance of coherence within this signifier, the adherence to normative expectations of femininity depicted by the protagonist of *Andréïda (El tercer sexo)* (Andréïda: The third sex; 1938) by Asunción Izquierdo Albiñana offers a productive counterpoint.

In this fictional work, Izquierdo Albiñana crafts a "third gender" in an attempt to dismantle patriarchy, yet the protagonist ultimately fails and reverts to the "second sex."[6] The fiction serves as a reminder of what it means to be attached to a gender norm by desire, habit, or survival. Thus, *Andréïda* adds another layer of complexity to the stories of gender dissidence, one that forces us to rethink essentialist representations of the feminine and their relationship with histories of survival and resistance. Moving fast-forward in time, I conclude with "La inquietante [e internacional] semana de las mujeres barbudas" (The Unsettling [and International] Week of Bearded Women), a series of online and offline cultural *acciones* organized by Cristina Rivera Garza and Amaranta Caballero Prado with the collaboration from Spain of Sayak Valencia in June 2005. Organized by women with multiple positionalities and identities, this cultural intervention aimed to disrupt gender norms in a ludic manner by mischievously taking up public space with their prominent beards in a performance of cuir dissidence.

With these examples, I trace a history of gender dissidence in Mexico, which acknowledges both the malleability of gender and the risks associated with the dematerialization of conflicts between subjects, identities, and genders.[7] With the rise of transexclusionary social movements and discourses in the second decade of the twenty-first century, I believe it is crucial to develop a model of cuir cultural criticism capable of contextualizing its objects of study while anchoring them in the present. This involves avoiding simplistic applications of contemporary understandings to the past while ensuring that these insights remain grounded in their sociocultural specificity. Drawing insights from the past not only elucidates current challenges but also embodies a political standpoint that denaturalizes the transexclusionary present by showing what we know and cannot know about the long past of various practices of gender dissidence. My archive shows a cultural history of gender dissidence that allows me to pinpoint transexclusionary discourses as a result of the coloniality of power that mobilizes a colonial/modern gender system born in a different context that does not correspond to our reality.[8] This highlights another important aspect of practices of restorative criticism: an ethical commitment to avoid reinforcing existing power structures, even when we are fully aware of the impossibility of an outside of power. In other words, even in failure, the hopeless yearning represents an affective form of cultural criticism that illuminates cuir routes full of possibilities, or at the very least, raises some messy questions.

The *Puerquitos'* Joyful Cult: An Early Laboratory of Gender Dissidence

With the help of Luis Cervantes Morales and Eduardo Delhumeau (a former attorney general of Mexico), Jurado/Balmori builds a solid reputation as a character outside of their time by performing their "raro laboratorio de psicología experimental" (rare experimental psychology laboratory) at as many private parties as possible in Mexico City.[9] The experiment tried to establish up to what limit a person could resist receiving a large sum of money (and/or other financial privileges) without making ethical or moral concessions. The acciones begin on June 23 of 1926 and lasted until Jurado/Balmori's death on November 27, 1931. During this time, Jurado performed exclusively as Balmori to the point of confessing Balmori's sins during the sacrament of penance on their deathbed.

Ostensibly, Balmori was a rich Spaniard man traveling the world with their fortune, seeking financial opportunities and romantic partnerships. Dressed entirely with men's clothing, wearing a hat to hide their long grey braids, a fake mustache, spectacles, and carrying fake checkbooks from a variety of world banks, Balmori was able to convince people to engage in situations of dubious morality. The structure of the Balmoreadas was quite simple. Through a network of journalists and friends, Jurado/Balmori, Delhumeau, and Cervantes Morales organized parties to lure in and trick their victims, who would later become part of the inner circle—the *"puerquitos"* (the "little piggies")—that helped with the planning and execution of further parties and additional pranks: "they become something of a cult, sworn to secrecy about Balmori's identity and eager to trap the next victim."[10] Among the *puerquitos*, there were generals, politicians, writers, journalists, artists, and surgeons—rumor has it that more than three thousand people were victims of the Balmoreadas.

This experiment plus the gender playfulness of Jurado/Balmori was so unique that after their death, their assistants along with a group of their male friends and fans organized a society of worshipful dupes that in the years to come would honor Jurado/Balmori's achievements and would take on the task of documenting their life. The group's activities began with setting up the grave and led to later publishing their memoirs under the titles of *Don Carlos Balmori, su extraordinaria vida y hazañas* (Don Carlos Balmori, his extraordinary life and deeds; 1938) by Delhumeau and *Memorias de Don Carlos Balmori: Escritas por su secretario particular* (Memoirs of Don Carlos Balmori. Written by his personal secretary; 1969) by Cervantes Morales. While it is true that without their efforts to document the Balmoreadas we would hardly know about this character, it is also necessary to recognize Jurado/Balmori's memoirs as a process of fictionalization mediated by their male friends. While indeed this can be viewed as an example of how the elusiveness of gendered cuir archives is sometimes related to the difficulty gender dissidence subjectivities face in telling their own stories, I am not interested in questioning if this mediation affects the veracity, and therefore the value, of the memoirs. Instead, I believe that the instances of Jurado/Balmori's agency manifested throughout the memoirs plus the affective imprints their story left in the Mexican imaginary of the following decades gives the Balmoreadas enough cultural capital to entertain my idea of this event as one that admits a counter-history of the sociohistorical processes of gender dissidence in Mexico.

Jurado/Balmori's acciones provoked so much joy (and noise) that not only their friends were preoccupied with documenting their story. The pranks also appeared in the major newspapers of the time such as *El universal gráfico* and *Excélsior* and are indexed in the most important reference books of the time, like the *Enciclopedia de México* (1966). Over time, their case also inspired several creative re-writings of their life, like *La ambición del diablo* (The devil's ambition; Ediciones Botas, 1962) by Martín Gómez Palacio; *El increíble Carlos Balmori* (The incredible Carlos Balmori; Editorial Universo, 1981) by Fernando Martí; *Vida y milagros: Novela teatral* (Life and miracles: A theatrical novel; Nueva Imagen, 1999) by Héctor Anaya; *Don Carlos Balmori: El genio forjador de ilusiones* (Don Carlos Balmori: The genius who forged illusions; Palibrio, 2014) by Joel López Zepeda; and *Más vale robar que pedir* (It's better to steal than to beg; 2010), a book published under the forged label of the independent publishing house Almadía by authors claiming to be Jurado/Balmori's heirs. Moreover, Silvia Pinal also dedicates an episode to Balmori on her famous telenovela *Mujer: Casos de la vida real* (Woman: Real-life cases), while Raúl Quitanilla and Julián Antuñano devote one episode of *Curiosidades históricas* (Historical curiosities) to these parties. Although the documentation surrounding the Jurado/Balmori case is extensive and diverse, it has not received much critical attention. Akin to the notable episode of the dance of the 41, which has garnered considerable attention from scholars and the mainstream audience since the early 2000s and even became the theme of Pride 2019 and a Netflix movie in 2020, the Jurado/Balmori episode remains overlooked. Maris Bustamante, Esther Gabara, and Gabriela Cano are the major scholars who have investigated the case. Besides, what remains of the Balmoreadas in the everyday Mexican imaginary is next to nothing: their alleged property—the Balmori building—is still intact on Álvaro Obregón street; a fancy rooftop bar bears their name in the middle of the Colonia Roma, paying homage to their dissidence. And perhaps, as the episode of *Curiosidades históricas* suggests, the colloquial expression "lo agarraron de su puerquito" (they made them their little piggy), which means making someone the frequent object of ridicule and abuse, is a remainder of this period. Even when their story and *acciones* left a considerable amount of information and material evidence that speaks about their popularity and significance, the passage of time—one that tends to favor heteropatriarchal structures—hides their joyful presence in history.

My restorative endeavor begins by pointing out that Jurado/Balmori's story suggests that the emergence of *travesti* practices as a political tool did not start in the eighties and nineties, decades that scholars tend to view as the point of emergence of *travesti* aestheticization—mainly male-to-female—as a political tool in Latin America.[11] Beyond putting into question this chronology, the Balmoreadas also complicate the idea of *travesti* aesthetics as primarily a male-to-female political practice. However, for Gabriela Cano, the Balmoreadas do not have a political or pragmatic sense since it was all about having a good time.[12] As she explains, the Balmoreadas are ludic spaces of sociability where the manifestation of sexual and gender dissidence is encouraged as well as the coexistence of people of all ages and between different social classes.[13] I disagree with Cano precisely because I view the ludic component as an embodied political practice with a long tradition in spaces of cuir/queer sociability inside and outside Mexico (i.e., the ludic performance of the Contemporáneos or the famous dance of the 41). The so-called affective turn and the recuperation of the emotional as an analytical category are precisely responses to the limitations of epistemological traditions that enthrone reason at the expense of the body.[14] Thus, I argue that the ludic component is a form of affect that puts into circulation a cuir mode of body politics that is simultaneously a personal and collective endeavor: Jurado/Balmori uses these ludic spaces to explore their nonheterosexual desire while simultaneously proposing a re-articulation of gender dissidence with their *travesti* practice.

There is a whole body of scholarship and activism that addresses the uses of the term *travesti* in the Latin American context. Here I am thinking of the *acciones* of *Las yeguas del apocalipsis*, the activism and writings of Lohana Berkins, Marlene Wayar, and Camila Sosa Villada; and scholars like Nelly Richard, Ben Sifuentes-Jáuregui, Lawrence La Fountain-Stokes, Vek Lewis, Marcia Ochoa, Verónica Gago, Lechedevirgen Trimegisto, among many others. What is more, *TSQ: Transgender Studies Quarterly*, has even dedicated at least two full issues—*Trans Studies en las Américas* (2019) and *The Transsexual/Transvestite Issue* (2021)—to the discussion of the geopolitics of the uses of terms such as *trans*, *trava*, and *travesti*. All agree that in Latin America *travesti* continues to be used as a form of self-identity, as a political positionality, and/or as a form of collective mobilization. Furthermore, since the word *travesti* is generally associated with male-to-female gender crossing, Cole Rizki brings up an important issue when considering the tensions between *trans* and *travesti* as identificatory categories. Rizki points out that few trans men would claim *travesti* as a term of self-identity and wonders, "what sorts of recourse do trans men have to localized identification if not *trans*?"[15] Since the widespread recognition of Paul B. Preciado's work, whose influence in Latin American cuir/queer thought is undeniable, drag has been more often associated with female-to-male gender crossings in the Hispanic world, where drag kings are a visible practice of gender dissidence. Furthermore, *travestismo* in Mexico both informs *travesti* and drag practices. *Travestismo* tends to be viewed as a time-delimited action, either because it happens within the constraints of a scenario (like drag), or because it is used as a strategy of survival by gender non-confirming people who cannot or do not want to embrace travesti practices as a quotidian embodiment. Sometimes *travestismo* is translated as cross-dressing but cross-dressing, to me, is the practice of gender bending for a variety of reasons, though not necessarily attached to a positionality or identity of gender nonconformity.

Since my interest is not in defining *travesti* practices or highlighting the differences between this practice and drag or identificatory categories such as *trans*, I have limited myself to a simplified definition of *travesti* and *travestismo* stemming from Balmori's case. I understand these practices as a form of gender dissidence that involves playing with the malleability of gender as an aesthetic practice while also emphasizing the corporality of the performer as a site of trouble. This practice is a political standpoint that consciously implies challenging the normativity of gender and sexuality with a ludic and/or irreverent tone. *Travestismo* is the temporal embodiment of *travesti* practices.

The case of the Balmoreadas is perhaps the first documented instance of female-to-male *travestismo* in Mexico. However, its uniqueness relies on the type of gender insubordination Jurado/Balmori is performing. One of the few times in which Cervantes Morales and Delhumeau quote Jurado/Balmori directly is at the end of each Balmoreada when Balmori reveals themselves as Jurado:

> pues yo ni soy grosero, ni enamorado, ni conozco de caballos, ni me intereso por su señora, ni le puedo regalar un coche; en una palabra, ni siquiera soy hombre, y por lo tanto, mucho menos puedo ser el archimillonario español Don Carlos Balmori. Me contento con ser una mujer débil, anciana, común y corriente, muy parecida a la mamacita de usted, a quién conozco de cerca y la quiero mucho.[16]

Well, I'm neither rude nor in love, nor do I know anything about horses, nor am I interested in your wife, nor can I gift you a car. In a word, I'm not even a man, and therefore, much less could I be the Spanish multimillionaire Don Carlos Balmori. I'm content with being a weak, elderly, ordinary woman, very much like your dear mother, whom I know well and care for deeply.

Each prank reaches its climax when Jurado/Balmori removes their mustache and hat to reveal the long grey braids that reminds us that we are facing a type of gender dissidence that is exercised both in the materiality of the body—a postmenopausal body living in poverty—and in the heteropatriarchal discourses that surround it. Thus, unveiling their corporality to the public troubles even further an already troubled idea of gender.

Let me elaborate on this by unpacking their decision to perform as a rich Spaniard man. Jurado is frequently described as weak, fragile, and innocent, while Balmori is portrayed as strong, seductive, clever, and rich. This juxtaposition calls into question the regulatory practice of gender identity itself by playing with normative ideals frequently associated with femininity and masculinity. Yet, Balmori's performance is not simply an imitation of hegemonic masculinity but a parody of it, traversed by other markers such as class and colonialism. By choosing to mock masculinity through a parody of the perfect image of hegemonic masculinity—that of the Spaniard conqueror—Jurado/Balmori reinforces gender as a playful imitation, highlighting *travestismo* as a parody of a parody of a parody, as suggested by Nelly Richard when theorizing *travesti* aesthetics.[17] In other words, Jurado/Balmori's *travestismo* is a political endeavor aimed at troubling gender without obscuring corporality or the historical layers that surround it.

Their case stands out due to the possibility that without Balmori's disclosure of their disguise, their gender trouble might remain undetected, potentially undermining the effectiveness of their *travesti* aestheticization as a tool of gender dissidence. Instead, what guarantees that their gender dissidence is perceived as a deliberate act of troubling gender is the act of revealing themselves as a poor, old woman, a revelation that leaves the *puerquitos* in a state of confusion and shock. Without revealing their corporality, their disguise would not be coded as a *travesti* practice at all. Thus, the subversiveness of their *acciones* lies not in revealing the repetitive iterations that create gender in the first place, but in demonstrating that the possibility of a "woman" assuming control of the public sphere—as suggested by Gabara—is still perceived as a threat, even when the category of "woman" is already embraced as a performative reiteration.[18]

The following passage helps clarify the gender trouble produced by Jurado's corporeality:

> Y los amigos llegaron pronto a una conclusión: habían perdido el concepto de tiempo y lugar, en un solo momento se había borrado de su mente la historia de sus vidas, por segundos habían olvidado en donde se hallaban, quienes eran y el porvenir que les esperaba; en sus propias narices aquel gran HOMBRE se les transformó en mujer provocando horrendo desequilibrio mental, y en estos pensamientos y hondas disquisiciones se les fue el sueño, y vuelta y vuelta en el Paseo de la Reforma, entre el Caballito y Chapultepec, buscando el por qué del SER de BALMORI material e inmaterial, los sorprendieron los trinos de los pajarillos que alababan al Señor en la madrugada del miércoles 24 de junio de 1926: Así terminó la primera jornada de esta verídica historia.[19]

> And the friends quickly reached a conclusion: they had lost the concept of time and place. In a single moment, the history of their lives had vanished from their minds; for seconds, they had forgotten where they were, who they were, and the future that awaited them. Right under their noses, that great MAN turned into a woman, causing a horrendous mental imbalance. In these thoughts and deep musings, sleep eluded them, and round and round they went on Paseo de la Reforma, between the Caballito and Chapultepec, searching for the reason behind the being of BALMORI, both material and immaterial. They were surprised by the chirping of the birds, praising the Lord in the early hours of Wednesday, June 24, 1926. Thus ended the first day of this true story.

Unveiling their *travestismo* is described as an act disrupting time and space quite literally, creating an atmosphere of obfuscation. The confusion is such that it leads the *puerquitos* to question the material and immaterial reasons behind the existence of a character such as Balmori. A search that ends up questioning, even just for a brief moment, how gender operates as a regulatory discourse that cannot be separated from material conditions such as age and class. Furthermore, failing to comprehend what is happening with this character provokes such an affective disorientation in the *puerquitos* that it prevents the understanding of the signifier "woman" as a sign close in itself. Thus, in Jurado/Balmori's *travesti* aestheticization, "woman" operates not as a biological entity nor as an ontological foundation, but as something to remind us that "woman" is already a parody of a parody full of *potencia* and in permanent dispute.[20] Their *travestismo* is traveled by a dissident alterity that keeps changing according to the situation, which prevents them from fully subscribing to a fixed gender signifier—this is why on their deathbed, for example, Jurado insists on confessing as Balmori despite the risk of dying in sin. Jurado/Balmori's *acciones* advocate for instances of gender trouble as political interventions that highlight the materialization of bodies and their territorialization.

The political gesture of the Balmoreadas is expressed in several ways throughout their performances. At the end of each Balmoreada, Jurado/Balmori carefully underlines their old age and refers to their impoverished economic status as elements that not only protect them from the possible rage of the *puerquitos* but also function as the reason for their success since no one can believe that an old "woman" could fool a group of young and middle-aged successful men. Considering poverty and age, Cristian Cabello has thought about the relationship between post-menopause and drag, suggesting that both operate similarly by understanding gender dissidence as materiality and discourse. Thinking through the becoming-male of their mother, the author suggests that the postmenopausal body is already a subversion of the ideal body and an opening of the signifier "woman," capable of questioning gender norms:

> Mi madre, cuando se casó, pesaba alrededor de 50 kilos. Ahora pesa casi 100, gracias a su adicción a la Coca-Cola y a que vende marraquetas en el almacén de Pedro Aguirre Cerda.... Mi madre en el año 1988 se sacó el útero, los ovarios, las trompas de Falopio. Por miedo a quedar embarazada.... Usa el pelo corto, porque es más cómodo: no hay chasquilla, no hay *glamour*; ropa holgada, buzos de mi hermano y zapatillas, creo que ya no recuerdo si usó tacos alguna vez.[21]

> My mother, when she got married, weighed around 50 kilos. Now she weighs almost 100, thanks to her addiction to Coca-Cola and to selling bread rolls at the Pedro Aguirre Cerda store.... In 1988, my mother had her uterus, ovaries, and fallopian tubes removed, out of fear of getting pregnant.... She wears her hair short because it's more convenient: no bangs, no glamour; loose clothing, my brother's tracksuits, and sneakers. I don't think I can remember if she ever wore heels.

The type of becoming-male described in this passage is not restricted—according to Cabello—to gender insubordination and calls for a broader definition of drag.

One way of amplifying the concept of drag for Cabello is for it to be considered as "un dispositivo disidente y terrorista que cuestione y demuestre la vulnerabilidad de cualquier construcción sexual de ficción o no ficción" (a dissident and terrorist device that challenges and exposes the vulnerability of any sexual construction, whether fictional or nonfictional).[22] While I disagree with the return to the tedious distinction between "fictional" and "real" gender, which is nothing more than a theoretical disguise for the old debate between the biological and the ontological, Cabello adds the value of vulnerability as a layer that is not necessarily always implied in the performative act. Jurado/Balmori reveals themselves as a poor "woman" to ensure that their gender dissidence is also interpreted in the context of the physical constraints of a postmenopausal body. This revelation leaves them vulnerable; a vulnerability that is mobilized by Jurado/Balmori as an affective mode of cuir politics that makes explicit the failure of binary ideology without giving up the signifier "woman." As long as this signifier continues to operate in our political and social reality, as their vulnerability shows, with the tactical mobility of a sign in permanent dispute of interpretation—as their postmenopausal body in poverty suggests—the category "woman" is still a useful signifier against regulatory discourses of the body and the binary ideology.

The political gesture of Jurado/Balmori is not only a collective endeavor against these regulatory discourses but also an individual form of survival that underscores the inseparability of *travesti* practices and *travestismo* from nonheterosexual desires, inseparability noted by Ben Sifuentes-Jáuregui in *Transvestism, Masculinity, and Latin American Literature*.[23] In my opinion, this might explain why the weddings are the most repeated type of prank—rumors suggest that Balmori was "legally" married 108 times. It is at the weddings—a type of ceremony saturated with affect—when the reader perceives with greater clarity that their *travesti* practice is an embodied form of cuir dissidence deployed very consciously by Jurado/Balmori as a political tool.

Let me briefly refer to an example that takes us back to the years before the golden age of the Balmoreadas. Born in Mexico City in 1864 or 1865, Concepción Jurado was the daughter of Don Juan Jurado and Doña María de Martínez de Jurado, a working-class couple living in what was called at that time Necatitlán, a predominantly working-class and immigrant neighborhood situated on the outskirts of the city. As a man of many trades and very limited resources, Don Juan urged his daughter to get married. As a response to this pressure, however, Concepción Jurado dressed up as a man to ask their own hand in marriage. This ludic way of resistance to an oppressive social convention pays off since Jurado never gets married and instead Carlos Balmori is born. In the years to follow, Jurado stays at their parents' house and occasionally dresses up as other characters.[24] Beyond this, we do not know anything about their life until the so-called golden age of the Balmoreadas at the end of the 1920s when Jurado/Balmori was already in their sixties. What the example illustrates is the beginning of their *travestismo* as a ploy against marriage, an institution that for Jurado/Balmori was an enterprise of capitalism and compulsory heterosexuality that deserves to be mocked and exploited for their own cuir joy. Later on, their *travestismo* became closer to *travesti* practices, as it became a more quotidian embodiment.

The memoirs suggest that Jurado/Balmori had such a soft spot for wedding pranks to the point that if the initial prank was about something else but the opportunity for a marriage proposal arose, Jurado/Balmori would deviate from the script regardless of whether they put the Balmoreada at risk. It seems to me that the desire for marriage pranks is driven in part by sexual desire. This is the case when Balmori is invited to make fun of the communist party. The purpose of this Balmoreada was to teach a lesson to a group of communists by seducing them with Balmori's money to show them that without the green product of capitalism their socialist enterprise cannot exist. Yet Balmori deviates from the original script to propose to Laura del Cielo—the leader of the communist press and the most beautiful woman Balmori has ever seen. The idea was that Balmori would give del Cielo the necessary money to keep the press alive, and their protection to the communist group if she agrees to a civil and religious wedding. In the meantime, del Cielo has the following inner monologue:

> Como lo habían dicho sus mismos compañeros revolucionarios, nada podía hacerse sin el dinero, nada podría buscarse en el combate contra el capital sin

el capital mismo ... han caído las rancias teorías de la monogamia y del matrimonio. La humanidad exige lealtad de uno para todos, jamás lealtad de uno para uno. Esta forma de ver las cosas ha caído en desuso y el amor libre se impone; de manera que no había mejor camino que rendirse ante el magnate y aceptar sus rancias fórmulas de matrimonio civil y la mucho más rancia todavía del matrimonio religioso.... ¡Cuántas mujeres en el mundo hicieron virar el camino de las grandes luchas por una decisión tomada a tiempo! En México no estaría obligada una gran mujer a pasar el Rubicón, sin pedir consejo, sin titubeos, sin temor al mundo ni temor al cielo.[25]

As their fellow revolutionaries had said, nothing could be done without money, nothing could be sought in the fight against capital without capital itself.... The outdated theories of monogamy and marriage have fallen. Humanity demands loyalty from one to all, never loyalty from one to one. This way of seeing things has fallen out of use, and free love prevails; thus, there was no better path than to surrender to the magnate and accept his stale formulas of civil marriage and the even staler religious marriage.... How many women in the world have redirected the course of great struggles with a timely decision! In Mexico, a great woman would not be forced to cross the Rubicon without seeking advice, without hesitation, without fear of the world or fear of heaven.

At the end of this Balmoreada, Laura del Cielo emerges as the only one willing to sacrifice her own personal beliefs in the name of a greater good, while the communist party is left embarrassed and humiliated by Balmori, who is simply happy to have kissed del Cielo without forcing her to sacrifice her political vision. This interior monologue is an example of the mediated fictionalization of the memoirs done by Cervantes Morales. However, and perhaps just because of this mediation, the passage can be read as a small political manifesto against the institution of marriage, a manifesto that also criticizes monogamy and the normative idea of love as central to the doings and un-doings of the Balmoreadas. This type of criticism is very frequent in the memoirs.

Another example highlighting the significance of the wedding pranks is the episode where Jurado/Balmori selects their target, contrary to the typical collective selection of the *puerquito*. In this instance, Jurado/Balmori opts to play a prank on their best friend, María Sánchez, by orchestrating a fake marriage proposal. Described as one of the most intense Balmoreadas, this episode is imbued with an atmosphere of nonheterosexual erotic desire: "Terminó el primer beso y comenzó el segundo, y así el tercero y otros muchos, hasta que el aprovechado novio dejó en paz a la boca de su esposa" (The first kiss ended, and the second began, followed by the third and many others, until the eager groom finally left his bride's lips in peace).[26] Despite being one of the episodes where the eroticism between Balmori and their victim is described with great intensity, in every wedding, Jurado/Balmori touches and kisses their brides with intense passion. Sometimes, this erotic affection was so daring—even for a "heterosexual couple"— that it caused discomfort among the *puerquitos*, who could not perceive the implicit cuir nuances due to the act of *travestismo*. However, Jurado/Balmori rarely acknowledges this discomfort, and it seems that the purpose of this vivid manifestation of sexual desire is no other than their own pleasure— rumor has it that Jurado/Balmori felt attraction for women. Regardless of the rumors, the memoirs clearly manifest that Jurado/Balmori takes advantage of the ludic atmosphere to enjoy pleasures that would have otherwise been challenging to display publicly without repercussions. I feel compelled to clarify that despite the nonconsensual overtones of this type of act, none of the female victims felt inclined to condemn Balmori's audacity, as they themselves were deemed "immoral" at the time of accepting the marriage solely for economic reasons (what a bold and elaborate way to get laid in heteronormative times!).[27]

I would like to close this strange episode of cuir history with a failed Balmoreada that once more highlights the relation between *travestismo* and cuir desire. An engineer named Armengol wants to teach his nephew a lesson for "sus claras aficiones al sexo feo" (their clear fondness for the unattractive sex) and implores Jurado/Balmori to punish the nephew for his same-sex erotic desires with their acciones.[28] The prank is simple: Balmori will ask for the hand of the nephew who in turn will think that he will finally be able to fulfill his desire to live publicly with a man to later embrace the "humiliation" of being married to Conchita. In the eyes of his uncle, this will teach the nephew a lesson. However, Jurado/Balmori deviates from the original plan and seduces the only woman in the room. After the engineer complains, Balmori announces that they will also take the nephew as their lover who, less excited with this role, is comforted by the idea of spending unlimited time inside Balmori's huge library. When Jurado/Balmori reveals themselves as a poor woman, Jurado expresses the possibility of marrying the "'efebo' . . . porque aunque anciana, me gustaría conocer el matrimonio" ('ephebe' . . . because, although elderly, I would like to experience marriage).[29] The nephew, while disappointed, ends up declaring with "un coqueto movimiento" (a flirtatious gesture) that he will always prefer "al jefe del Tercio Español Don Carlos Balmori" (the chief of the Spanish Third, Don Carlos Balmori).[30] At the end, the nephew is not the one making ethical nor moral concessions—after all, he is not hiding his cuir desires.

During this prank, however, Jurado/Balmori expresses several times their feelings of discomfort and uneasiness, which I believe leads them to deviate from the plan and marry the woman as a way of relieving the pressure they are feeling. On one hand, Jurado/Balmori's prioritization for their own self-comfort shows once more their agency. On the other, this Balmoreada serves as a window into the differences experienced between masculine and female dissident experiences when exploring their non-normative desires in the Mexican post-revolutionary era. These differences are intersected by other identity markers such as race, class, and age, as I have been arguing. For a postmenopausal female body living in poverty to express their cuir desire with the confidence and flirtatiousness of the young man of this Balmoreada, they had to resort to the possibilities of the playfulness of *travesti* practices.

A Paranoid Reading of Asunción Izquierdo Albiñana's Third Gender

While the Balmoreadas exemplify a joyful disruption of gender relations during the post-revolutionary era, the anxiety and paranoia that these new relationships evoke, especially among white, middle- and upper-class societies, is much more palpable than their playful possibilities. The modern woman is the most visible example of this type of gender disruption. A woman willing to challenge the limits previously imposed to their gender—across both their personal and the professional lives, including their appearance and style—was considered a threat to the established order and caused discomfort among Mexican society.[31] Since the androgynous style of the modern woman (short hair, athletic bodies) blurs visual distinctions between genders, the concept of a "neutral gender" or "third sex" begins to circulate during this time and quickly becomes a euphemism used to describe anyone who falls outside normative expectations of gender and sexuality: "este modelo de mujer lograba subvertir los términos del binarismo normativo, resignificándolos y abriendo el espacio de posibilidad a un nuevo, tercer sexo.... El tercer sexo podía ser la feminista marimacho, la mujer emancipada, la coqueta, la garçon, el homosexual, la sufragista solterona, la lesbiana" (This model of woman managed to subvert the terms of normative binary thinking, resignifying them and opening up the space of possibility for a new, third sex. ... The third sex could be the feminist tomboy, the emancipated woman, the flirt, the garçon, the homosexual, the spinster suffragist, the lesbian).[32] As the quote illustrates, the concept of the third gender—and by extension, the modern woman—embodies a subtle gender revolution that simultaneously reveals the anxieties such rebellion provoked. While this upheaval ultimately gave rise to new normative ideas of femininity, it also sparked hopes for a future marked by greater gender troubles.

The tension between the desire to redefine gender ideas and the sometimes-needed attachment to the norm is capture by Asunción Izquierdo Albiñana's debut fiction *Andréïda (El tercer sexo)* (Ediciones Botas, 1938). Despite being published by one of the largest publishing houses of the time, Izquierdo Albiñana's fiction did not receive and has not received much critical attention regardless of being an important piece of cuir history with a unique standpoint about gender dissidence.[33] Inspired by *L'Ève future* (1886) by the French writer Auguste Villiers de L'Isle-Adam, *Andréïda* tells the story of a young woman that becomes "el monstruo ejemplar primero del Tercer Sexo" (the exemplary monster first of the Third Sex).[34] Described as pure artifice and as a mechanized self-construction, Andréïda is a character that challenges strict gender roles in the hopes of dismantling the heteropatriarchal structures that, according to her views, have made women mere machines of reproduction and pleasure. With a terrifyingly conventional beauty and an intelligence that scares anyone that surrounds her, Andréïda is the envy of all women and the being that every man wants to possess. But Andréïda has no interest in worldly values nor mundane pleasures such as smoking cigars or being available to men. Andréïda's sole goal is to trouble gender roles and achieve women's emancipation. And yet, at the end of the novel, the protagonist returns to the second sex.

One of Andréïda's suitors, named Raúl, coerces the protagonist into having sex that results in pregnancy. This coercion is not the first instance of emotional abuse since Raúl often blames Andréïda for the suicide of a former admirer and continuously tries to manipulate her into having a "formal" relationship. Throughout the novel and until her pregnancy, Andréïda wants to pursue her idea of the third gender, an idea that does not include a man by her side. On the contrary, Andréïda hopes for a life under the same roof with Nelly—her former professor and closest friend. But with her pregnancy and the consequent fear of not being able to support themselves financially,

Andréïda accepts the marriage proposal of Raúl, and the story ends with a "Fueron felices y tuvieron muchos hijos" (They were happy and had many children)—a return to the second sex.[35]

An epilogue written from the author's point of view dismisses this happy ending and imagines a different future for Andréïda:

> Gustosamente hacemos constar que en la feliz solución a la magnífica vida de la sin par Andréïda, influyó, no poco, la cobardía de la mano femenina que la plasmara en letras. Mano cobarde que, espantada de su audacia, se apresuró a alargarle la rehabilitación, la suprema redención a su heroína, dentro de una forma suave y rosada, destinada a estremecer al mundo con un débil vagido de infante...
>
> Pero, ¿quién nos dice que en el futuro, en el pavoroso futuro, esta docilidad de hoy de Andréïda, ésta su concesión a la frase, no se ahogue en el lago letal y sin fondo al que la arroja fatalmente la rebeldía a la injusticia y de la cual nació...?[36]

> We gladly acknowledge that in the happy resolution to the magnificent life of the incomparable Andréïda, the cowardice of the feminine hand that rendered her in writing played no small part. A cowardly hand that, terrified by its audacity, hastened to offer her rehabilitation, her ultimate redemption, within a gentle and rosy form, destined to shake the world with a weak infantile cry...
>
> But, who can tell us that in the future, in the dreadful future, this current docility of Andréïda, this concession to the phrase, will not drown in the bottomless and lethal lake to which it is inevitably thrown by the rebellion against injustice from which she was born...?

I read this epilogue as restorative gesture within Izquierdo Albiñana's own paranoid writing—a type of writing concerned with depicting the darker side of the cuir life while also representing the author's disjointed conjunction of ideas, that I have elsewhere called a "coherent incoherence" aesthetic.[37] This "coherent incoherence" manifests itself in several of Izquierdo Albiñana's female characters as paranoid attitudes revolving around their desire for a gender revolution. Their paranoia constantly forces the characters to detach themselves or move away from this desire due to concerns or fears about what the detachment from the norm really means. Other times, paranoid writing can even manifest itself as a delusional depiction of reality (for example, an android made of organic matter). I am interested in showing how this paranoid writing becomes an example of restorative criticism that provides insights on how gender revolutions happen, knowledge that can be useful to, for example, understand the transphobic rise in sentiment of the second decade of the twenty-first century.

For Eve Kosofsky Sedgwick, queer studies has a distinctive history with paranoia because paranoia reflects the repression of same-sex desire while also—and more significantly—functioning as a site for illuminating how homophobia and heteropatriarchal structures work.[38] In her discussion of paranoid readings as way of seeing things differently, this scholar sketches paranoia as a "strong theory" of "negative affects" that is anticipatory, reflexive, mimetic, and has faith on exposure.[39] Following these ideas, I read Izquierdo Albiñana's novel as a restorative practice that emerges from the cuir experience of the protagonist that then becomes illegible or invisible under her own paranoid writing. Thus, the epilogue plus other characteristics of *Andréïda*—such as the intimate relationship between Nelly and the protagonist, the intertextuality of the text, her critique of marriage, and the rushing pace of the end—require a paranoid reading to make legible her restorative motives.

The way literary scholars have approached Izquierdo Albiñana's fiction illuminates the illegibility of these motives. In the few paragraphs that Robert McKee Irwin dedicates to *Andréïda*, he argues that Izquierdo Albiñana "chooses to employ the popular trope for male homosexuality to combat feminist ambition."[40] In his analysis, the third sex is a trope of same-sex masculine desire and there is no possibility for a restorative reading with cuir nuances, since the purpose is to conquer "unnatural feminism" by way of maternity.[41] This scholar concludes that *Andréïda* is an example of how the social anxiety caused by different manifestations of gender trouble at the beginning of the century still carried weight at the end of the thirties. In a similar vein, Emily Hind argues that "instead of the cruel, dehumanized, asexual third sex," Izquierdo Albiñana suggests that it "is better to embrace the sexualized, inferior but normative second sex," decision that for Hind exemplifies a tension between the figure of the intellectual woman and the maternal.[42] However, in a more recent article, this same scholar proposes a different reading by alluding to the epilogue: "Izquierdo Albiñana no se imagina a una mujer intelectual normativa y tampoco se traga el giro hacia la domesticidad" (Izquierdo Albiñana cannot imagine a normative intellectual woman, nor does she buy into the shift toward domesticity).[43] Perhaps, a case of paranoid reading? Lastly, Paul Fallon takes Hind's ideas further to sustain that in the novel, Izquierdo Albiñana encourages the troubling of binary gender conceptions and the legal institution of marriage while exploring an everyday type of activism that can lead to change.[44] So, what is it then? A normative view of gender or a feminist-cuir restorative intervention?

If scholars and literary critics have agreed on a reading for the work of Izquierdo Albiñana, it is the one that emphasizes her style as contradictory. Manuel Pedro González observes that the plot of her novels tends to be "caprichoso y carente de lógica y raíz humana" (whimsical and lacking in logic and human grounding).[45] Emmanuel Carballo highlights her characters as always denied the possibility to "trascender las páginas y convertirse en seres posibles" (transcend the pages and become possible beings).[46] Vicente Leñero argues that *Andréïda* follows "todas las convenciones de la novela tradicional de principios de siglo" (all the conventions of the early twentieth-century traditional novel) to later affirm that her nontraditional "audacia moral" (moral audacity) and "crudeza de sus escenas eróticas" (crudeness of its erotic scenes) are the book's main attributes.[47] Most critics suggest that her coherent incoherence is the result of an immature literary project or a tedious personality; and some even venture that if she had stopped writing as the way she did, she could have been a great writer.[48] With a more benevolent and feminist look, Hind imagines that if she had a "supporting cohort of feminist intellectuals" maybe she would have been more radical.[49] Perhaps the issue to address here is the urgent need of better tools to interpret the implications of an aesthetics that highlights the coherent incoherent aspects of a cuir reality instead of imagining harmful hypothetical scenarios.

I do not want to expand on the life of Asunción Izquierdo Albiñana because I have already done it elsewhere and so the scholars I have mentioned.[50] More importantly, writing about her life is also inevitably running the risk of reproducing the gender-based violence she suffered at the hands of her husband because it is difficult to omit details that, although they provide certain reading guidelines, also arouse a morbid curiosity that I would rather avoid. Suffice it to say that he did not approve her intellectual ambitions, even when Izquierdo Albiñana contributed financially to support the family with her writing before her husband's appointment as senator of San Luis Potosí in 1940, a moment in which he decides to ban her from writing.[51] Before this ban, she writes *Andréïda* at the age of twenty-seven and two years later *Caos* (Chaos) (Ediciones Botas, 1940)—the only two books published under her name out of fear for spousal reprisals. After this, she continues to publish using different pseudonyms and exploring different genres, such as theater, short stories, and poetry.[52] As she explains in one of her personal letters, she also wrote most of the political discourses of her husband and even for some of his friends.[53] She won literary prizes and organized secret gatherings with some of the intellectuals of her time.[54] She spoke German, Russian, English, French, and Italian. As her close friend Anna Murià recalls, she felt trapped in her normative life but did not have the courage to walk away from her economic privileges nor her house in Las Lomas.⁵⁵ All this to say that she is a Mexican intellectual and a professional writer living a life of strong coherent incoherencies while dreaming with a more hopeful future that sadly she never got to experience herself.

Going back to the idea of paranoid writing, one of the first things the reader of *Andréïda* notices is how the book performs this coherent incoherence or paranoid writing through the omniscient narrator and the actions of the protagonist. A suggestive way of perceiving this, has to do with how time is understood in relation to gender dissidence and how this knowledge relates to the pace of the plot. Right at the beginning of the story, the narrator clarifies that "Andréïda no es un ser de transición" (Andréïda is not a being of transition) but "un ser de porvenir que se adelantó por designio inexplicable, a ese extraño elemento problemático que llamamos Tiempo" (a being of the future who, by an inexplicable design, advanced ahead of that strange problematic element we call Time).⁵⁶ The word "transición" is frequently used to evoke both to the transience and to the incompleteness of the modern woman as a figure trapped between the past and a future that has yet to fully arrive. Hence, the urge to clarify in the first few pages that Andréïda is a complete being that is here to stay and not the result of a fad—she is a being of the future.

In a similar vein to José Esteban Muñoz, who views queerness as something always already in the horizon, Andréïda's gender dissidence functions as a utopic impulse performed in the quotidian.⁵⁷ That is why Paul Fallon notices that, in the novel, a special emphasis is placed on daily activism as a tool for change.⁵⁸ When there are no adequate structures to support more radical changes, the everyday disruptions perform by Nelly and Andréïda (i.e., their work as journalists that leads them to, for example, document and discuss the feminist labor movement; or to write about cases of gender-based violence) enact a certain surplus that contains the promise of a future change. As I mentioned before, this way of feeling temporality affects the pace of the plot given that the narrator frequently and extensively rambles on topics such as marriage laws, women's emancipation, labor movements, US imperialism, etc. But other times the narrator hastily describes what the reader would think are passages more relevant to the plot of the story, such as the discovery of the pregnancy and the subsequent outcome that are condensed into a couple of pages. Because of this pace and long digressions, *Andréïda* sometimes feels more like an example of nineteenth-century realistic novels than a text from the post-revolutionary period. This strange pace feels dangerously backward and out of tune in relation with the novelty of the third gender that *Andréïda* proposes. I believe this pace is an example of how Izquierdo Albiñana is attentive to the past for the purpose of critiquing a present to make room for a future chance of troubling gender.

The utopian impulse of queerness is related to Sedgwick's reparative hermeneutics in the sense that paranoia is anticipatory.[59] In this case, I see Izquierdo Albiñana's back-and-forth on gender ideas as an example of paranoia that seeks to eliminate future surprises. One of the first issues that Andréïda faces while embracing her gender dissidence is to gain her independence which, in this case, means finding a job that gives her financial stability. Even though women in the thirties were already part of the labor force in Mexico, they did not enjoy the same rights as men. For example, if a woman was married, she required her husband's permission to work and it was assumed that if she became pregnant, she would return to being the angel of the house.[60] Thus, Andréïda is forced to confront the fact that to remain independent—a nonnegotiable characteristic of the third sex—she cannot succumb to any marriage proposal. Furthermore, she realizes that the system itself prevents the reshaping of gender roles with their outdated laws.

Andréïda is anticipating the various types of material constraints faced by gender dissidents. The book places special emphasis on the risk of pregnancy and the lack of a legal identity for women as the main reasons for women's dependency. As exemplified in the novel with several cases, this dependent status facilitates instances of gender-based violence: Marisabel suffers from physical violence at the hands of her husband and remains at his side out of fear of economic hardship.[61] After being extorted by her lover, María Luisa kills him to protect the daughter from scandal to later confess that the real criminal should be the husband—a sadistic man that controlled her financially so that she wouldn't leave him.[62] *Andréïda* suggests that it is more dangerous to not anticipate the obstacles of troubling gender than to embrace a third sex without facing any of the possible challenges.

Another way of perceiving paranoia in *Andréïda* is to think through the book's mimetic motions via intertextuality. Sedgwick argues that a practice of paranoid knowledge is essential to understanding paranoia and the way paranoia understands anything is "by way of imitating and embodying it."[63] To make sense of gender roles, Izquierdo Albiñana rewrites the main plot of Villiers's book. In *Tomorrow's Eve*, a man tired of his wife's personality receives an offer from Mr. Edison, an engineer who proposes to build him an android that imitates the woman's affections and body without her tedious personality. Named Hadaly, the android is a prototype of Edison's project to control, destroy, and replace women's identities with machines. What puts an end to Hadaly's life, however, is not Mr. Edison's himself but nature (she drowns in a sinking ship during a storm). The story's ending points toward the failure of the project because ultimately the engineer cannot control when or how the android gets dismantled. Villiers's book provides Izquierdo Albiñana with the knowledge that gender can be troubled; and therefore, the discourse of gender as something fixed and natural can be refuted. I argue that the protagonist in *Andréïda* embodies this knowledge to try out other possibilities.

In her early work as a columnist and under her pen name Psique Hadaly—an obvious reference to Villiers' android's mind—Izquierdo Albiñana addresses her female readers to instruct them in the goals of the modern woman. If men have an ideal woman, then the modern woman must claim this ideal back to create a new version—one where they constitute themselves as subjects of their own desire and develop their own personalities.[64] This idea continues to be tested in Andréïda's character. Instead of science and in difference to Villiers, what matters is the reiterative practice of artifice, suggesting that identities are constituted through an artificial imitation that sets itself up as the origin of all imitations. Andréïda imitates an ideal gender—that of the third sex—exposing the fragility of the gender binary by emphasizing this maneuver as an invention of herself that has nothing to do with nature.

The question of agency becomes a singular point of Izquierdo Albiñana's thought on gender. In *Tomorrow's Eve*, Alicia (the wife of the unhappy man) is depicted as completely deprived of agency. In contrast, Andréïda exercises agency by actively choosing to perform differently: "me he creado a mí misma" (I have created myself) or "mi poderosa voluntad ha variado la naturaleza" (my powerful will has altered nature) are phrases that our protagonist is constantly repeating to herself and others.[65] By the end of the novel, Andréïda realizes that choosing is not as uncomplicated as she thought, because identities as social constructs are also affected by material conditions as I pointed out earlier. Andréïda's return to the second sex could be read as an anticipatory recall of the messy relation between gender performativity and body matter that still haunts our political present. In the end, Andréïda is unable to rectify the violence of gender because her body constitutes a constraint that she is not able to deconstruct in her present time. Even when she cannot sort out a cuir present for herself and other women, her reflexive and mimetic process unravels new layers of theoretical problems that even today's feminists are still juggling with.

The last point that I want to address is that of paranoia and its faith in exposure. The narrator as well as the protagonist advocate for exposing their readers to knowledge as an efficient way of countering future gender violence. Andréïda's recurrent lectures on marriage laws and the documented cases of domestic abuse are examples of the trust placed on exposure as a preventive method for gender-based violence. However, it seems to me that Izquierdo Albiñana's faith in the practice of education, raises the question of paranoia as normative hermeneutics because it fails to recognize and problematize the positionality of the paranoid writer and that of the one who is being exposed. Additionally, it also obscures the ways in which exposure itself can be an act of violence. Thus, paranoia can turn into a "weak theory."[66] In this case, by exposing their readers to a monolithic education centered on gender struggles, Andréïda fails to address distinct forms of oppression and her own privileged position as an educated woman of the middle class. As a case in point, every time Andréïda finds herself in front of a racialized woman she is incapable of recognizing their differences and denies them any capacity of agency with her patronizing views. For Andréïda, the root of all oppressions lies in the category of gender; thus, solving gender disparities will result in all women's emancipation. The dissemination of this universalizing perspective is an example of how exposure can be violent.[67] In *Andréïda* the possibility of an intersectional or situated future is never envisioned. In other words, Izquierdo Albiñana is unable to anticipate the problems of what today is akin to white and neoliberal feminism. I see this lack of anticipation (and in consequence, the absence of the utopic impulse) as stressing suspicion or doubt as one of the qualities of paranoid writing that prevents a normative and universalizing becoming. Thus, the persisting feeling of doubt of the paranoid is what opens the possibility for a restorative criticism.

If Izquierdo Albiñana never shows herself as suspicious of the universalizing vision of female emancipation, she doubts all the time when it comes to exposing the possibility of a cuir experience as I suggested with the analysis of the third gender and the return to the second sex. Another way Izquierdo Albiñana shows her paranoid suspicions about the possibilities of cuir dissidence is by means of Andréïda and Nelly's relationship. Often the narrator hints the possibility of same-sex female desire between the two friends while also affirming their relationship as a case for a lesbian continuum—a range of woman-identified experiences beyond erotic desire.[68] At the beginning of the story, Andréïda is living in an all-girls boarding school in the US where Nelly—who has the habit of dressing in a tailored suit and never expresses sexual interest for man—is her teacher and superior. During that time, the narrator recalls Andréïda's reaction to a "escandalosa amistad" (scandalous friendship) between two of the students: "Lejos de Andréïda estaba el poseer una mentalidad mezquina y malintencionada, puesto que sus múltiples lecturas y su propia especial naturaleza la colocaban en un plano de la más alta compresión humana. Es más, en ocasiones, ella había criticado duramente la incomprensión de muchos pedagogos ... y reconocía que su criterio acusador ... no tenía razón de ser. Andréïda proclamaba rotundamente que este amor era natural, sano, puro, biológico" ("Far from Andréïda was the possession of a petty and malicious mentality, since her numerous readings and her own special nature placed her on a plane of the highest human understanding. Furthermore, on occasion, she had harshly criticized the lack of understanding of many educators ... and acknowledged that her accusatory judgment ... had no reason to exist. Andréïda proclaimed unequivocally that this love was natural, healthy, pure, biological").[69] Andréïda goes beyond proclaiming same-sex desire as something natural and positive by recognizing that she has gone through "esa etapa" ("that stage") with Nelly.[70] After confessing her erotic desires, she quickly turns this erotic affection into a case of lesbian continuum by highlighting their relation as frugal and fraternal. But time reshapes "ese afecto un poco exaltado" (that somewhat exalted affection) into "el puro y fraternal que hoy las unía" (the pure and fraternal one that united them today) to the point of buying and sharing a house together.[71] If by now my reader is still not convinced by these cuir nuances, perhaps a last example that returns us back to the idea of cuir erotic desire will make me sound less or (even better) more paranoid.

In one of Raúl's multiple and tedious attempts to conquer Andréïda, she declares: "Me parecía el único hombre que, de haber sido mujer ... hubiese amado" (He seemed to me the only man who, had he been a woman ... would have loved).[72] The sentence's ambiguity highlights Andréïda's cuir attitudes and gender dissidence, as it can be interpreted in two ways: if Andréïda were a woman, she could fall for Raúl; or if Raúl were a woman, Andréïda could love them. Whether the statement refers to Raúl or Andréïda herself does not matter; both interpretations imply same-sex desire. It is important to remind that Andréïda sees herself as a third gender, which is often used euphemistically to refer to lesbianism, bisexuality, and female masculinities. María Jesús Fariña Busto suggests looking at the third gender as part of a *ginealogía*—a term that speaks of the historical uses of silences, euphemisms, and other forms of marginalization endured by lesbians throughout the twentieth century in Spain.[73] This scholar mentions *Andréïda* as an example of how *ginealogía* can be trace to other geographies, such as Mexico, where is also palpable the historical use of the third gender as an indirect word to substitute the "bluntness" of different sexual and gender dissidences.

It is not possible to know with certainty why Izquierdo Albiñana goes back and forward when it comes to Andréïda's erotic desires. Perhaps it has to do with the risk of repression and censorship when it comes to making visible same-sex desire, or with Andréïda's own indecision when thinking about erotic desire, female emancipation, and the attachment to the norm. Whatever the case is, the point is that I read this uncertainty as a way of anticipating the possible problems of exposing cuir desire in a heteronormative world. It is also a way for Izquierdo Albiñana to express her own attachments to the norm as a survival mechanism. It seems that her paranoia haunts the writer into believing that the price for embracing same-sex desire and a cuir life ultimately will be paid by the feminist struggle (sound familiar?). And yet, she refuses to succumb to fear and marks the way for those who dare to follow it—*Andréïda* is full of cuir references demanding paranoid readers.

On one occasion, Andréïda mentions being dissatisfied with her beauty. She relates this feeling to Oscar Wilde's *The Picture of Dorian Gray*, a book that although it had yet to become the potent centerpiece of gay male desire that it is today was already a benchmark of queer culture by the 1930s. After imagining herself as a third gender version of Dorian, Andréïda concludes that her sadness is not due to her beauty complex but to the fact that she misses Nelly (she has been staying alone outside of Mexico City for a couple of months to recover from the scandal of her suitor's suicide). Of course, one can read nothing out of this reference, but would not that be reproducing the "it didn't happen," "it didn't mean anything," "it doesn't have interpretative consequences," "stop asking" repressive and conservative ways in which literary criticism sustains homophobic understandings of canonical and non-canonical cuir/queer literature?

The question is rhetorical since Sedgwick already answer yes in a very eloquent section of her landmark book *Epistemology of the Closet*.[74] The infinite contradictions of Izquierdo Albiñana's paranoid writing suggest that no one can know where the limits of a cuir-feminist inquiry are to be drawn. *The Picture of Dorian Gray* is among the texts that have set the terms for a modern homosexual identity, and Izquierdo Albiñana is very cautious and clever in the ways she uses this reference. Thus, addressing these nuances posits *Andréïda* as one of the books which, if it had not been ignored, could account for the emergence of female same-sex desire and gender dissidence at the beginning of the twentieth century in Mexico.

Perhaps the question that deserves a more detailed answer is what makes paranoid writing a restorative practice? I am afraid that my response might sound too simplistic. After all, it is the desire for restoration that transforms paranoid writing into a restorative practice—desire that, in this case, is loudly manifested through the epilogue. As *Andréïda* shows, this desire also needs to be a form of praxis; in this case, Andréïda intervenes with her daily activism her present reality even when she is aware of its immanent failure. To set into motion the restoration process, a collaboration also needs to happen. In this case, Izquierdo Albiñana puts her faith into future paranoid eyes willing to interpret all the contradictory forces of the text to anticipate, ponder, and embody future gender troubles with their own new normativities and possibilities. After all, restorative criticism is the practice of asking the questions, claiming it happened, embodying the meaning, and defending the interpretative consequences that can be as significant as we want them to be.

In this case, one of the reparative moves is to affect canon formations by introducing forgotten episodes or texts that cultural history has condemned as illegible or insignificant. The practice of disrupting a universal canon is a reparative move with a long history in cuir/queer and feminist methodologies. But the intention is not to create different minor canons or a new set of centerpieces that go back to the lettered city or to the stagnant idea of the nation. Rather, this cultural production has the capacity of doing something for our present social movements; it offers unique access to knowledge that illuminates epistemological gaps that today are being used to sustain normative views without the possibility for future restorations. *Andréïda* embodies a gender revolution that always operates in a continuum of feeling an attachment to the norm while performing as always suspicious of this norm for the sake of lo cuir. The invitation of restorative criticism is to bring these affects to our present revolution.

A Mischievous Archive: The Future of the Bearded Women

In March 2005, an open invitation to participate in a playful and mischievous project starts to circulate through the blogs of Cristina Rivera Garza, Amaranta Caballero Prado, and Sayak Valencia. To partake in the joke, one simply had to send a photo to the troublemakers to be modified by Caballero with a beard or mustache to later be posted online. Labeled as "La inquietante [e internacional] semana de las mujeres barbudas," this project culminates with an event at Casa Refugio Citlatépetl held from June 18 to 25 of the same year. Curated by Abril Castro, "La inquietante . . ." included the photos intervened by Caballero as well as a series of professional portraits of the bearded women taken by Mariano Aparicio and Yvonne Venegas. It also involved an on-site photographic studio for the bearded public, video art, multiple texts from different genres, and an onstage adaptation of *Plagio de palabras* (Plagiarism of words; 2000) by Elena Guiochins.[75] Beyond this art exhibition, the bearded women took to the streets, gave their lectures, and visited cantinas with their prominent mustaches. Rumor has it that part of the archive was lost in a cantina where they played dominoes and drank alcohol. As the cantinas are usually male-dominated spaces, their presence was received with strange looks from uncomfortable men without daring to say anything—word on the street suggests that Adriana González Mateos said, "Barbonas porque rima con cabronas" (Bearded women because it rhymes with bitches), words that condense the affect of the mischievous act. These women sought to promote a ludic and transgressive reflection of the meaning of gender in a compulsively heterosexual and patriarchal society where female bodies tend to be often policed to the degree that hairiness is deem unacceptable and even monstrous.

The bearded women were made up of a mix of artists, writers, professors, and feminists from places like Tijuana, Monterrey, Barcelona, Uruguay, and Mexico City. In addition to the already mentioned some of the participants were members of the Colectivo La Línea and individuals like Cristina Peri Rossi, Mónica Mayer, Myriam Moscona, Ana Clavel, Francesca Gargallo,

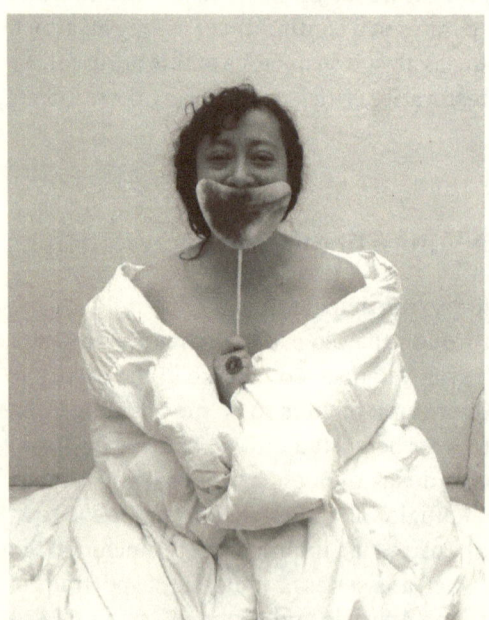

Figure 2.5. Ana Clavel, wrapped in a duvet, poses against a plain background, holding a stick with an oversized mouth cutout in front of her face, resembling a hairy pubic area and creating a playful, provocative effect. She wears a ring with a flower on her finger, adding a subtle pop of color to the minimalist composition. Courtesy of Ana Clavel.

Adriana González Mateos, Eve Gil, Clarissa Malheiros, Carla Faesler, Mónica Nepote, Bárbara Colio, Rocío Cerón, Marta Lamas, Juliana Faesler, Ishtar Cardona, Vizania Amezcua, Patricia Vega, Gabriela Cano, Amelia Suárez, Mónica Zsurmuk, plus all the mischievous collaborators that contributed with their online submissions such as Pedro Ángel Palou, Víctor Lerma, and Luis Felipe Lomelí since the invitation was also extended to include male peers. Similar to the acciones of Jurado/Balmori, this group of troublemakers uses humor to transgress heteropatriarchal structures from a transfeminist standpoint. Their mischievousness is another remnant of the archive of gender playfulness explored throughout this chapter.

Arjun Appadurai has argued that the archive is built on accidents that produce traces to help with the search of collective memory.[76] For this author, the archive is a tool "for the refinement of desire."[77] On the other hand, the production of archives as movable tools that produce lines of deviation is central to Cristina Rivera Garza's work.[78] As an example, Roberto Cruz Arzabal finds in *Viriditas* and *La muerte me da* (*Death Takes Me*) the production of "archivos potenciales" ("potential archives") defined as movable spaces that do not seek to contain but to map tensions.[79] Following their ideas, the archive of gender playfulness comprised by the Balmoreadas, Izquierdo Albiñana's fiction, and "La inquietante . . ." helps me map my desire for tracing genealogies of gender dissidence in the search of collective memory with the hopes of producing potential deviation routes in the face of the rise of transphobic discourses.

This archive shows that there is an older history of feminist insurrection in Mexico built on gender as a nonbinary discourse. If gender dissidence has a long feminist history in the context of Mexico, transexclusionary movements can be viewed as a contemporary example of the coloniality of gender. Explained by María Lugones as an encompassing phenomenon that permeates all control of sexual and gender access, the coloniality of power has a light and dark side: the light side reorders gender hegemonically while the latter erases gender dissidence; that is why understanding the place of gender in precolonial societies is pivotal in Lugones's thinking.[80] I believe transexclusionary discourses are trying to operate in a similar way by reorganizing gender in hierarchical terms while also ignoring deep histories of gender nonbinary thinking. It is also important to mention that transexclusionary discourses are somehow foreign since their theoretical support comes from other geopolitical contexts such as the United States and Spain. If, in the year of its production—and as some of their collaborators recalled—"La inquietante . . ." was merely intended as a simple joke for amusement, here, the archive of gender playfulness emerges to disrupt essentialist discourses of gender and creates a geopolitical space for future subversions.

This archive also highlights how the category of "woman" has been deployed strategically in Mexico as political positionality without being rigidly defined or fixed in meaning. In *Feminismo bastardo* (Bastard feminism), María Galindo contends that beyond the compelling validity of questioning gender binaries posed by queer theory, there is the political option of choosing the social position or the place from which to build alliances.[81] For Galindo, women as a "universo complejo" (complex universe) represent "un lugar histórico en explosión" (a historical place in explosion) from which to address and position ourselves.[82] She continues to explain that speaking from the positionality of women does not entail embracing a "condición biológica, quirúrgica o identitaria" (biological, surgical, or identity condition) but rather a "espacio metafórico, poético y político" (metaphorical, poetic, and political space) that is open to the edges of nonbinary thinking.[83] Within my archive of gender playfulness, we witness nonbinary thinking in action as the bearded women, Andréïda, and Jurado/Balmori engage in acts of gender dissidence from the metaphorical and political standpoints of women, refraining from imposing either biological or ontological definitions on this gender category. The affective results of this choice on spectators, ranging from laughter to disgust, anxiety, and fear in the case of the bearded women or the Balmoreadas, and Andréïda's paranoia, demonstrate that positioning ourselves politically this way still generates discomfort, thereby continues to offer a political advantage that we can exploit. In one of the manifestos for "La inquietante . . ." and later reposted on her personal blog under the title "Welcome to hairy tales," Sayak Valencia writes, "No somos drags vaciadas de contenido, ni fashionistas extremas. No somos kitsch-optimistas, ni exhibicionistas vulgares. Somos lúdico-práctico-críticas. . . . Cuestionamos cualquier lógica de la identidad a través de la acción (performance) para así re-trazar al ser y al sujeto" (We are not empty-content drags, nor extreme fashionistas. We are not kitsch-optimists, nor vulgar exhibitionists. We are playful-practical-critics. . . . We question any logic of identity through action (performance) in order to re-trace the being and the subject).[84] This sentence summarizes the history of gender dissidence found within my restored archive. Through ludic interventions, it gathers a critique of identity categories while also strategically employing them in practice to redefine their meanings. It is a practice of restorative criticism because it does not break from the category of woman but reformulates it as an open metaphor ready to be restored.

A long-term memory that traces gender dissidence within the context of Mexico is necessary and urgent to illustrate how the discourses of identity and essentialist understandings of womanhood are a very recent phenomenon, often imported from other geopolitical contexts. In the context of Spain, Lucas Platero argues that transexclusionary discourses are recent and primarily fueled by social media and individuals unaware of transfeminist histories, solidarities, and resistances.[85] Platero demonstrates how feminism has embraced queer criticism and has begun to seek a less essentialist political subject by tracing various instances throughout history, identifying moments when "hay que arriesgar el sujeto político del feminismo" (we must risk the political subject of feminism).[86] In the case of Latin America, Galindo uses the metaphor of a can to describe the identity logics of the "enlatado gelebetoso" (slimy canned LGBTQ+) as a neoliberal fashion imported from abroad. According to Galindo, the purpose of this can is to confine the Latin American gender and sexual dissidence within an identity ghetto, aiming for easy classification and organization for better exploitation and exportation management.[87] Galindo advocates for a feminist praxis that always bothers with its rejection of classification and coherence.

In the case of Mexico, my archive of gender playfulness serves as a time capsule to observe the various moments when women have risked the subject of feminism while using their own corporality as a territory for gender disidentification. This, in turn, provokes a critical ludic discourse based on a praxis that troubles binary thinking. The different episodes of gender dissidence scattered through time in this chapter reveal the layers upon layers of gender troubling in Mexico. The appearances of bearded women, the *travesti acciones* of Jurado/Balmori, and the paranoid feelings of Asunción Izquierdo Albiñana complicate the subject of feminism from a cuir perspective.

Indeed, the genealogy of gender dissidence presented in this chapter can be seen as a reparative exercise in long-term memory. It sheds light on the historical existence of gender dissidence and its alliances with feminism, revealing that the feminist transexclusionary discourses are a relatively recent development. If the transexclusionary discourse of promoting essentialist ideas of gender to mask transphobia is a very recent layer on the history of gender in Mexico, then, transexclusionary discourses are a very fragile and superficial layer. Restoring various archives of gender playfulness denaturalizes the transexclusionary views as inherent in the history of gender, downplaying their relevance in our geopolitical context. If the past is marked by numerous mischievousness acts that trouble gender norms by strategically employing the category of "woman" from a feminist and cuir political positionality, the likelihood of a future full of bearded women is still on the horizon.

CHAPTER 3

Snap, Snap, Snap!

Toward an Affective Cuir Method of Literary Critique

Have you ever rolled your eyes while reading a book? Or perhaps you sighed as a physical way to express weariness in the face of a lamentable situation? These physical reactions are typically interpreted in our society as signs of losing control of our emotions, leading to behaviors or reactions that may be irrational, impulsive, or extreme. It is a common belief that when one fails to effectively control their emotions, it impacts our ability to think clearly or make rational decisions. Of course, these reactions are gendered and at some point, they were even interpreted as a medical condition called hysteria. I mention this because my relationship with Mexican literature can be described as a series of physical reactions that tend to convey the overwhelming or uncontrollable reaction toward a book, a critique, or a situation that becomes unbearable almost always due to some comment that hides (or not) a heteropatriarchal bias. For example, in March 2020, I attended a conference on contemporary Mexican literature where I presented an early version of this chapter. During that time, my emotions were all over the place. I received two job rejections while traveling to El Paso, and the odds of finding an academic position were very slim. Additionally, it was also the weekend when people started talking about lockdowns due to COVID-19 in the United States, and everyone was feeling uneasy about traveling back home after the conference. In my case, I decided to change my plans. Originally, I had intended to attend the Women's March in Ciudad Juárez since it promised to be one of the most important ones, and I had never attended one before. However, I changed my flight out of fear of getting trapped in the area and being forced to pay for a place to stay. All this to say, I remember feeling cranky, disappointed, and weary. After all those years of graduate school, I was going to be jobless (I got a job), and my advisors were already talking about the possibility of moving my PhD defense online, which the sole idea felt nerve-racking (it happened). So, sitting at a table for over an hour to present about lesbian writers complaining about the state of lesbian literature seemed even more absurd than normal. I had zero mood for performing the proper academic role that one is supposed to perform, especially as a graduate student.

Naturally, during the Q&A session, someone inevitably felt compelled to raise those perennial questions that never fail to test my patience. The first one, "and what about men?" veiled in pseudo-provocation, lacks sophistication, and deserves little consideration. (One might amusingly respond with "Why not elephants or flamingos?" as a cheeky rejoinder). The second query, though seemingly poised for a deeper response, framed women's writing as an anomaly and exception, suggesting it only emerges when one delves into unfamiliar territory with sufficient vigor: "But how did you find out about the work of all [two] these lesbian writers?" Perhaps I am being unfair because, as I have referred to in the introduction, the canon is a magnificent tool that serves to obscure the work of others. Since the moderator was taking multiple questions before the panelists could answer, another attendee requested clarification about what I meant by "snapping" as a method of literary critique. When it was my turn to answer, I asked the audience who could mention the names of five gay male Mexican writers. After the majority raised their hands and some even began recalling names, I asked how many lesbian writers they could mention besides the two names I had already provided. A couple of people recalled Nancy Cárdenas, and someone mentioned *Infinita* (Infinite; 1992) by Ethel Krauze, a novel about lesbian desire written by an author who does not identify herself as a lesbian writer. Bisexual writers? Trans? Silence. Rolling my eyes, I asked, "Does that answer your question about why not men?" Perhaps I was being snappy, but the improvised exercise of recalling names was an excellent moment to explain what I mean by snapping as a method of literary criticism. It is the moment when losing control of our emotions represents a breaking point that potentially reorients our interpretative strategies to less damaging practices. Asking how you found your corpus is not inherently a bad question, but when that is the only question that you keep hearing and normally it is a question that only surfaces when we talk about women writers and other so-called minorities, it becomes a problem because it implicitly signals women's writing as something obscure instead of pointing to, perhaps, our own reading biases as the problem.

In the late 1980s, women writers began to document and fictionalize the experiences of women who chose to live outside the confines of heterosexuality. During this period, they did not adhere to the fashionable aesthetics of the time and often faced various degrees of censorship, resulting in a form of erasure that has kept them on the margins of Mexican (cuir) cultural histories. This obliteration is still felt today; the presence of so-called lesbian literature in Mexico is still questioned, and cultural histories of sexual and gender dissidence tend to focus on the masculine experience. In the face of this systematic erasure, lesbian writing can be viewed as a collection of breaking points—or snaps—where women writers use their frustration to experiment with literature.

In this chapter, I propose a feminist and cuir methodology that utilizes affect as a category of literary analysis. Affect is an unrecognized force which can later translate into emotions and feelings. Sara Ahmed provides an example of this affective force in the concept of the "snap," which she sees as a creative and productive way to approach feminist breaking points. In her work *Living a Feminist Life*, Ahmed frames breaking points as positive openings for feminist praxis. She coins the term "feminist snap" to describe these fractures.[1] By treating *snap* as a verb, Ahmed identifies a sensation that captures the moment of sudden rupture, often evoking a crisis, which in turn creates space for change. The figure of the feminist killjoy, someone who disrupts the status quo in response to misogynist or racist remarks, exemplifies the concept of the feminist snap. Thus, the snap emerges as an affective assemblage that challenges normative discourses and seeks "to bind subjects together."[2] Its affective force lies in the potential stickiness of the emotions it generates. I explore the snap as a writing and interpretative methodology through the analysis of two fictional pieces that engage with negative aesthetics, foregrounding the unstable nature of gender and sexual dissidence and expressing frustration against canonical formations: *Amora* (Beloved; 1989) by Rosa María Roffiel and *La reinita pop no ha muerto* (*The Little Queen of Pop Is Not Dead*; 2013) by Criseida Santos Guevara.

My hypothesis is that the relationship between women's writing, aesthetics (especially experimental forms) and canon (un)building is expressed through an affective assemblage—the snap—that legitimizes both their aesthetic choices and their political views. Since the snap is fueled by a physical reaction that later transforms into a recognizable emotion, the reader can also mobilize their own affective reactions into a different direction, resulting in something totally unrelated to the affective assemblage proposed by the writer. Analyzing the ways in which affect is captured and its lines of deviation, allows for a re-description of canon formations and the processes of historicizing Mexican literature that explains the biases in which cuir literature has been understood as well as reorienting the perceived definition of canon—as a more or less fixed list of masterpieces reproducing hegemonic cultural value—to a body that has the capacity to affect and to be affected.

In her book *Women's Experimental Writing: Negative Aesthetics and Feminist Critique*, Ellen E. Berry proposes the notion of negative aesthetics as a form of critique to innovate in the ways in which literature and feminism have been linked in literary studies by primarily using a corpus of fiction and nonfiction written in English. I found her ideas compelling for my project because Berry enumerates a set of textual features and political commitments—ranging from thematic concerns to self-conscious and theoretical awareness—"deployed in such a way that normative structures of perception and representation are rendered unstable, in the process revealing their limits or crisis points."[3] Berry is interested in examining the negative aesthetic modes promoted by her corpus that—as the author argues—can shape political expressions in unique ways, especially those in relation to feminism.[4] Following her lead, I am intrigued by the use of negative aesthetic modes in *Amora* and *La reinita pop no ha muerto* to innovate in the ways in which literature and cuiridad have been linked in Mexican literary criticism. The negative aesthetics employed by these writers allow me to trace snap moments to show how affect is used to rethink literature in a way that counteracts the power dynamics of dude lit.[5] These snaps manifest through genre, book reviews, cuir bonds (or feminist winks), aesthetic choices, and even through performing authorship and readership as I will address in the last chapter. I am particularly interested in the snaps caused by uneasy feelings (such as failure and refusal) and those that relate to issues of canonicity, the critical possibilities of cuiridad, and experimental writing.

I begin this chapter by analyzing *Amora* as a failed fiction because I believe it sheds light on the relationship between affect and the processes that render Roffiel's writing unintelligible to their male peers, or those adhering to traditional notions of masculinity, and the subsequent consequences of this unintelligibility. Sara E. L. Bowskill has identified these processes, suggesting that woman-authored novels often face negative criticism due to interpretative strategies that favor dominant literary discourses, consequently excluding them from the canon.[6] On the other hand, María Elena Olivera Córdoba and Artemisa Téllez have traced a genealogy of Mexican lesbian literature that proves helpful in illustrating how *Amora*'s unintelligibility impacts future representations of the lesbian experience. Both authors identify Roffiel's fiction as pioneering and opening the space for lesbian existence in Mexican literature.[7] Téllez also proposes a periodization that positions *Amora* as a work seeking positive—even utopic—representations of feminist lesbians, while later literary texts explore lesbian positionalities outside normative frameworks.[8] An example of this is Artemisa Téllez's graphic novel *Crema de vainilla* (Vanilla cream; 2015), which delves into BDSM representation and lesbian relationships. While Téllez's analysis of *Amora* differs significantly from the reading I propose in the following pages, her periodization still sheds light on this fiction as a narrative that initiates different modes of writing lesbian literature.

In this sense, *Amora*'s failure can be viewed as an opening for contemporary writers like Criseida Santos Guevara. Emily Hind has expressed the point I want to convey here by highlighting feminist criticism as always being "busted criticism."[9] If being perceived as a failure is almost inevitable for feminist critics and writers, perhaps we should embrace the analytic malfunction, as Hind argues, rather than proving their success. Roffiel and Santos Guevara exploit the unintelligibility of cuir women's writing to challenge the canon and gender representations by deploying extreme negative aesthetics, such as those identified by Berry. Together, these writers show how uneasy feelings reorient literature toward cuir methods of interpretation.

Before jumping into the analysis of *Amora*, I want to insist on the erasure and censorship that lesbian literature still faces in the first decades of the twenty-first century. During the research of this project, I interviewed several lesbian writers with horror stories of blunt censorship and discrimination. Some of the cases have been discussed publicly such as the one described by Artemisa Téllez in her aforementioned essay "'A Chloe le gustaba Olivia': Implicaciones de una literatura que quisiera llamarse lésbica" ("Chloe liked Olivia: Implications of a literature that would like to be called lesbian"). Others have become cautionary tales like the case of Sara Levi Calderón, who had to go into exile after publishing *Dos mujeres* (Two women; 1990) for fear of reprisals by her family. Beyond just censorship, the erasure is palpable within a publishing industry that still does not make much room for this kind of literature. Most lesbian writers are self-published, circulating through independent publishing houses with small distributions, and those few who do get picked out by commercial publishing houses rarely get a second edition.[10] The panorama is even bleaker for bisexual and trans* writers and/or topics. In this context, the publication of *Versas y diversas: Muestra de* *poesía lésbica mexicana contemporánea* (Verses and Diverse: A sample of contemporary Mexican lesbian poetry; 2021) edited by Paulina Rojas and Odette Alonso, as well as the re-edition of *La reinita pop no ha muerto* (2022) by Random House, and the very recent publication of *Crucé la frontera en tacones: Crónicas de una TRANSgresora* (I crossed the border in high heels: Chronicles of a TRANSgressor; 2023) by trans activist Alexandra R. DeRuiz and Almadía's publication of *Transporte a la infancia* (Transport to childhood; 2023) by Frida Cartas—a book that circulated as an *edición de autor*—are rare events in the history of the representation of gender and sexual dissidence of women.

In contrast to this pattern of erasure, there is a significant disparity within gay literature. Numerous anthologies exclusively feature texts authored by men exploring gay desire. What troubles me about these collections is not their focus on documenting gay desire; such emphasis is understandable given the enduring homophobic biases present in our literary traditions. Rather, the issue lies in the marginalization of cuir women's writings, dismissed as an anomaly of the past, as exemplified in *La síntesis rara de un siglo loco* (The rare synthesis of a crazy century; 2017) by Sergio Téllez-Pon. This anthology, which traces the history of homoerotic poetry, begins with the works of Sor Juana Inés de la Cruz, only to be followed by fifty-seven male authors delving into themes of gay desire.

Another form of dismissal is ignoring the existence of any cuir positionalities except that of gay men. One example is the much-needed project of revisiting and reediting *De amores marginales* (On marginal love; 1996) edited by Mario Muñoz, a collection of short stories about nonheterosexual desire. The new edition is entitled *Amor que se atreve a decir su nombre* (Love that dares to speak its name; 2014) also edited by Mario Muñoz and León Guillermo Gutiérrez. This re-edition not only reduces the number of woman-authored texts but also promotes gay identity exclusively in terms of same-sex erotic practices, resulting in the erasure of cuir characters that appeared in the first edition that do not fit this new representational approach.

Some literary critics excuse themselves by arguing that increasing the visibility of women's writing within the cuir community should be the responsibility of women alone. They dismiss any interrogation of whether women and other feminized bodies are granted equal space for this task. Even when women writers do manage to carve out spaces for themselves, they are often overlooked by the same critics who insist that it's solely our duty to create our own platforms. Unfortunately, lesbian literature is frequently perceived as inherently flawed, destined to fail—an assumption exemplified by an unresolved case highlighted by Artemisa Téllez.[11] In the face of these entrenched heteropatriarchal biases, lesbian literature often reaches breaking points and fractures. The role of the feminist killjoy literary scholar is to identify these fractures and transform them into new interpretative frameworks that make room for a broader spectrum of cuir possibilities.

Snap One: *Amora's* Failure and the Unacceptable Bisexual Lesbian

In 1986, at the Jornadas Culturales Gay in the Museo del Chopo, Roffiel presents a paper entitled "¿Existe o no la literatura gay?" (Does gay literature exist or not?), which was later published by the prestigious feminist journal *Fem*. Dismissing the question that the title posits and considering it an idle debate, Roffiel discusses the importance of gender and sexual dissident writers producing "good literature." In this context, what Roffiel means by "good literature" is a form of writing that challenges problematic representations of dissidence and their systemic negative outcomes. As a case in point, Roffiel mentions how her readings of lesbian canonical pieces, such as the novel *Figura de paja* (Straw figure; 1964) by Juan García Ponce, have been "desagradable" (unpleasant) because such literature often depicts lesbianism as a futureless path—Leonor, the protagonist of García Ponce's novel, commits suicide in the narrative.[12] After the publication of *Amora* and during the first Encuentro de Escritoras Mexicanas (1995), Roffiel addresses the question differently. This time, the writer ponders whether Mexican lesbian literature exists or not. Once again, Roffiel shows no interest in debating definitions or categories such as "the lesbian writer." Her intention is to emphasize that, regardless of how one defines Mexican lesbian literature—"¿La que habla de lesbianas aunque las autoras o los autores sean completamente heterosexuales (si es que tal cosa existe), o bien la escrita por lesbianas aunque sus textos no toquen el tema lésbico?" (Is it the one that talks about lesbians even though the authors are completely heterosexual [if such a thing exists], or the one written by lesbians even if their texts don't touch on the lesbian theme?)—this corpus is almost nonexistent.[13] Roffiel speaks abruptly not only about the representational issues of Mexican literature but, more importantly, by arguing that defining what constitutes lesbian or gay literature only serves to further obscure this literary tradition. Throughout these essays, the tone of her words crackles with irritation and exhaustion. Roffiel's frustration is rooted in the portrayal of the crisis in the first essay—the lack of gay/lesbian literature—and her disappointment expressed in the second essay, where despite some publications, such as her own novel, the panorama remains unchanged. I propose that despite this stagnation, *Amora* can be seen as a breaking point. The novel materializes the moment when Roffiel snaps and decides that the damage wrought by the canon is too great—it's time for the emergence of a complex lesbian character with the potential for a future life.

Amora tells the love story between Lupe, a feminist lesbian by choice who works at a rape crisis center, and Claudia, a petit bourgeois *buga*.[14] Published a decade after Luis Zapata's *El vampiro de la colonia Roma* (*The Vampire of the Colonia Roma*; 1979), *Amora* stands as the first Mexican novel to deeply explore lesbian existence and a diverse array of woman-identified experiences. In the backdrop of the seventies and eighties, a group of lesbians, sexual assault survivors, and women tired of compulsory heterosexuality build a feminist community. They grapple with what it means to be a lesbian feminist, especially one that gives way abruptly under pressure. With the exception of Claudia, all the characters of *Amora* are feminist killjoys inhabiting a contact zone where they continually confront sexual violence and homophonic micro- and macro- aggressions.

The women in *Amora* are sharp-tongued not due to a lack of happiness, but as a response to the pervasive heteropatriarchal violence they endure daily. Thus, *Amora* can also be interpreted as the writing of a collective snap. Through the conversations among these friends, Roffiel presents the reader with a series of snapshots portraying the women's responses not as isolated breakdowns, but as a culmination of pressure from accumulated situations. The telling of *Amora* requires using a snap not only as an action but also as method of distributing information and emotions, to convey this snap as a wake-up call, making the violence of gender visible to the reader, and as a possible moment to break the cycle.

The story begins with a snap as Lupe speaks abruptly and smartly upon overhearing the following statement: "¡Los hombres son una subcategoría!" (Men are a subcategory!) to which she responds with a feminist killjoy smile, "¿Todos, o solo los machos?" (All of them, or just the macho ones?)[15] This marks the first conversation between Lupe and Claudia, initiating their love story. The outset of *Amora* underscores the significance of the snap as a literary device setting the narrative tone and shaping the reader's encounter—either embracing the killjoy moment with laughter or bracing for discomfort. As readers, our interaction with this dialogue elicits sensations felt in our bodies, later recognized as emotions. For a feminist killjoy, the sensation of the snap is familiar, provoking responses such as eye-rolling, squirming in chairs, or a knowing smile. The affective response transitions into emotional reactions, ranging from joy at Lupe's sharp retort to anger provoked by the pressure of heteropatriarchy, which her sharpness signals.

If affective experiences do not translate easily onto an existing "emotional map," then, instead of registering the encounter as a feminist killjoy moment, the reader may feel uneasy.[16] Rather than recognizing these feelings for their potential change—breaking the bond with the canon, heteropatriarchal violence, and even with literary genres as I will address later—literary critics simply dismissed the novel as poorly written. According to the interpretative strategies followed by these critics and through book reviews, *Amora* does not have much literary value beyond the "fluke" of being the first lesbian novel. There is a consensus that the novel needs work. Characters with little psychological depth, formal carelessness, excessive clichés, the autobiographical, and *panfletario* tone seem to be the most popular issues that explain—according to literary criticism—its "clear failure."

After carefully analyzing two book reviews, Claudia Schaefer-Rodríguez concludes that critics "judge Roffiel's first attempt at a novel a failure, owing to her taking too many 'liberties' ... with structure and style."[17] However, most critics have mixed feelings. Admitting enjoyment while reinforcing the negative aspects of the book, Pablo Salvador Martínez feels an "atracción fatal" (fatal attraction) toward *Amora*.[18] For Antonio Marquet, the novel is simultaneously "un relato provocador y letargosamente convencional" (a provocative and lethargically conventional story).[19] Even reviewers change their minds overtime. In their initial interpretation published in 1989, Ignacio Trejo Fuentes concludes that *Amora* is merely a literary pamphlet without any literary essence; while twelve years later, he gives a different opinion: "[*Amora*] es una obra bien hecha, a secas, decorosa, llevada con amenidad, con un ritmo cercano a lo periodístico, y por eso se lee con agrado" (It is a well-done work, plain and simple, decent, carried with pleasantness, with a rhythm close to that of journalism, and that's why it is read with pleasure).[20] At the end of the nineties, and with the emergence of gender studies, the interpretative strategies of scholars underwent a positive change that resulted in the implementation of different lenses of analysis for these types of novels. This shift may explain Trejo Fuentes's change of heart. However, what I want to convey with this brief recall of *Amora*'s reception is that while critics can explain why the novel fails in "rational" terms (formal carelessness, clichés, etc.), they cannot pin down their attraction. The affective aesthetic encounter produced by *Amora* is not easily translated into prefixed modes of interpretation or emotions, which leads to declaring the novel a failure.

As these reviewers show, *Amora* appears to be an autobiographical fiction cited often as lacking literary ambition with an emphasis on Roffiel's self-explanatory form of writing. Despite this negativity, two feminist reviews help clarify the positive aspects of the novel—one published anonymously by the revista *Fem* and the second one written by Elena M. Martínez and published in *Letras femeninas* (Feminine letters).[21] While Martínez does not give a value of judgment, the anonymous reviewer recognizes the problems of Roffiel's narrative while also claiming that the book deserves attention for being the first feminist-lesbian novel published in Mexico. Both reviewers argue that one of the positive features of the book is the way in which Roffiel complicates the meaning of feminism and lesbianism to avoid essentializing views and coherent identifications. One can argue that *Amora* is an experimental novel in the most literal way. In it, Roffiel deconstructs clichés about lesbianism, feminism, love, compulsory heterosexuality, and gender violence. The intimacy created by the novel's first-person point of view invites the reader to experiment with multiple possibilities before identifying/dis-identifying ourselves with one form of feminism, lesbianism, or another—hence the experimental nature of the text.

The negative reviews and the inability to explain why *Amora* seductively fails, along with the experimental nature of the novel, suggest "an encounter between text and reader for which there is no ready formula for interpretation."[22] When discussing experimental forms of writing in women's literature in English, Berry enumerates thematic concerns and formal strategies that evidence the experimental nature of women's writing as highly self-conscious and theoretically aware texts. Collectively, these textual characteristics and political affiliations form a profound critique of all systems of control and inequality, thereby producing a kind of extreme or limit feminism not easily assimilated within conventional rational frameworks.[23] *Amora* is a highly theoretically aware narrative that subverts feminism and lesbianism from a personal standpoint, demonstrating the novel's theoretical awareness. Thematically, the narrator delves in extreme descriptions of sexual assault and rape, as well as the pathological nature of heteronormativity, in search of alternative ways of practicing love and building communities of care to counteract the pedagogies of cruelty imposed by heteropatriarchal forms of relationality. Furthermore, *Amora* lacks closure, adopts an antiliterary emphasis with Roffiel's self-explanatory writing style, utilizes the snap as a writing method, and remains ambiguous about its genre. These formal strategies collectively point toward *Amora*'s experimental nature, which I believe is valuable as it offers a novel approach to writing and representing lesbianism in Mexican literature. Literary critics have failed to recognize this value.

In *Amora*, Roffiel uses strategies from the manifesto and from feminist pedagogies (the snap), fiction, nonfiction, pamphlets, and autobiography to write a text that exceeds genre definitions. With the rise of nonfiction and so-called *escrituras geológicas* (geological writings), these types of texts have become more accepted and gained attention from literary critics and scholarship in the second decade of the twenty-first century.[24] At the time of publishing *Amora*, as the book reviews show, nonfictional texts did not fit into molds and were dismissed very negatively. Despite this negativity, it is interesting to perceive that *Amora* continues to build a strong community of readers due to its complicated structures of representation. Since the book complicates what a fiction is and shows the political implications of this type of literature, *Amora* continues to affect our present. It does so by illuminating the incomprehensible strategies of cuir literature and their relationship with contemporary forms of writing. This shows the experimental form of the novel as a valuable feature in our present.

Perhaps the most incomprehensible characteristic of *Amora* that still lingers in contemporary readings of the novel is Lupe's positionality as a bisexual woman, which means that the first lesbian fiction ever published in Mexico is not quite about a lesbian. Lupe's bisexuality is not hidden, nor is it expressed in metaphors that only people *de ambiente* can understand. It is expressed very openly with statements like "seguiré abierta a una relación heterosexual hasta el último de mis días" (I will remain open to a heterosexual relationship until the last of my days); or "[Claudia says] Tienes razón, Amora, la humanidad avanza hacia la bisexualidad. (La humanidad no sé. Yo ya llegué hace rato)" (You're right, Amora, humanity is moving toward bisexuality. [As for humanity, I don't know. I arrived there a long time ago]).[25] Nonetheless, Lupe continually refers to herself as a lesbian and explains her decision in a relational way:

> —¿Por qué te refieres a ti [*sic*] misma como lesbiana si también tienes relaciones amorosas con hombres?
> —Es una forma de militar. La gente tiene una imagen muy estereotipada de la lesbiana: marimacha, de pantalones, chamarra de cuero y pelo rasurado. Cuando te les presentas, femenina, dulcecita, cariñosa y amable, pues les rompes los esquemas y, a veces, hasta llegan a agarrar cierta conciencia. Yo creo que la moral es cuestión de épocas y de necesidades políticas, y que lo clandestino y "terrible" deja de serlo cuando se habla de ello y se vuelve lo que es: parte de nuestra cotidianidad.[26]

—Why do you refer to yourself as a lesbian if you also have romantic relationships with men?
—It's a way of militating. People have a very stereotypical image of the lesbian: tomboy, in pants, leather jacket, and shaved hair. When you present yourself as feminine, sweet, loving, and kind, you break their molds, and sometimes they even start to become somewhat aware. I believe that morality is a matter of eras and political needs, and what is clandestine and terrible stops being so when you talk about it and it becomes what it is: part of our everyday life.

Lupe's attachment to lesbianism as a "forma de militar" was commonly held within global lesbian and feminist communities of the 1980s, as bisexuality was perceived as not radical enough to fully commit to a lesbian feminist praxis and theory.[27] This view was compounded by the extreme gender violence Lupe faced daily at the rape crisis center. Choosing not to engage with men should be understood as a relational decision, one that does not necessarily imply sexual or romantic preferences but rather signifies a political stance against heteropatriarchy. After all, *Amora* is a product of its time—a period when bisexuality was not considered a useful political positionality.

Lupe's eloquent explanation about her decision to occupy a lesbian positionality illuminates why *Amora* has been read exclusively as a lesbian fiction both at the time of publication and in the present (María Elena Olivera Córdova, Artemisa Téllez, Claudia Schaefer-Rodríguez, Cynthia Duncan, Antonio Marquet, Bladimir Ruiz, and César Cañedo). For some critics treating the novel as a lesbian fiction is a political act, while others only confirm their damaging stereotypes by highlighting the lesbianism portrayed in the novel as a stable category. Both readings dismiss bisexuality as a political positionality and contribute to a normative understating of sexuality where bisexual people are rendered a middle ground that has no enduring context of its own; or by discursively positioning bisexuality (in particular, bisexual women) as merely sexual and embodying heterosexual privilege rather than political figures or possessing subcultural knowledge; or simply by erasing or reproducing an outdated view of bisexuality as "the apolitical cop-out for those that are not radical enough to fully commit" to a lesbian life.[28] However, one of the aims of Roffiel's experimental writing is to challenge restrictive ideas. Therefore, not embracing the complicated positionality of Lupe as a bisexual woman who chooses to situate herself in lesbianism is another example of how literary criticism continues to fail in its readings of the novel.

Perceiving books affectively means that texts become sites of feelings and display political investments and emotions mobilized by the readers, including my own. Snapping is a highly contagious form of affect among feminist killjoys, and I too was infected. I confess that I became interested in this fiction simply because I was tired and frustrated with the continued erasure of bisexuality, especially by literary critics and readers who are part of the community of dissidence, though it does not surprise me. The systemic erasure of Lupe's bisexuality is not only imbued with biphobia but also serves as another example of the laziness of literary critics when it comes to reading texts that break established bonds. In other words, my reading of *Amora* is another form of snapping, not against the canon per se, but rather against interpretative frameworks that reproduce normative ideas about literature and gender, and sexual dissidence. During a personal interview, I broached the topic of Lupe's bisexuality with Roffiel, expressing my desire to reclaim this aspect for the protagonist.[29] With a feminist killjoy smile, she met my gaze and remarked: "I'd love to see how people take it. I imagine it won't be easy." I interpreted her words as a validation of my urge to snap—after all, *alborotar el gallinero* (stirring up the henhouse) is a feminist killjoy tool. Setting jokes aside, *Amora*'s insight suggests that character identities are not fixed but are dynamic positions shaped by the reader's political perspectives and temporalities. I believe it is time to underscore that the protagonist of the first lesbian novel also embodies bisexuality, signaling the need to reclaim political spaces for bisexual narratives and representation.

Bisexual people acknowledge "in themselves the potential to be attracted romantically and/or sexually to other varying genitalia, and or varying genders, not necessarily at the same time, not necessarily in the same way, and not necessarily to the same degree."[30] Lupe feels more attracted to women, and her attraction oscillates over time. She identifies herself as a bisexual lesbian to unmake dominant structures of gender and sexuality. Erasing bisexuality or lesbianism simplifies the experimental nature of *Amora*, which—as I have been arguing—is what makes the novel so valuable. *Amora* dislocates readers from consistent or untroubled identification or disidentification with sexual dissidence. At the same time, the intimacy created by the autobiographical tone and the first-person point of view, combined with the narrator's descriptions of herself as a bisexual lesbian, invites readers to not view these positionalities as contradictions but as possibilities in the horizon. The snap, as a feminist method, is a way to approach creatively and positively breaking points, signifying the start of something different.[31] In this case, Lupe embraces the political value of occupying a troubled positionality.

Once more, this indetermination was perceived as a failure:

Amora es una novela de denuncia social, con un deseo de mostrar que las lesbianas también "comen tacos." Sin embargo es una obra de la que es evidente la ausencia de motivaciones literarias, de una voluntad de estilo, lo cual no deja de lamentar el lector. Esta novela-testimonio, por ejemplo, hubiera ganado mucho como novela corta. Extirpando divagaciones y algunos capítulos, sus propósitos originales tendrían mayor fuerza. Después de todo, no es gratuito que esta novela haya ocupado el tercer lugar en ventas el año pasado (sólo superada por *El general en su laberinto* y *Como agua para chocolate*).[32]

Amora is a novel of social denunciation, with a desire to show that lesbians also eat tacos. However, it is a work in which the absence of literary motivations and a sense of style is evident, something the reader cannot help but lament. This testimonial novel, for example, would have benefited greatly as a short novel. By cutting out digressions and some chapters, its original purposes would have had more impact. After all, it is not coincidental that this novel was the third best-seller last year (only surpassed by *El general en su laberinto* and *Como agua para chocolate*).

There are several things to unpack from this quote. Some literary scholars have denounced that the absence of Mexican lesbian literature is the result of self-censorship without seriously considering the interpretive prejudices to which lesbian literature is subjected nor the precarious conditions lesbian writers face in the publishing and literary sphere.[33] Considering this context, to suggest a kind of self-censorship to "fix" *Amora* is wicked but also reveals the lack of interpretative strategies to comprehend the experimental nature of the book. Marquet's suggestion of removing chapters gets even more twisted if we consider the editorial history of *Amora*. The commercial success of *Amora*—comparable to Gabriel García Márquez's and Laura Esquivel's sales and popularity—motivated a prompt second reprint only to be kept it in storage rooms despite the demand.[34] Even with the support of the readers, the novel was taken out of circulation resulting in censorship. And yet, the book became a rite of passage and circulated in photocopies around the lesbian and sexual dissidence communities until independent publishing houses reprinted the book at the end of the nineties.

Marquet's negative criticism also highlights lesbian misinterpretation as one of the major problems of *Amora*. The aforementioned fragment includes a footnote on the word *tacos*. The footnote reads "Es de toda evidencia un acto fallido el que comete la narradora al utilizar como argumento que la vida cotidiana de la lesbiana poco difiere de la vida de muchos heterosexuales. En efecto esta afirmación que activa la vagina dentada—siendo el taco símbolo del pene—, nos lleva al universo de la castración." (It is clearly a failed act committed by the narrator when she argues that the everyday life of a lesbian is not much different from that of many heterosexuals. Indeed, this statement that activates the concept of the toothed vagina—with the taco being a symbol of the penis—takes us into the universe of castration).[35] Marquet attaches the failure of the novel to the image of the lesbian. The insistence on interpreting "tacos" as "penis" followed by the statement that *Amora*'s failure consist in situating lesbianism in the "universe of castration," suggests a very pervasive reading that reproduces a normative view of sexuality like the one produced by the erasure of bisexuality. As an example of this normative view, the image of the *vagina dentata* contains the implication that feminist lesbians promote emasculation. Evoking the image of a misogynistic cautionary folktale reveals more about the anxieties of the critic than the value of the novel. It also reproduces the pervasive idea of the snap as a form of gender hysteria without any positive traits.

Marquet brings one last point to support his argument regarding the low value of *Amora*—that is, its long-winded discourses that break with the central argument of the plot, namely the lesbian story. Regarding these incoherent digressions, Roffiel has stated that their book turned out to be a "libro de superación que ha ayudado a las propias mujeres lesbianas y, a quienes las aman, a ver estas relaciones como positivas y bellas" (A self-help book that has helped lesbian women themselves, as well as those who love them, to see these relationships as positive and beautiful).[36] Other scholars have argued that the fragments of social denunciation are meant to deconstruct our affective education. This is why readers have approached the text as a self-help manual.[37] This affective deconstruction forces the reader to disidentify the novel as a lesbian love story rather than as a move toward cuir relationality, which Marquet fails or refuses to understand. Even when the novel's ending gives the illusion of a resolution between Lupe and Claudia—who get back together after a series of ups and downs due to Claudia's own process of discovering her sexuality—there is no closure to their love story. The ending highlights that Lupe's fulfillment is not limited to Claudia but extends to other forms of relationality, such as her community of friends and her political activism. In fact, the last chapter reads less as the culmination of a love story and more like a premonitory statement on the difficult times ahead for gender and sexual dissidents.

Amora ends in 1983 when the AIDS crisis has already wreaked havoc in the world and the first cases are beginning to appear in Mexico. A wave of homophobia and gender violence ventures, while Lupe also senses the upcoming separation of the feminist and lesbian political agendas. The novel's final pages reflect on love, happiness, and futurity, and simultaneously loss, negativity, and disembodiment. Thus, the last chapter "Vida, nada me debes; vida, estamos en paz" does not end up idealizing love nor life. Instead, the novel remakes the normative love story as a forever unfinished site. For Lupe, uneasy feelings—those that are hard to process into established emotional maps—are what make life so valuable because they represent moments of change. In the last line of *Amora*, Lupe wonders if "¿Se puede ser tan feliz sin sentirse un poquito culpable?" (Can one be so happy without feeling just a little guilty?)[38] Once more, this ending suggests that the interpretative key proposed in the novel lies in Lupe's indeterminacy as an affective strategy that forces the reader to experiment with lesbian literature beyond problems of representation. *Amora* opens the space for unacceptable bisexual lesbians, undetermined genres, highly theoretical narratives, self-referential literature, the snap, and affective encounters as cuir methods of literary critique.

In conclusion, *Amora* is the experimental writing of a series of snaps—against the canon, normative views of sexuality, genre, and heteropatriarchal formations—that highlight the potential of cuiridad to reorient our affective encounters with literature and our emotional education to more ethical interpretations. The affective assemblage of *Amora* puts into motion a series of sensations that have an impact in the way we interpret the novel. The task of the literary critic is to read these sensations—and their impossibility to be pinned down as clear emotions—as potential instead of literary failure. For these reasons, I argue that *Amora* is an experimental piece of writing that challenges outmoded ways of interpreting literary works and aesthetic conventions—as well as normative discourses of sexual dissidence—whose literary failure is productive to think cuir modes of writing and interpreting literature. As Jack Halberstam has demonstrated in *The Queer Art of Failure*, failure can be a good way of critiquing heteronormativity and can open creative ways of thinking.[39] The lack of success experienced by *Amora* generates snaps as approaches for understanding and conveying affective readings through writing. Authors in the early twenty-first century respond to the perceived inadequacies of lesbian literature by formulating a negative aesthetics that challenges the canon in a more direct manner, a theme I will now explore in *La reinita pop no ha muerto*.

Snap Two: The Unfulfilled Promise of an Impossible Cuir Canon

In the twenty-first century, lesbian literature experienced a postfeminist shift as writers began to delve into sexual representation from uncomfortable positions.[40] This shift coincided with the emergence of queer theory and the widespread influence of Judith Butler's theoretical proposition to trouble gender norms and permanently problematize categories of identification.[41] In this context, Mexican women writers capitalized on the inherent ambiguity of lesbian literature and its perceived failure to explore negative aesthetics. They endeavored to remap affects, offering a pathway to comprehend gender and sexual dissidence and their interconnection with literature in ways that diverge from normative emotional narratives, historical perspectives, and interpretations. In other words, writers used gender trouble to also trouble practices of representation in Mexican literature.

One example is the work of Cristina Rivera Garza, specifically *Nadie me verá llorar* (No one will see me cry; 1999) and *La cresta de Ilión* (*The Iliac Crest*; 2002). Based on her research of early twentieth-century testimonies of patients at Mexico City's insane asylum named La Castañeda, Rivera Garza writes a novel that complicates representations of illness while also snaps at the canon. The protagonist, Matilda Burgos, befriends and becomes the lover of La Diamantina, a fellow sex worker at the same establishment. They read together *Santa* (Saint; 1903) by Federico Gamboa and react as follows: "Cuando la Diablesa y la Diamantina leyeron el pasaje juntas, no sólo no pudieron evitar las carcajadas sino que además hicieron el amor sobre las páginas del libro. ¡Ay, pobre embajador Gamboa, tan cosmopolita y tan falto de imaginación!" (When the Diablesa and the Diamantina read the passage together, not only could they not avoid laughing, but they also made love on the pages of the book. Oh, poor Ambassador Gamboa, so cosmopolitan and so lacking in imagination!)[42] This interaction is an example of a feminist killjoy moment—both lovers mock Gamboa's poor representation of female sexuality. While Rivera Garza criticizes early traces of lesbian representation, she also writes an experimental fiction that integrates historical research, archival practices, and theories of illness and gender into the plot. This experimental method helps the writer suggest that the representation of illness—and lesbianism, which can also be understood as an illness given the time period—may only be "represented" by unmaking what a fiction is. Unintelligibility and experimentation are trademarks of Rivera Garza's writing, as well as exercises in rewriting the canon from a cuir-feminist standpoint. This is also the case with *La cresta de Ilión*, which I will analyze in the last chapter of this book.

Other examples of troubling representation can be found in the poetry of Yolanda Segura and Sara Uribe. In her book *Un montón de escritura para nada* (A bunch of writing for nothing; 2019), Uribe includes a poem in which the poetic voice mocks an editor who requests a "poema neutro" (neutral poem)—a text purportedly neutral that can manipulate an affective landscape predetermined by the editor and the market:

> Primero me preguntó si mi poema quería salir vestido de poema;
>   de poema mexicano; de poema mexicano contemporáneo; de
>   poema
> mexicano contemporáneo escrito por una mujer; de poema
> mexicano contemporáneo escrito por una mujer bisexual.
> Después aseguró enfático que era preferible que lo desvistiéramos.
> Que al público le sería más atractivo si podía arroparlo a
> contentillo. Como aquellas muñequitas de papel a las que les
> fabricábamos ropa hecha para fijarse al cuerpo con minúsculas
> pestañas.
> Los más desnudo posible. Dijo. Sin tatuajes. Sin marcas.[43]

> First, he asked me if my poem wanted to come out dressed as a
>   poem; as a Mexican poem; as a contemporary Mexican poem;
> as a contemporary Mexican poem written by a woman;
> as a contemporary Mexican poem written by a bisexual woman.
> Then he emphatically assured me that it was preferable to undress it.
> That the audience would find it more attractive if it could be dressed
> at will. Like those paper dolls we used
> to make clothes for, attaching them to the body with tiny
> tabs.
> The more naked, the better. He said. Without tattoos. Without
>   marks.

The poem fails to meet the editor's request and instead is presented as a satire highlighting the impossibility of achieving neutrality in literature, particularly for a bisexual woman. I read this poem as another example of snapping in the face of the unintelligibility of bisexuality in the literary sphere. Conversely, in *Estancias que por ahora tienen luz y se abren hacia el paisaje* (Rooms that for now have light and open to the landscape; 2018), Segura utilizes the Kinsey test to explore the notion of writing from a lesbian perspective while avoiding the reproduction of normative lesbian ideals. The poetic voice in the text suggests this task is inherently impossible and lists examples of texts that have "failed" to capture cuir/queer positionalities: "no existe el poema en que sor juana salió del clóset no / existe el poema en el que plath se reconcilia con su padre / no existe la canción en que juan gabriel usa las palabras / coger mayate identidades queer" (There is no poem in which sor juana comes out of the closet / there is no poem in which plath reconciles with her father / there is no song in which juan gabriel uses the words / fuck dung beetle queer identities).[44] Both poets navigate the ambiguity of cuiridad and the emotional impact of failure to articulate their perspectives on aesthetics, writing, and the literary landscape.

In the following pages, my focus is directed toward *La reinita pop no ha muerto* (2013) by Criseida Santos Guevara. In this book, the author employs negative aesthetics and uneasy emotions to narrate the story of a new Lupe, aiming to finally fulfill the unmet promise of introducing a "good lesbian" character in Mexican literature, thus potentially securing a triumphant entry into the canon. Rather than successfully completing this task, however, *La reinita . . .* embraces a radical refusal of the canon and traditional reading practices. What I found unique about *La reinita . . .* is the centrality of the literary canon and the snap in the development of the story of Lupe.

La reinita pop no ha muerto is a story that doesn't progress. The protagonist, a lesbian, shuttles between Monterrey and Houston in an endless pursuit of stable income. It's also a love story between Lupe and her boss, Inés, a Chilean migrant fixated on Hispanic art. The narrative touches on plagiarism—Lupe rises as a successful rap singer but falls into disgrace after plagiarizing a song by Eminem. Additionally, it's a tale of reclaiming Monterrey's identity as a "machorra closetera" (closeted butch) in a globalized world that tries to mold the border city into something it's not—an industrial hub devoid of precariousness.[45] It's also an endeavor to finally document Monterrey's lesbian history while creating the quintessential "personaja lesbiana" (lesbian character) with sculpted legs that Mexican literature has lacked.[46] These narratives, interwoven with a short fiction and a soundtrack, stagnate without progress or resolution. Ultimately, *La reinita . . .* concludes as it began—with Lupe perpetually failing at her aspirations. This book intrigues me due to its lack of progress. If the experimental aesthetics of *Amora* don't fully embrace negativity, Santos Guevara's formal techniques hinge on radical rejection and the unsettling sensations of frustration, apathy, and reluctance. This makes the novel an ideal subject for examining how failure and negative aesthetics are employed by lesbian writers to create "good lesbian" literature.

One of the characteristics that the reader perceives from the first pages is Lupe's negative attitude: "Mi vida es una especie de serpientes y escaleras. Conforme más escapo, conforme más avanzo, cuántas más veces lo intento, cuando más cerca estoy de lograrlo, llego a la maldita casilla que me regresa al inicio" (My life is a kind of snakes and ladders. The more I escape, the more I advance, the more times I try, the closer I get to achieving it, I end up at the damn square that sends me back to the beginning).[47] This quote is followed by a description of Monterrey as a "pozo sumido" (sunken well) where the "pinchurrienta humedad" (miserable dampness) is unbearable, and later, her birth and abandonment are portrayed as the beginning of her traumas.[48] Throughout the novel, Santos Guevara emphasizes the pathological nature of human relations by highlighting Lupe's toxicity, as she constantly repeats negative patterns of heterosexual relations such as harassing Inés and displaying jealousy. The author has claimed in several interviews that in *La reinita . . .* she recycles the characteristics of heteronormative relations to parody and laugh at the collapse of current structures of relationality.[49] At the same time, Santos Guevara satirizes neoliberal culture and the market—after all, Lupe is exposing herself in a reality show.

The narrative unfolds during the drug war promoted by Felipe Calderón, amid Mexico already bearing the burdens of the global neoliberal regime. Thus, the trauma and violent situations Lupe faces in her everyday environment—such as *feminicidio*, forced migration, and precarious living conditions—are constantly highlighted. This violent context exposes the crisis points of any social or political discourse, revealing the impossibility of embracing ethical modes of relationality. Despite Lupe's political views and cuir attitudes, she continually finds herself forced to choose among various questionable and unethical options to survive. Unlike the activist Lupe from *Amora*, this Lupe represents an individual subject who harbors no belief in escaping the disaster wrought by Calderón and the neoliberal system. Consequently, she may resort to colonizing children for financial gain: "Mi nivel de estrés bajo pero volví a batallar para encontrar empleo. Estuve vagando unos cuántos meses hasta que la suerte me llevó por Madero y Platón Sánchez, a un edificio de la SEP que convocaba a profesionistas con buen nivel de inglés para dar clases en las escuelas públicas. Ema y yo nos apuntamos. Nos metimos a colonizar a niños en zonas marginadas" (My stress level dropped, but I battled again to find a job. I wandered for a few months until luck took me to Madero and Platón Sánchez, to a building of the SEP (Secretary of Public

Education) that was calling for professionals with a good level of English to teach in public schools. Ema and I signed up. We went to colonize children in marginalized areas).[50] The quote and the narrative of the book illustrate Lupe's mockery of progress narratives intertwined with heteropatriarchal capitalism and colonialism, all while acknowledging her own complicity in these problematic structures. Lupe embodies the role of a feminist killjoy but rejects the snap as potentiality. The darkly humorous tone consistently underscores the protagonist's skepticism and emphasizes their ability to wield negative emotions as disruptive forces, serving as reminders of the limitations of affirmative discourses. Through the combination of humor and refusal, an intimate bond forms between the text and the reader, resisting attempts to neatly categorize these emotions and redirect discourses toward more positive or simplistic interpretations.

Besides the pathological nature of Lupe, who is even described as an unfaithful bipolar lesbian, Santos Guevara employs formal strategies to experiment with negation as cuir aesthetics.[51] The lack of closure, progression, fragmentation, and ambiguity serve as formal strategies utilized by Santos Guevara to resist sexual representation. These strategies not only hinder the reader from employing reading strategies capable of comprehensively deconstructing literary value but also prevent closure and progression. If Roffiel's method revolves around indeterminacy as a possibility, Santos Guevara's approach leans toward refusal. This refusal becomes more perceptible to the reader through the (un)representation of lesbianism and genre undoing.

Similarly to *Amora*, *La reinita* . . . is neither a fiction nor an autobiography but incorporates elements of both. However, one distinction is that *La reinita* . . . lacks the necessary theoretical awareness to be categorized as nonfiction. In an interview, Santos Guevara explains that,

> Un libro como este le puede interesar a un lector que no sigue las reglas de la ficción. No es una autobiografía ni una novela que se clave mucho en llorar porque le va mal en la vida amorosa; al contrario, decide parodiar y reírse, analizar desde otro punto de vista este colapso de las estructuras. Va al hueco intergeneracional, o sea, los que no se quedaron tan convencidos del paradigma y los que apenas están viendo de qué se trata este cotorreo.[52]

> A book like this might interest a reader who doesn't follow the rules of fiction. It's not an autobiography nor a novel that dwells too much on crying over a bad love life; on the contrary, it chooses to parody and laugh, analyzing from

another point of view this collapse of structures. It goes to the intergenerational gap, meaning those who weren't so convinced by the paradigm and those who are just now seeing what this whole thing is about.

As the quote suggests, the book explores the collapse of all interpretative strategies and genre rules. This collapse induces anxiety in the reader, who finds themselves confronted with their affective experience without any guidance on how to navigate their emotions. I interpret the negative aesthetics of *La reinita* ... as an expression of Santos Guevara's rejection of any framework of critical interpretative mastery. Berry defines texts like these, which undermine our critical sophistication, as "limit texts."[53] Limit texts resist conventional reading practices of identification and disidentification. While *Amora* proposes indeterminacy as a potentially positive quality, *La reinita* ... rejects any politicized interpretation, which, in itself, constitutes a political stance.

Another significant contrast between *Amora* and *La reinita* ... lies in the theoretical consciousness conveyed by the texts. Feminist and experimental writing not only challenge stylistic norms but also interrogate established modes of representation that tend to favor fragmentation and disrupt identities, ultimately resulting in opaque texts. Scholars examining these aesthetic forms have criticized them for their perceived inaccessibility. For instance, Rita Felski argues that realism advocates for a "populist stance, aiming to connect text with everyday life practices in the pursuit of direct social change," a quality she believes is absent in experimental writing.[54] What distinguishes my chosen case studies is their shared experimentation with a form of negative aesthetics intended to catalyze a direct shift in how lesbian literature is perceived, without becoming obscure. While Roffiel employs nonfictional strategies to tether *Amora* to everyday experiences, *La reinita* ... explores the effects of pop songs to broaden its audience. The novel's soundtrack fosters a different kind of connection with the reader, one not tied to scholarly discourse but rather to the emotional responses evoked by our bodily reactions when we sing along to "para hacer bien el amor hay que venir al sur" (to make love well, you have to come to the south), a popular song by Raffaella Carrà. Even as *La reinita* ... recycles familiar narratives, its textual playfulness and subversion of genre conventions exemplify Santos Guevara's steadfast refusal to conform to established literary norms. This blend of recycled content and innovative form creates a disorienting effect, compelling readers to engage with subtle nuances they might otherwise overlook.

One nuanced aspect concerns Lupe's lesbian identity. If Roffiel's portrayal of Lupe is perceived as an unacceptable bisexual lesbian, forever confined within heteronormative frameworks by literary critics' normative tendencies, the Lupe depicted in *La reinita* . . . embraces this unacceptability. She harnesses its power to explore the process of rejecting the stereotype of a "good lesbian." In other words, Santos Guevara anticipates that Lupe will be automatically labeled a failed lesbian due to the historical reception of lesbian literature. Rather than contesting this flawed analysis, Santos Guevara embraces the creative potential of resisting the development of a conventional lesbian character. Consequently, the novel does not introduce new representations of sexual dissidence or pursue liberation, as doing so would undermine the inherent value of lo cuir as an ever-elusive concept. If lo cuir continues to defy straightforward depiction of its political potency and emotional resonance, then perhaps there still lies political significance in this discourse.

The same argument can be applied to the necessity of crafting a compelling lesbian protagonist, as expressed by both Roffiel and Santos Guevara. Both writers resist the urge to create such a character, fearing that doing so would prescribe a singular definition of what constitutes a "good" lesbian character. However, acknowledging the need for a well-developed lesbian character suggests a direction for progress, while the deliberate avoidance of this character generates a negative impact, revealing the presence of cuiridad while simultaneously indicating the absence of lo cuir. Guadalupe never conforms to the archetype of a "good" lesbian; instead, the novel can be interpreted as a guide on how to shed such labels. Simultaneously, Lupe emerges as the nuanced lesbian character that Mexican literature has long lacked, precisely because of her refusal to conform to stereotypes.

What particularly captivates me about Santos Guevara's novel is her use of the snap as an affective method, offering insight into the construction and perpetuation of canonical forms. Following the humorous episode detailing the colonization of children through English classes, Lupe, the protagonist, yearns to express her "joterías" (queerness) through her writing: "Volvieron con más fuerza mis ánimos de escribir las joterías de Monterrey. Ratificar a Monterrey como una machorra closetera y a partir de ahí contar esta historia. Machorra Monterrey, Machorra yo. México se escribe con J. Monterrey con M de Machorra. Guerra en las calles y yo streetfighter" (My spirits to write the queer stories of Monterrey returned with more strength. To reaffirm Monterrey as a closeted butch and from there tell this story. Butch Monterrey, Butch me. Mexico is written with a J. Monterrey with an M for Butch. War in the streets and I'm a streetfighter).[55] Lupe continually asserts her intent to write "Monterrey se escribe con M de Machorra." The title of Lupe's envisioned book echoes that of *México se escribe con J* (Mexico is written with J; 2010), one of Mexico's first gay cultural histories, which predominantly focuses on the experiences of gay men in Mexico City. This anthology, along with its re-edition, suggests that urban gay men are still positioned as the custodians of national cuir/queer culture. Frustrated by the lack of representation, Lupe decides to craft a new cuir history from the vantage point of a sexual and geographical periphery—that of a lesbian from Monterrey. Yet, much like other aspirations in the novel, Lupe never fulfills her ambition to write "Monterrey se escribe con M de Machorra." She snaps at the canon but also refuses the canon as a tool for building cuir histories and literatures.

With her unfulfilled promise of writing "Monterrey . . .," Lupe proposes something quite simple yet complex about canon formations and their relation to cuiridad. A cuir canon needs to be perceived in terms of potentiality to secure the value of lo cuir as something that cannot be fully grasped in the present. Lupe snaps at the sight of *México se escribe con J* as she interprets the book as a form of canon building that uses a national framework to assemble gay cultural history without leaving much room for other types of methodologies or representations of sexual dissidence. With her refusal to transform her snap into "Monterrey se escribe con M de Machorra," Lupe enables the reader to perceive canon formations not as a set of prefixed norms that give value to literature in relation to the nation or identity, but as something that is "produced only as an effect of its circulation."[56] By refusing this circulation, Lupe maps the impossibility of a cuir canon when the political value of lo cuir lies in its ungraspable nature in the present moment. Lupe's unsuccessful attempt at canon building needs to be read in tune with her refusal to engage in progressive narratives and literary methods that foster literary value rather than annihilating it. That is why her snap does not materialize into a new book to recount the history of cuiridad in the borderlands.

Reading lesbian literature as a series of snaps collectively shows how affective reactions can be a cuir method of literary critique. Roffiel uses the snap to reorient the reader's sentimental education while also proposing new forms of writing to better "represent" the unrepresentable aspects of cuiridad. On the other hand, in *La reinita* . . ., Santos Guevara takes advantage of the pre-ascribed failure of lesbian representation to snap at the canon without reinscribing lesbian literature in it. While canonicity is a marker that allows literature to live longer and circulate, this is not always the case with lesbian literature. Therefore, what *La reinita* . . . proposes is to snap, build resentment, plagiarize anything and everything to never write the lesbian character that Mexican literature owes us. The impossibility of representation also becomes the impossibility of a cuir canon. That is the fulfilled promise of lesbian literature: to circulate among feminist killjoys as an accumulation of snaps to keep articulating what Mexican cuir literature is and can be.

CHAPTER 4

Communal Writings and the Canon Hoax

The Glu-Glu Fear and Other Elegant Emotions

Desaparecidas las dos, aunque cada cual a su manera,
daban la impresión de estarse obligando
a entrar en un estado de aparición
que las volviera reales otra vez,
aunque esto solo ocurriera en el escenario
    que formaban ellas mismas

Both disappeared, though each in her own way,
they gave the impression of forcing themselves
into a state of appearing
that would make them real again,
even though this only happened on the stage
    they themselves created

CRISTINA RIVERA GARZA

In *La cresta de Ilión* (*The Iliac Crest*; Tusquets Editores, 2002), Cristina Rivera Garza engages in a strange dialogue with the Zacatecan writer Amparo Dávila, whose haunting presence torments the narrator and disrupts Rivera Garza's own plot.[1] At the beginning of the twenty-first century, Dávila was a little-known writer, and her books were not readily available. Thus, at first glance, *La cresta de Ilión* could be described as the story of rescuing Amparo Dávila's presence and manuscripts. Fast-forwarding to 2021, the lesser-known Mexican writer Didí Gutiérrez publishes another rescue—this time, of a group of writers who wrote the first collective novel of Mexican literature in the eighties. *Las elegantes* (The elegant ones; Paraíso Perdido, 2021) is not only a book that makes this novel accessible to readers but also a critical anthology that explains the recovery process carried out by Gutiérrez to find the pioneering work of these women writers. Gutiérrez and Rivera Garza share the idea of literature as a communicating vessel that exposes writing as a collective experience, uncovering the past while blazing paths into the future.

Rivera Garza theorizes this form of writing as "disappropriation," an aesthetic that embraces writing as communal labor. A text is not the result of mere inspiration or individual genius, but of "el proceso de producción, reapropiación y desapropiación a través del cual se genera, en contacto corpóreo y constante, el mismo [the text]" (the process of production, reappropriation, and dispossession through which [the text] is generated, in corporeal and constant contact).[2] According to Rivera Garza, this approach to writing also involves an ethical dimension that "haunts the closed hierarchical systems of literary production," which often prioritize privilege, prestige, and market dominance.[3] As a process that exposes the mechanisms creating hierarchies and unequal literary histories, the poetics of disappropriation share with restorative criticism the need to work with authors from the past—who are often lost in the crevices of literary history—to expose the damage caused by the canonical tale of "force disappearance" to which, among other things, cuir women's writing has been subjected.[4] In this sense, *La cresta de Ilión* and *Las elegantes* serve as exercises in restorative criticism.

As one progresses through both narratives, however, it becomes clear that the rescue involves the use of force, creating a sensation akin to an uncomfortable invasion or an aggressive up and down movement in the digestive tract. In the case of *La cresta de Ilión*, the invasion is not a metaphor. A false Amparo Dávila violently occupies the narrator's house, leaving them in a state of terror. The narrator also stresses, multiple times, the indigestibility of their experience. In *Las elegantes,* the initial source of discomfort arises from the idea of consuming everything to regurgitate their own fictional work, as stated in the "manifesto elegante" (an elegant manifesto) by its members. This insatiable appetite results in the mobilization of a cuir image of the woman writer—an obese figure with a fashion design addiction. This dissonant image produces unease in the reader, leaving them to confront their own preconceptions and prejudices. Both books overwhelm the reader with the accumulation of dissimilar images, like the one described earlier, perpetually leaving them uncertain about what is truly unfolding within these fictions.

La cresta de Ilión and *Las elegantes* confront the reader and the writer with fear, anxiety, and distrust. This emotional negativity defies interpretation since these emotions are often not based on concrete and clear information, but rather on a gut feeling. These types of affects are more likely to generate aesthetic or political ambiguities compared to more canonical passions, since we have already been emotionally educated with them. So far, I have referred to reparative criticism as an interpretative tool that shows how women writers dissent. However, I argue that *La cresta de Ilion* and *Las elegantes* embody a subtle desire to resist the idealization of reparative criticism as a more "ethical" or "better" way of interpreting the works of women writers with the circulation of these ambiguous affects. These books exemplify what I see as breaking the bond with canonicity. The authors are not interested in posterity but in communality as an inherent value of writing literature.

La cresta de Ilión and *Las elegantes* present themselves as objects of feeling, employing strategies similar to reparative criticism, including meticulous curiosity, the circulation of affect, and a certain nostalgia for the literary past. The key distinction lies in their communal aspect: they aim to involve everyone in constructing a horizon that ensures "the collective re-appropriation of the material wealth available," specifically that of the canon.[5] In other words, these books not only focus on restoration through listening but also demand to be shared and participated in, fostering "communalities of writing." This form of writing is always carried out in cooperation with others, resulting in a collective work that is felt in the author-reader-text assemblage and experienced communally though messy relationalities.[6] I am drawing upon the feminist practice of "solidarity in difference" when referring to messy relationalities. This practice, which gained momentum after the significant mobilizations of 2016 known as the Primavera Violeta in Latin America, encourages us to perceive our connections to the world through the optic of difference.[7] Verónica Gago defines this type of connectedness as "a mode of solidarity that does not appeal to similarity so much as to difference—but in a way that understands difference as 'exteriority,' something inherently foreign to our own experience."[8] I am interested in exploring how these communalities of writing and their messy connections generate affective responses that can reshape the normative framework of literary value into a strategy of cuir dissidence.

In the era of the poetics of disappropriation, a challenge arises when considering the problem of canon formation because new technologies not only alter the conditions of the production of literature (e.g., from print books to transmedia to performance) but also reshape the relationship between author, reader, and text. One of the most notable consequences of these changes is the diminishing significance of the individual author in favor of "plural authorship."[9] Traditionally, canon formations have been understood as processes of selection or exclusion, culminating in a set of representative literary works. For example, Harold Bloom, in his book *The Western Canon*, states his intention to "isolate the qualities" that made certain authors canonical, "that is, authoritative in our culture."[10] John Guillory, in *Cultural Capital*, reiterates that this selection is often based on either the authority of the individual author or the literary pieces that perpetuate hegemonic cultural values.[11] Ignacio Sánchez Prado brings to our attention the case of Mexico, where the literary canon has been viewed through a Bourdieusian lens, emphasizing the acquisition of symbolic capital, and focusing on the conditions of literary production and reception.[12] While the poetics of disappropriation still concern themselves with the material conditions of production and readership, they are less focused on capital accumulation and more centered around communality, citational practices, and the mobilization of emotions as value.

If the canon, as an organizing principle of literary quality, has been in decline, the canon as a reference system for reading different forms of writing is still a "sticky "concept.[13] The syllabus, the lists of best books, awards, reviews, and conferences are systems of reference and citational practices that create a canon through circulation and repetition, accumulating affect and generating tensions. The stickiness of the canon makes it difficult to transform, much less eliminate, because it operates as an affective economy. Sara Ahmed uses this concept to describe how affect can work as an economy that moves around shaping individuals, objects, and communities.[14] Considering the canon in terms of sticky affect explains why it is so hard to break with the concept without simply reproducing the same exclusive and selective processes of canon formation.

However, there is a possibility of intervening in the types of affect that the canon produces through its circulation and the temporality shaped by the affective encounter. Unlike writings concerned with literary posterity or transcendence, Rivera Garza insists in the production of the present as a defining feature of disappropriation.[15] Communal writings prioritize their historical moment and embrace the present, which means that whatever circulates today can change tomorrow and this does not detract value from the work itself. The present, in this context, serves as a "quotidian impulse" that offers a glimpse into the future.[16] Thus, one must not only learn to read differently (reparative criticism) but also to reference and share what we read in more creative ways that do not uphold canonical standards of quality, authorship, authority, and posterity in the hopes of transforming our future.

I propose that these communal writings are reference systems for sharing and building what Diana Taylor refers to as "archives" and "repertoires" of diverse forms of writing and reading.[17] This reference system can include individual objects such as books and photos (the archive) but also embodied memory such as performances and other acts that are considered ephemeral (the repertoire). This framework uses ambivalent affects as forces to redistribute the economies that have created the stickiness of the canon as a normative concept in the first place. It is not about a body of works considered exemplary or authoritative, typically deemed to possess enduring value. But about a body of works that functions as a body-to-body system of communication, rooted in our immediate present and the communal. Its purpose is to amplify the emotions that have made certain works stick within a community by actively involving the community itself in the dissemination of these affects.

The feelings I am interested in are inherently ambiguous and disorienting, that is cuir feelings in the sense of indeterminacy. Since these types of emotions can be unreliable, they cannot easily reproduce authoritative figures. If an object of feeling promotes a state in which one feels confused about what one is feeling, then, it becomes harder to reinforce dominant or normative perspectives. Works such as *La cresta de Ilión* and *Las elegantes* demand an active reader willing to solve the puzzle, even when aware of the missing pieces and the impossibility of their recovery. The task is to embrace the mess and reevaluate the canon in terms of the communal and the circulation of affects.

Fear to Digest or the Anxiety of Cuir Potencia: The Communality of the Emisarias

La cresta de Ilión is an experimental work of fiction that easily defies categorization in terms of thematic summary, propositional content, or identification. Various scholars have approached Rivera Garza's formal experimentation in different ways, such as Juan Bruce-Novoa, who identifies it as a literature of "la desidentidad" (disidentity); Oswaldo Zavala, who sees it as an effect of the "radicalización de la alteridad" (radicalization of otherness); Oswaldo Estrada, who views it as writing against representation; and Emily Hind, who describes it as "no-consumible" (non-consumable).[18] Furthermore, *La cresta de Ilión* meets all the criteria for Ellen E. Berry's negative aesthetics, as discussed in the previous chapter, often eliciting various discomforting feelings in the reader.[19] Consequently, it comes as no surprise to me that nearly every scholarly piece published on *La cresta de Ilión* mentions, in one way or another, the challenging nature of the reading experience.

Instead of solely explicating or interpreting the meaning of *La cresta de Ilión*—a task already undertaken by numerous scholars—I am embracing Rivera Garza's invitation to participate in collective production, which I view as an emotionally driven response to the evocative nature of the text.[20] I posit that the narrator's overt expression of fear and anxiety throughout the narrative overwhelms the reader, drawing them into the disappearance of Dávila (or infecting them with the epidemic of disappearance) and the language conspiracy (or enlisting them in the resistance of the Emisarias [Emissaries]). These unsettling emotions give rise to various versions of Amparo—la Falsa, la Verdadera, la Emisaria, la Huésped (the False One, the True One, the Emissary, the Host) Rivera Garza's Amparo, my Amparo, and yours. This type of recovery work does not reinforce conventional narratives nor politics of representation, which prompts a reevaluation of Dávila that results in a communal effort to rethink not only her presence but what this type of recovery means for the formation of canons.[21] The communal invitation plus the complexity of Rivera Garza's collaborative endeavor is akin to Roland Barthes's concept of the writerly text, texts that turn the reader into a writer, which defies the commercialization and commodification of literature.[22] In the case of *La cresta de Ilión*, both the writers (Dávila and Rivera Garza), the reader, and the circulation of affect are needed to defy the literary establishment.

Two epigraphs, serving as a citation and an invitation, warn the reader about the disconcerting encounter they are about to embark upon. The first epigraph is taken from *Panopticon* (1984), an experimental text by Canadian writer Steven McCaffery.[23] This citation alludes to the act of reading as a relational practice, "a minuscule act of collective production."[24] Cheyla Samuelson views this reference as an invitation for the reader to be "*created* as a reader through the experience of the text;" to become the kind of reader the text intends.[25] To assume this role, one must embrace two premises: the notion that reading (and writing) is a communal practice and that language is a "conspiracy in operation," as implied by the epigraph. The concept of language as a "conspiracy in operation" points toward the tacit agreement that words merely represent reality (e.g., a tree is just a tree, a man is only a man). In contrast, McCaffery's work emphasizes the materiality of the signifier and its endless possibilities of organization, creating networks of signification. In other words, language is understood as a set of performative utterances, which cannot be simply "consumed by a 'comprehending' reader" or a passive reader.[26] Meaning is generated by an active reader through the movement, accumulation, and circulation of words. Hence, the epigraph indicates that the difficulty of reading *La cresta de Ilión* arises from the lack of access to the author's interpretative code, leaving room for infinite signification. As a result, the act of reading becomes a ritual of "sadistic voyeurism."[27] Despite Rivera Garza's enjoyment of insane and unsafe forms of play—continuing the BDSM metaphor—she is aware of the dangers and offers a safe word: Amparo Dávila.

The second epigraph is a quote from "Patio cuadrado" (Square courtyard), a short story written by Dávila and published in 1977 as part of *Árboles petrificados* (Fossilized trees).[28] Accompanied by the title "Invitación primera" (first invitation), the quote implies that the reader has been invited to rescue Dávila's books by immersing themselves in a pool full of water.[29] From the very beginning, the reader senses that Dávila will play a significant role in the plot, providing a sense of reassurance. However, deciphering Amparo as an anchor point relies less on the significance attributed by the reader or the author to this writer, and more on the intensification and persistence of the unsettling emotions and sensations she evokes. In the words of Hind, Rivera Garza "puede interpretar a Dávila a través del contexto de *La cresta de Ilión* sin dañar el texto precursor, porque el significado plasmado en un orden particular de señas no importa tanto como la serie de búsquedas por el sistema detrás de estas marcas" (they can interpret Dávila through the context of *La cresta de Ilión* without damaging the precursor text, because the meaning embedded in a particular arrangement of signs matters less than the series of searches within the system behind these marks).[30] In this case, the system behind the mark is revealed to the reader as the atmospheres created by Dávila and taken up in *La cresta*.

Part of what makes Dávila's work so compelling, particularly for feminists and cuir readings, is her mastery at using atmospheres as motifs to guide readers toward understanding the importance of sensations and emotions in the act of reading. Adriana Álvarez Rivera explains that

> Los cuentos de Dávila no son transgresores por sus temáticas ni tampoco subvierten, como las vanguardias o el absurdo, a través de las rupturas formales y de la lógica interna que presentan: violan las consignas porque confrontan al lector con la incertidumbre, obligándolo a realizar hipótesis para encontrar "respuestas" en el texto, pero también forzándolo a asumir que el mundo, tal

como lo conocemos, revela rendijas tras las que se oculta, como afirma Dávila en sus entrevistas, otra realidad, oscura, misteriosa, honda e inexplicable.[31]

Dávila's stories are not transgressive due to their themes, nor do they subvert, like the avant-gardes or the absurd, through formal ruptures and internal logic: they violate the dictates because they confront the reader with uncertainty, forcing them to form hypotheses in order to find "answers" in the text, but also forcing them to assume that the world, as we know it, reveals cracks behind which another reality hides—one that is dark, mysterious, profound, and inexplicable, as Dávila states in his interviews.

Rivera Garza herself asserts that what is intriguing about Dávila's writing is her ability to create these atmospheres.[32] I find that the magic of Dávila's settings lies in the bodily sensations they provoke in readers, such as the goosebumps on my arm when the protagonist of the short story "El huésped" (The guest) carefully approaches the door that holds the petrifying guest, or the upset stomach I feel when the main character of "El pabellón del descanso" (The pavilion of rest) decides to take the pills to rest for eternity. Therefore, Dávila's transgression is writing short stories with and for the body.

La cresta de Ilión begins with an unknown woman who the narrator lets into their house on a stormy night. What follows is the narrator's exploration of their reasons for allowing a stranger in: boredom, the woman's powerful gaze, and desire. The first fragment ultimately assures the reader—differentiated by the narrator as a female or masculine reader—that an uncontrollable desire was the cause. The second fragment, however, begins by refuting this assertion:

> no sentí deseo, sino miedo.
>
> Supongo que los hombres lo saben y no necesito añadir más. A las mujeres les digo que esto pasa más frecuentemente de lo que se imagina: miedo. Ustedes provocan miedo. A veces uno confunde esa caída, esa inmovilidad, esa desarticulación en deseo. Pero abajo, entre las raíces por donde se trasminan el agua y el oxígeno, en los sustratos más fundamentales del ser, uno siempre está listo para la aparición del miedo.[33]

> I did not feel desire, but fear.
>
> I suppose this is something that men will understand and that I don't need to expand upon. To the women, I'll just say that this happens more often than you might think: fear. You provoke fear. Sometimes we confuse this

collapse, this immobility, this disarticulation, with desire. But underneath it all—among the roots through which water and oxygen filter, in the most fundamental substrata of being—we are always prepared for the appearance of fear.

From this statement, the atmosphere of *La cresta de Ilión* is one of fear, anxiety, and terror.

Fear is an emotional reaction to an identifiable threat—la Falsa Amparo. In other words, fear arises from the proximity of an object. According to Sara Ahmed, fear moves between objects, restricting certain bodies (such as the narrator's) through the expansion of others (like the multiple Amparos, pelicans, trees, ourselves, etc.). And yet, fear is not merely fear but a symptom, a defense mechanism, or an alert to a greater danger.[34] The narrator's fear of Amparo itself stems from a fear of femininity, which conceals a fear of castration, ultimately linked to the fear of disappearing. This is why Ahmed argues that fear intensifies through the displacement between objects.[35] In Ahmed's model, there are two types of displacement. The sideways movement "works to stick objects together as signs of threat" and it is "shaped by multiple histories."[36] The narrator associates fear with women, a sign that sticks with other images such as emasculation and fading. At the same time, these images are the result of multiple histories, such as the narrator's relationship with La Traicionada and the story of Juan Escutia, a man who in the novel loses his life due to his rebellious attitudes, echoing the historical episode of the Niños Héroes.[37] In *La cresta de Ilión*, the multiplication of histories cause fear to reside momentarily within the female body.

The second type of displacement is a backward movement, which explains how objects of fear are substituted over time. In *La cresta de Ilión*, the fear of the narrator intensifies every time the Falsa Amparo states that she knows the narrator since long before her arrival. The sentence "Te conozco de cuando eras árbol" (I know you from when you were a tree) becomes a trigger of fear because it signals this backward movement, connecting the narrator to a past history.[38] As the narrative progresses, an active reader begins to associate the word "tree" with a "cosexual" past temporality, which is the origin of the narrator's fear.[39] To be clear, the fear does not stem from losing their penis—the narrator frequently touches themselves to ensure it's still intact—but from the fear of losing their sense of self:

> Fear creates the very effect of 'that which I am not,' through *running away from an object*, which nevertheless threatens as it passes by or is displaced. To this extent, fear does not involve the defense of borders that already exist; rather fear makes those borders, by establishing objects from which the subject, in

fearing, can flee. Through fear not only is the very border between self and other affected, but the relation between the objects that are feared (rather than simply the relation between the subject and its objects) is shaped by histories that 'stick,' making some objects more than others seem fearsome.[40]

The fear experienced by the narrator is what causes Amparo to be fearful, and it also establishes differences between genders, being the fear of castration—from Sigmund Freud to Felipe Garrido—a sticky story.[41]

Another example of how fear does not involve the defense of borders that already exist but the making of those borders is the strange language in which La Falsa and La Traicionada communicate, which separates the narrator from their world. On the night the narrator opened the door to La Falsa, they were expecting one of their ex-partners, La Traicionada. When La Traicionada finally arrives, she develops an instant connection with La Falsa, who takes care of her ailing body. "Ma glu nemrique pa, glu?"–explains La Falsa.[42] The narrator initially believes that the women created their own language but later discovers that the director of the hospital where the narrator works also speaks this language. It is fear that segregates the narrator and not their language. Upon hearing them speak for the first time, the narrator feels a sense of horror, saying: "Me sentí aislado y débil como el exiliado que vive en un país que nunca le resultara familiar" (I felt isolated and weak, like an exile living in a country that will never feel familiar).[43] By the end of the plot, after drinking water (from the pool, perhaps?) provided by La Traicionada, the narrator no longer fears them. The narrator exclaims, "Glu hisertu frametu jutyilo, glu-glu," with a fearless desire for more.[44]

Throughout the narrative, the narrator attempts to persuade the reader to join forces with them. Regardless of the attempts, the reader is suspicious of the narrator's intentions. It anticipates a vague threat, although, not contained within an object or La Falsa. Instead of fear, the reader experiences a state of uneasy suspense commonly known as anxiety. Anxiety, defined as a feeling of worry, nervousness, or unease about an uncertain event, is closely linked to gender (the castration hypothesis) and intellectual histories. Some scholars even suggest that anxiety is "the intellectual's signature sensibility."[45] Consequently, Rivera Garza disidentifies the narrator from this tradition by invoking fear. In *La cresta de Ilión*, the narrator, due to their unreasonable fixation with Dávila, does not possess the power of knowledge. Instead, the novel presupposes that the reader is the one who has the intellectual sensibility needed to decipher the meaning of the plot. And it is the communal act between reader(s) and the plural authors that allows the manipulation of language to redraw intellectual histories. In this case, the intellectual is not a figure of authority that guard's knowledge, but a reader who recognizes the necessary and intricate work between writers, readers, and affects those texts such as *La cresta de Ilión* demand. At first glance, this communal language manipulation can cause anxiety because is an infinite process that feels like an unsuccessful search for the real or an interpretation of reality—the reader never knows who the "real" Amparo is, what is real and what is not.

Ahmed argues that the difference between fear and anxiety lies in terms of the status of the object. Anxiety is an approach to the object, while fear is produced by an object being approached.[46] If anxiety functions as an orientation, we, as readers, can orient ourselves differently by accepting that language lacks the inherent capacity to explain the meaning of *La cresta de Ilión*. Yet, whether this statement produces anxiety, or a sense of relief, depends on the type of reader. Adriana González Mateos is the first scholar to note this difference. According to González Mateos, the "pesadilla" (nightmare) of *La cresta de Ilión* "puede ser muy divertida para quiénes la presencian sin estar atrapadas en ella" (can be very amusing for those who witness it without being caught in it).[47] This nightmare represents the hidden horror of "la posibilidad de que *ser hombre/ser mujer* sea solo un disfraz" (the possibility that being a man/being a woman is just a disguise).[48] In response to Christopher Domínguez Michael's rhetorical question about who fears Rivera Garza, the type of reader that fears Rivera Garza is the one who is terrified of disappearing in the face of uneasy relationalities, whether feminist, cuir, or both.[49] Those who believe that literary value is an inherent property of texts and still advocate for the singularity of the writer as a marker of canonicity might view *La cresta . . .* as a nightmare as well. With this book, the displacement of fear can be infinite. It's not about who fears Rivera Garza but rather what this fear conceals with its displacements: the horror of the potential disappearance of the compulsory codes that produce the norm—the vanishing of national borders, the blurring of gender binaries, the dissolution between sanity and madness, the reimagination of Literature with a capital L . . . For the rest who are unafraid, we are offered the alternative to burst out laughing.[50]

Through her dialogue with Amparo Dávila, Cristina Rivera Garza expresses her desire to change everything with *La cresta de Ilión*. In an interview, the writer explains that instead of paying homage to Dávila—a practice whose "verticalidad" (verticality) and "distancia" (distance) resembles more the strategies of dude lit than the ethics of disappropriation—she works with her: "trabajé algunas de sus estrategias de escritura: con ella, quiero decir, no sobre ella" (I worked on some of her writing strategies: with her, I mean, not about her).⁵¹ According to Christopher Domínguez Michael, Amparo is not a character, but a motif: "pues Rivera Garza hizo de Dávila, de sus textos, de sus fotografías en las cuartas de forros, de su leyenda (si es que la tiene) una potencia" (For Rivera Garza, Dávila—her texts, her photographs on book covers, her legend [if she has one]—became a force).⁵² Hind adds that the most stable aspect of *La cresta* . . . is Amparo Dávila as a "no-consumible" motif: "Mientras los lectores no logren atrapar y asimilar a Amparo Dávila en la novela de Rivera, ambas escritoras están a salvo de haber producido una narración consumible, aunque sí se atrevan a ser olvidadas" (As long as readers fail to capture and assimilate Amparo Dávila in Rivera's novel, both writers remain safe from having produced a consumable narrative, even if they dare to be forgotten).⁵³ On the other hand, Felipe A. Ríos Baeza, argues that the female characters and the works of Dávila suffer from the epidemic of disappearances, "por lo que desean combatir el olvido haciéndose presentes en el contexto actual pero requieren 'hacerse espacio' en un entorno que las tiene *a priori* distanciadas" (they seek to fight oblivion by making themselves present in the current context, but they need to "make space" in an environment that has them distanced a priori).⁵⁴ This presents another case of cruel optimism: Amparo Dávila and Cristina Rivera Garza produce a literature that is not easily digested, thus shielding them from being forgotten, while simultaneously their literature "resiste la memoria de los lectores-personajes" (she resists the memory of the reader-characters), which can condemn them to oblivion.⁵⁵ But time is a funny thing. If, in the early 2000s, critics and scholars felt that the experimental nature of *La cresta de Ilión* caused the book to stick little to the memory of the readers, during the second decade of the twenty-first century, the successful career of Rivera Garza and the popularity of *La cresta* . . . may suggest otherwise. As the same critics argue, the key to overcoming what can be felt as a conundrum lies in the collaborative work between Rivera Garza and Amparo Dávila, which manifests itself as *potencia* contained in the fictional figure of Amparo.

In Latin American transfeminist theory, which I would confidently assert is not the starting point for Domínguez Michael, the word *potencia* refers to a different form of power. "In Spanish, there are two words for *power*: *poder* and *potencia*, which derive from the Latin *potestas* and *potencia* respectively," as explained by Liz Mason-Deese, the translator of *Feminist International* by Verónica Gago.⁵⁶ While the word *poder* underlines a "static, constituted power," *potencia* represents a "dynamic, constituent dimension," defined by Mason-Deese as "our power to do, to be affected and to affect others, while *poder* refers to power over, a form of power with the mechanism of presentation that separates the bodies being represented from their own *potencia*."[57] In the case of Rivera Garza's novel, Amparo Dávila represents an alternative theory of power based on our collective capacity to act.

Verónica Gago argues that *potencia* can never be detached from the body that contains it. Therefore, "feminist potencia is the potencia of the body that is always individual and collective and that also always exists in variation, that is, singular."[58] On the other hand, Rivera Garza theorizes the poetics of disappropriation as a form of writing that is not solely the result of "una inspiración tan inexplicable como individual sino una forma de trabajo material de cuerpos concretos en contacto—tenso, volátil, irresuelto—con otros cuerpos en tiempos y lugares específicos. Las escrituras, en otras palabras, son cuerpos en contexto" (an inspiration as inexplicable as it is individual, not just a form of material work of concrete bodies in contact—tense, volatile, unresolved—with other bodies in specific times and places. The writings, in other words, are bodies in context).[59] If *potencia* is a "desiring capacity," Rivera Garza's dream to change everything is not impossible but rather the force "that drives what is perceived as possible" because it depends on the affects that either stick or slip away from the individual that is already always collective.[60] Amparo Dávila—the writer—represents an individual body, a piece in a bricolage, that reveals the history of the struggles against heteropatriarchal forces inside the so-called lettered city. Amparo Dávila, as a motif, embodies a situated form of writing that, even when individual, contains the collective (the body-to-body system), and operates as a driving force for Rivera Garza's dream of recovering the figure of Amparo Dávila without producing more harm. This recovery dream conceals the feminist mission of las Emisarias, which is to perform a hostile invasion in the hopes of creating a utopia where women writers will not be forgotten.

My own personal cuir affects drive me to a particular space in the novel that makes me feel that this utopia is possible in the present. The most tangible space in the story is the room where La Traicionada and La Falsa spend their hours together. One of the first narrator's tantrums occurs when they realize that the women are sleeping together, breaking with compulsory heterosexuality.[61] It is also at this point that the narrator fully embraces their role as a spy, desperately seeking the reader's complicity. At this juncture, what the reader and the narrator have in common is being outsiders, separate from the intimate cuir bond between these women. We may never be fully welcomed into this intimate cuir space, but accepting the challenge that lo cuir puts forward—as an indecipherable code in the present, as a quality not contained within *La cresta* ... but enacted though the circulation of cuir affects—offers a way out of the nightmare with its promises of pleasure and communities of care.[62]

The narrator never enters this room, yet, by the end of the narrative, they are able to remember the time when they were a tree. The narrator's gender has been a point of discussion among scholars who have written about *La cresta de Ilión*.[63] This is because their gender is portraited as a process of becoming—becoming woman, man, and tree—which prevents fixation, driving scholars either into an imaginary scavenger hunt to apprehend the "real" gender or to the impossibility of identity representation. While gender is socially constructed, sex tends to refer to the material differences between bodies, commonly associated with biological and physiological characteristics. The narrator's material body is also expressed as a process of becoming—sometimes they touch their own penis, while other times they feel their iliac crest, the bone that most effectively differentiates (anatomically) between sexes. For Cristina Rivera Garza there is no language that can fully encompass gender or any normative framework. Therefore, the narrator oscillates between the penis and the iliac crest—that is, gender and sex can only be understood as *potencia*.

La cresta de Ilión ends with a temporal displacement to the tree's era. In *Escrituras geológicas* (Geological writings), Rivera Garza investigates a temporality through a geological language explored by critical theorists invested in queer and gender studies (Elizabeth Povinelli and Christina Sharpe) to imagine the present as "el sedimento más reciente y por ello, el más superficial que anuncia otros sedimentos" (the most recent sediment and therefore the most superficial, which announces other sediments).[64] The return of the narrator to the time when they were a tree literally links cuiridad to a future temporality. It is the past in the present that makes the narrator feel that the world they create is not enough: "Desde ahí, desde Ilión, desde su cresta, Ulises partió de regreso a Ítaca después de la Guerra. Sonreí al recordar también que la pelvis es el área más eficaz para determinar el sexo de un individuo. Todas las Emisarias debieron haberlo sabido para poder dar con mi secreto" (From there, from Ilion, from her crest, Odysseus departed don his return to Ithaca after the war. I smiled upon remembering, too, that the pelvis is the most definitive area to determine the sex of an individual. The Emissaries should have known this to be able to discover my secret).[65] Concluding with the image of the hip bone, a space of utopia, and the reference to las Emisarias as the ones that always had the code to decipher the narrator's secret, is not a confirmation of the "real" gender of the narrator. Felipe

A. Ríos Baeza argues that the invasion of Amparo causes the fracture of the performative masculinity and femininity, preventing the narrator (and the skeptical reader) from interpreting the narration "desde su anterior y rígida perspectiva de 'hombre razonable'" (from his previous and rigid perspective of a "reasonable man").[66] The iliac crest is just an object that contains the displacement of the narrator's toxic masculinity as the price to pay in order not to disappear. Two decades later, the cuir utopia presented in *La cresta de Ilión* continues to be a subject of debate (although I would like to imagine that the narrator's gender identity does not provoke so much anxiety today as in 2002), and the nightmare continues. The difference is that twenty years later the communality of las Emisarias continues to grow and their *potencia* can no longer be stopped.

Whet Your Appetite: A Little Taste of *Las Elegantes*

In *La cresta de Ilión*, Amparo Dávila is not the only intertextual reference to the work of women writers. An allusion to the first generation of Mexican women writers who practiced literary creation as a communal and scandalous exercise in autonomy slips through the pages of Rivera Garza's fiction. The group of "Las elegantes" briefly appears in "la Ciudad del Norte" ("The city of the North") inside a twenty-four-hour restaurant. With their characteristic air of moral and intellectual superiority, the narrator sits down to criticize the people dining at the neighboring tables: "Había mujeres gordas rodeadas de repletas bolsas de plástico en dos de las mesas. Un par de hombres de rostros ajados y dientes nejos miraban sin parpadear los ventanales iluminados. No me fue difícil imaginarlos en los camastros de mi hospital" (There were fat women surrounded by overflowing plastic bags at two of the tables. A pair of men with weathered faces and blackened teeth stared unblinkingly at the illuminated windows. It wasn't hard for me to imagine them in the beds of my hospital).[67] These women are not significant to the plot, and they only appear in this scene. Still their corpulence is enough to trigger chaos when police arrive, which confirms the narrator's suspicion:

> Se trataba de una patrulla nocturna a cargo de levantar vagabundos de las calles céntricas. Entraron al restaurante iluminado y, después de pedir el riguroso *carnet* de identificación, comprobaron lo que era evidente: la mayoría de los comensales en ese lugar no tenían oficio ni producían beneficio alguno a la Sociedad. Un equipo de cuatro oficiales uniformados de azul procedieron

a subir a los vagabundos a la parte posterior de su camioneta para transportarlos después, según fuera el casó, a la cárcel, a alguna institución de beneficencia, a los hospitales, o a mi moridero.[68]

It was a nighttime patrol tasked with rounding up vagrants from the downtown streets. They entered the brightly lit restaurant and, after demanding the obligatory identification card, confirmed what was evident: most of the diners in that place had no trade or contribution to Society. A team of four officers in blue uniforms proceeded to load the vagrants into the back of their truck to transport them, depending on the case, to jail, a charitable institution, a hospital, or my death Ward.

Besides being recognized as overweighted or obese, and by their addiction to designer clothes, "Las elegantes," were also constantly harassed by the police and ignored as producers of literature.[69] Perhaps I am overreading this passage, but if being an avid reader of Rivera Garza's work has taught me anything, it is that her use of transtextual strategies is subtle and conceals many of her theoretical arguments. More than an homage, this brief irruption situates "Las elegantes" as possible precursors of Rivera Garza's ideas of communality and disappropriation since they wrote the first Mexican collective novel.

In the 1980s, poet Leonor Enciso, who had recently arrived from Uruguay, started a literary workshop in Mexico City. This workshop would soon become an experimental laboratory for a group of writers determined to publish the first great Mexican novel as a collective enterprise. The novel was to be written by ten writers, with the fictitious space of Las bonitas serving as a common thread for the story. The group named themselves "Las elegantes" in honor of Guadalupe Dueñas (1910–2002), a writer from Jalisco who belonged to the same generation of Amparo Dávila. Dueñas's work has also been recovered from the obscurity in recent decades. Similar to the type of recovery work done by Rivera Garza, "Las elegantes" aimed to mobilize the image of Dueñas as a humorous and competent writer, qualities that, as Hind demonstrates in *Dude Lit*, women often struggle to perform successfully.[70] By envisioning "Las elegantes" as a tangible version of "las Emisarias," one can perceive their work as a desperate effort to manage the disappearance epidemic and its repercussions for women writers.

The members of this group were Leonor Enciso, Roberta Marentes, Susana Miranda, Aurora Montesinos, Fidelia Astorga, Alí Boites, Tania Hinojosa, Nora Centeno, Wendy Tienda, Lola Herrera, and Julia Méndez. They were working on the novel titled *Las bonitas*, which was on the verge of being published when the devastating 1985 earthquake struck Mexico City. The earthquake resulted in an imprecise number of casualties that remains unknown to this day, tragically including Leonor Enciso and Nora Centeno. After the earthquake and the deaths of two of its members, "Las elegantes" never reconvened. As a result, the book *Las bonitas* remained unpublished, their literary movement was forgotten, and their presence went unregistered in both the canon and Mexican literary history. Even when all the members—apart from Julia Méndez—continued their literary careers with considerable success. For example, Roberta Marentes won the Bernardo Ortiz de Montellano prize in 2008, and Aurora Montesinos the prestigious Arqueles Vela prize in 1993 with the experimental novel *La ruta nos aportó otro paso natural* (The route provided us with another natural step), a narrative palindrome that reads the same forward as backward. Following an invitation from Octavio Paz, Fidelia Astorga frequently collaborated in *Vuelta*, and Alí Boites created one of the most endearing characters in Mexican detective fiction, the famous Isolina del Toro. Despite their accomplishments, search engines still do not display any entries about these women beyond their association with the publication of *Las elegantes*.

In 2009, the writer and cultural advocate Didí Gutiérrez discovered the story "Buenas noches" (Good night) by Wendy Tienda in a Panamanian magazine. The text was accompanied by a note that mentioned the group "Las elegantes." This discovery led Gutiérrez to realize that the chapters of *Las bonitas* were published separately as short stories in zines or artisan editions outside Mexico, subverting the purely commercial circulation of their texts. Initially, the novel was intended to be a collective effort funded and produced by its authors—Susana Miranda had some printing knowledge and an old Heidelberg. Fearing the upcoming commercialization of women's literature and their consequent dismissal as "'easy literature' by many high-brown critics," Enciso believed that the only way for women writers to gain a foothold in the masculine literate sphere was if they owned the means of production.[71] It is worth noticing that the poetics of disappropriation are also attentive to the means of production, advocating for independent publishing houses, grating copyright permission to their creative work, among other things.

After the discovery, Gutiérrez embarked on the task of tracing the texts and researching this literary movement. The result of this archival research was published in 2021 under the label of Paraíso perdido, and after its commercial success, a re-edition of *Las elegantes* was published in 2024. This anthology brings together all the authors' texts in the original agreed-upon order. Additionally, it includes a prologue written by Gutiérrez, where she explains the scavenger hunt and its importance, as well as provides the biographical and bibliographical information about the authors that she was able to obtain. The book even includes a facsimile copy of the "Manifiesto elegante" (elegant manifesto), originally published in February of 1984.

This group of Mexican writers compels us to reconsider the ongoing historical debate on the concept of the author as a solitary figure reliant on individual labor, which is highly prevalent in contemporary literary studies. This debate is made possible through the work of writers such as Sara Uribe, Daniela Rea, projects like the collaborative essay of *Lucrecias*, and many others, besides the literary and scholarly project of Rivera Garza. The irruption of "Las elegantes" in Mexican literary history means rethinking the idea of the isolated writer who works alone without clear networks of support. "Las elegantes" would gather every week to write and read collectively, engaging in discussions about their writing and even began to embark on the task of constructing a group identity, which was rooted in their messy relationalities (mainly, in terms of nationality, sexuality, and corporality). Some members were exiles, others were not heterosexual, some had formal education and others did not.

Gutiérrez points out that "Las elegantes" sought to devour their predecessors, particularly figures like Gabriel García Márquez, Julio Cortázar, and Juan Carlos Onetti (rumors suggest that Enciso left Uruguay after falling in love with Onetti).[72] They also aimed to consume "universal" literary figures, including Honoré Balzac and William Faulkner. It is believed that "Las elegantes" planned a trip to the US to commemorate the publication of *Las bonitas* (another possible reference in Rivera Garza with 'la Ciudad del Norte'?). For obvious reasons the trip was never made. Nevertheless, according to the documents retrieved from the Elegante archive, this trip was intended to include a visit to Faulkner's grave. The exact purpose of this visit remains a mystery—was it to perform an act of vandalism, a display of public indecency, or an attempt to metaphorically (hopefully) consume Faulkner's remains? After their excessive consumption of literary patriarchs, "Las elegantes" gained considerable weight, transforming corpulence into an authorial performance.

With their bodies out of control and an apparent inability to resist the temptations of consumer culture, "Las elegantes" fracture the image of the intellectual as an authoritative figure who uses an exclusive criterion to define literary value. Their "lack of control" over their bodies implies a lack of refined taste, making their desire for consumption potentially dangerous. According to Margitte Kristjansson, the "proof" of fat people's lack of control is their corpulence, and for fat women, their fatness is taboo as

```
            MANIFIESTO ELEGANTE*
               (FEBRERO, 1984)

   1.Destruiremos la concepción
     tradicional de la práctica
     artística solitaria, al crear una
     obra literaria en equipo.

   2.Seremos Las Elegantes en honor a
     la escritora mexicana Guadalupe
     Dueñas, porque somos competentes
     y graciosas.

   3.Nos comeremos a nuestros
     antecesores, incluso a nuestros
     predecesores, para regurgitar
     una obra nueva ubicada en Las
     Bonitas, porque antes de ellos
     nosotras ya existíamos.
                Balzac, Faulkner, Onetti, Rulfo
   4.Para evadir los rígidos esquemas
     de la razón, pondremos la letra
     al servicio del cuerpo; lo
     alimentaremos hasta la saciedad
     con el fin de establecer los
     efectos del peso en nuestra forma
     de escribir.

   5.Trascenderemos en el tiempo a
     partir de un solo libro compuesto
     por nuestros cuentos dispuestos
     en el orden conveniente a lo que
     será la gran novela total, lo que
     sea que eso signifique.


    *Facsímil del original en archivo.
```

FIGURE 4.1. "Manifiesto Elegante" (February 1984). Courtesy of Didí Gutiérrez.

it is associated with inappropriate sexual desire.[73] This connection between fatness and sexual defiance explains why "Las elegantes" were constantly harassed by the police, as seen in the scene in *La cresta de Ilión*. By the way, this scene also evokes the narrator's disgust toward their fat bodies in contrast to La Falsa's desirable skinniness.

As a case in point, Julia Méndez faced multiple charges of misdemeanors, including public indecency, and disturbing the public order.[74] In *Las elegantes*, Gutiérrez explains that it is difficult to verify Méndez's possible lesbian identity since she passed away in 2009.[75] Given the absence of clear evidence regarding the sexual dissidence of Méndez, it is unproductive and possibly harmful to claim this cuir identity for them. However, in 2023, a photograph of Julia Méndez was discovered in a thrift store in the Escandón neighborhood, prompting Gutiérrez to collaborate with Paula Laverde Austin in creating a visual archive of Julia Méndez. As part of this project, Gutiérrez interviews one of Méndez's closest friends.[76] Going by the name of Rímel, a member of the trans* community in the colonia Portales, this friend not only confirms Méndez's sexual dissidence but also claims that they got to know each other at *El Azul*, a "bar de ambiente" (gay bar) in the late eighties. This bar was notorious for frequent police raids, and it was a place where the "madrinas" (godmothers) often waited hidden in the nearby streets to later detain dissident people who would then be charged and processed for being cuir in the Torito, a prison famous for violating human rights.[77] This interview lends credibility to the rumors about the sexual dissidence of some members of "Las elegantes."[78] In that case, the police harassment experienced by these writers would serve as one of the few references we have regarding the violence and persecution endured by dissident communities during the time of Arturo "El Negro" Durazo Moreno's tenure as the chief of police in Mexico City and the subsequent years.[79]

With their cuir performance of the fat-genius woman writer, "Las elegantes" question who has the right to write and who disappears from the literary sphere. As I mentioned earlier, the Mexican canon has often been viewed through a Bourdieusian lens, which considers taste as a form of cultural capital. According to Bourdieu, taste operates as a mechanism of distinction, arguing that "the body is the most indisputable materialization of class tastes."[80] However, our taste and distaste can also disguise cultural privilege: "taste is both an aesthetic and a moral category . . . a way of subtly identifying and separating 'refined' individuals from the lower, 'vulgar' classes."[81] In the realm of literature, having "good" taste implies possessing a refined sensibility that hides the sociopolitical structures that underlie it.

In their distasteful and indiscriminate consumption, "Las elegantes" quite literally engage with the canon on an affective level: the only way to select a set of literary masterpieces is by tasting as many predecessors as possible. In order not to choke on the volume of words or lose our sense of taste from the multiple flavors, the body needs to expel what is being consumed before deciphering any specific flavors. Therefore, I propose that "Las elegantes" not only perceive the author as plural but their consuming practices compel them and us to engage in a form of disappropiative writing, symbolized by the act of regurgitating what others have written. Their consumption and taste should be understood as a body-to-body system of communication that rebels against normative structures, such as the canon and the authoritative figure of the singular author.

Another example of this rebellion is their addiction to designer clothes, which, in most cases, are not designed for overweight women. Kristjansson explains that "Due to historically unequal access to clothing in fat sizes, the consumption of fat fashion has happened in very different ways than the consumption of what is often referred to as 'straight-sized' fashion."[82] If their indiscriminate consumption of literature fattens them to the point where their obsession with designer clothes becomes absurd, their insistence in consuming these clothes is an act of rebellion that contradicts their suppose lack of taste. As a group, "Las elegantes" had unique literary tastes. Their favorite writers included Asunción Izquierdo Albiñana, Guadalupe Marín, María Elvira Bermúdez, and Guadalupe Dueñas. These writers shared the commonality of having their work undervalued and thus excluded from the canon until very recently; three of them only began to circulate in the second decade of the twenty-first century due to the Colección Vindictas (Vindictas Collection), a series created by Socorro Venegas and Ave Barrera at Publicaciones UNAM to recover the works of women writers. The taste of "Las elegantes" suggests how women writers consumed literature in various ways, seeking a more flavorful and affective engagement with the canon to account for their cuir tastes.

This literary movement drives us to rethink the genealogy of the author's displacement, shifting from an individual who generates meaning to a collective author who embraces "las escrituras de otros dentro de sí de maneras abiertas, lúdicas y contestatarias" (the writings of others within oneself in open, playful, and confrontational ways).[83] "Las elegantes" not only cite other writers but they literally wrote together. Prior to the digital era, they authored the first communal and disappropiative novel in 1985, almost thirty years before the publication of *Los muertos indóciles* (*The Restless Dead*; 2013), book in which Rivera Garza coins the term disappropriation. The recovery work and the restorative criticism of Gutiérrez concerning this group of writers urge us to reassess the past four decades of literary criticism in Mexico.

Is the Canon a Hoax? To the Memory of Future Emisarias and Other Elegant Women

One of the most successful forms of intervention in the public and literary sphere in the second decade of the twenty-first century is the feminist and cuir movements. Mexican writers currently seek to foster an affective rearrangement among aesthetic practices, places of enunciation, and the constructions of the public and communal spheres. This rearrangement is productive in challenging ideas about the canon, the functioning of national literature, and the role of intellectuals and writers in the twenty-first century. An example of this is the recovery of forgotten women writers that I have documented throughout this book, which aims to reshape the understanding of literary history, as proposed by the anthology *Las elegantes*. Regardless of the importance of recovery work, it is key to note that women writers today are engaged in much more complex strategies that cannot be reduced to a mere reconstruction of a contra-canon based on a politics of representation. They are creating multiple affective assemblages that serve to legitimize both aesthetic concerns and an ethics of writing that diverges from the patters of male-dominated literature (dude lit). I propose that *Las elegantes* exemplifies this assemblage by mobilizing the authorial plural figure through a disappropiative performance that includes the elegant archive and their repertoire. This performance unravels the notion of the individual genius and reveals the debt that Mexican literature owes to women writers and other so-called minoritized groups.

As I mentioned before, Cristina Rivera Garza proposes reimagining the concept of authorship to avoid excessive worship of the author and the political and ethical implications that come with it. For instance, one consequence of the writer's cult is the perpetuation of male privilege in the literary sphere. Instead of emphasizing individual genius and exceptionalism, the concept of disappropriation implies the relinquishment of ownership over one's work through communal writing that breaks away from the cult of the writer. The writing of *Las elegantes* is disappropiative in at least two senses. On one hand, it is a collectively written novel with citational practices that point to the collectivity of the text as explained in the previous section. On the other hand, the texts were originally published by independent magazines and fanzines, subverting commercial circulation of books and their possible acritical reception. If the group of "Las elegantes" uses disappropiative techniques to write *Las bonitas*, the anthology of *Las elegantes* takes this into uncharted territory. *Las elegantes* is not a traditional print book, but a disappropiative performance that circulates through the affect of its readers and their responses.

Performance art, or *arte de acción*, is an artistic practice characterized by blurring disciplinary and artistic boundaries. It systematically and deliberately integrates experimentation, using the body as a vehicle for expression. Generally, it is a non-object-based art form. Despite this, I propose to consider Didí Gutiérrez's anthology *Las elegantes* as a literary object that, in itself, becomes a form of *arte de acción*, moving away from the book-object as its ultimate purpose. As *arte de acción*, the book-object becomes an affective assemblage that mobilizes other ways of understanding literature. And here's a major spoiler alert: the anthology of *Las elegantes* is a cuir-feminist hoax where nothing is as it seems.

In her essay "The Literary Hoax," Clara Sitbon argues that literary hoaxes are a genre that seeks to challenge the status, function, and credibility of the author. According to this critic, these literary scams or frauds reveal how the authorial figure operates in the public sphere and expose the flaws of the literary system. In this case, publishing an anthology about a nonexistent women's literary movement done by writers that never existed is an affective response to the epidemic of disappearances of women writers. If these writers never existed, my reader might be very confused by all the information provided in the previous section. This information comes from *Las elegantes* and the readers who decided to become part of the literary hoax by feeding the story new information and sharing the book without unmasking the project as a hoax.

Let me reiterate: "Las elegantes" are a fictional group of women writers created by Didí Gutiérrez with the help of many mischievous people to reflect about

> la herida inconsciente de la injusticia que tenemos desde siempre las que escribimos. Tenía curiosidad de saber cómo se despeñaban las escritoras en géneros literarios que se han relacionado más con los varones.... Desde la intuición percibí nuestra ausencia en el panorama de las letras y deseaba, sin saberlo, la existencia de un colectivo organizado de chicas inteligentes, divertidas, desobedientes, dueñas de sus cuerpos y sus decisiones. Se hizo realidad mi anhelo que, al final, es el de muchas.[84]

> The unconscious wound of injustice that we, as writers, have always carried. I was curious to know how women writers fared in literary genres that have traditionally been more associated with men.... From intuition, I sensed our absence in the literary landscape and, unknowingly, I longed for the existence of an organized collective of intelligent, playful, disobedient women, masters of their bodies and their decisions. My yearning became a reality, which, in the end, is the yearning of many.

As stated in the epigraph accompanying this chapter, women writers in the twenty-first century are creating a sense of solidarity and a *potencia* to become real, even if they exist only within the stage they constructed for themselves. In a way, Didí Gutiérrez is materializing the desires and dreams of literary scholars and readers eager to find a collective group of women writers with intelligence, autonomy, sense of humor, and irreverent attitudes—a group of friends daring to do the impossible.

The pedagogies of cruelty and the *editopatriarcado*, which refers to the set of prejudices and beliefs around women's writing, construct an assumption that literature authored by women lacks quality because "es floja, dulzona, poco original, romántica y boba" (it is lazy, sugary, unoriginal, romantic, and silly).[85] These prejudices permeate the Mexican editorial sphere and literary criticism, leading to systems that dismiss women solely based on their gender, thereby predisposing women and other gendered bodies to be marginalized and overlooked. Throughout the pages of this book, I have mentioned other perspectives, such as those of Sarah Bowskill and Emily Hind, who argue that writing perceived as feminine—whatever that may mean—is a priori judged as unintelligible and deemed a failed endeavor. Therefore, these scholars suggest leveraging the supposed analytical failure inherent in women's writing as means to rebel against the system as explained in Chapter 3. Taking advantage of the systematic erasure of women from the Mexican canon, Didí Gutiérrez orchestrates her brilliant deception.

Regardless of the circumstances, Didí Gutiérrez is not alone; she is accompanied by a comprehensive paratextual apparatus that supports the existence of the supposed group known as "Las elegantes." This apparatus includes biographical data, literary influences, and physical archives, all of which provide evidence of the allege tangible existence of "Las elegantes." After the publication of *Las elegantes*, Didí Gutiérrez mobilizes a different archive and repertoire with the assistance of her readers, including writers like Laura Baeza, Eduardo Huchín Sosa, and Laura Sofía Rivero; artists like Hilda Ferrer and Paula Laverde Austin; as well as scholars such as the philosopher Diana Fuentes and myself. This collective effort aims to honor the elegance of "Las elegantes" by celebrating in dialogue their ephemeral rebellion through the affective circulation of their existence and the supporting evidence.

Examples of this evidence include recovered photographs, a facsimile copy of the manifesto, maps of Las bonitas and their whereabouts, and printed publications about their work, such as the article for *Tierra Adentro* about Julia Méndez's sexual dissidence. Through my own research and writing, I continue with the hoax and contribute new points of discussion by tracing the influence of "Las elegantes" in *La cresta de Ilión*; or by positioning them as an important group of writers in women's cuir cultural production in Mexico. If it had existed, *Las bonitas* would have been the first Mexican lesbian novel—Julia Méndez's short story "Las tipas duras se lavan las manos"

FIGURE 4.2. Poster for "Magno Simposio Exprés: Las Elegantes 2021," an open call inviting participants to submit proposals inspired by Didí Gutiérrez's *Las elegantes*, published by Paraíso Perdido. The symposium, scheduled for November 21, will feature brief presentations limited to five minutes and emphasizes humor and creativity.

FIGURE 4.3. Program poster for "Magno Simposio Exprés: Las Elegantes 2021," held on November 21, 2021, from 18:00 to 20:10. The event features various playful and experimental presentations inspired by Didí Gutiérrez's book *Las Elegantes*. The listed participants include writers, philosophers, and cultural promoters, each offering unique performances such as ASMR sessions, readings, and interactive explorations.

FIGURE 4.4. Detailed program for "Las Elegantes 2021," featuring a diverse lineup of presentations from writers, academics, and cultural figures. The symposium takes place on November 21, 2021, with back-to-back sessions running from 18:30 to 19:50, concluding with a keynote speech.

ALL IMAGES ON THIS PAGE COURTESY OF DIDÍ GUTIÉRREZ.

(The tough women wash their hands) is about a lesbian couple ending their relationship. Besides lesbian representation, rumors suggest that the majority of "Las elegantes" were bisexual and practiced polyamory. Thus, *Las bonitas* would have been the cuir novel that Mexican literature still owes us.

As part of the repertoire, the publishing house Paraíso perdido announced a call for a virtual symposium dedicated to *Las elegantes* and "Las elegantes," with the aim of presenting more evidence and sharing new discoveries. Writer Eduardo Huchín Sosa participates in this symposium with a paper that discusses the limitations of literary interpretation when confronted with writings of disappropriation. Instead of conducting a close reading of *Las elegantes* to propose further details about the members, Huchín Sosa takes a spiritualist approach in his paper titled "¡Qué elegancia, la nicromancia!: Una lectura espiritista de Las Elegantes" (What elegance, necromancy! A spiritualist reading of *Las Elegantes*). With the assistance of a third party, Huchín Sosa reads tarot cards for a couple of elegantes. This performance is another example of disrupting the idea of value in literature. Instead of doing a close reading or finding the formal attributes of *Las elegantes* and "Las elegantes," Huchín Sosa proposes that only ghostly remnants and nontraditional tools can shed light on a path toward the future.

Before his participation in the *Magno simposio exprés: Las elegantes 2021*, Huchín Sosa reviewed *Las elegantes* for the cultural magazine *Gatopardo*. In this text, the author recalls the first virtual presentation of *Las elegantes*, which took place on August 11, 2021, and sparked a polemic discussion questioning the existence of "Las elegantes." Through Facebook, attendees either denied or provided new evidence that further confused the situation. For example, a Facebook comment states that one of the first translations of Ursula K. Le Guin's work was signed by L. E., initials that have remained a mystery for scholars of literature and perhaps correspond to Leonor Enciso. In the same Facebook thread, Huchín Sosa asks if Alí Boites will be a featured writer in the seminar on detective fiction organized by the Colección Vindictas.[86] The discomfort experience during this event serves as a symptom, according to Huchín Sosa, in response to what the book proposes—a debate on the boundaries between imagination and academic research.[87] He raises the following thought-provoking questions: "¿Cuántos de los escritores rescatados a últimas fechas no eran en realidad una proyección de quienes investigaban sobre ellos? ¿Era de verdad estrictamente necesario que los autores existieran *antes* de aparecer en una antología?" (How many of the writers recently 'rescued' were actually a projection of those researching them? Was it really strictly necessary for the authors to exist before appearing in an anthology).[88] Does it really matter if "Las elegantes" exist or not? I believe that the Emisarias and their multiple Amparos already answered the question. It is not about their existence, but rather about the affects they mobilize, and the type of conversations they generate without causing more harm to the "real authors," such as Amparo Dávila, Guadalupe Dueñas, María Elvira Bermúdez, Asunción Izquierdo Albiñana, and all the other voices contained in *La cresta de Ilión* and *Las elegantes*.

The literary hoax of *Las elegantes* emerges at a time when Mexican writers, weary of the oppressive practices of the literary world, continue to scream their opposition. However, perhaps for the first time in history, they have the necessary tools to express their disagreement without going unnoticed, such as the internet and social media. Without these tools, the book-*acción* of *Las elegantes* would be harder to pull off. The brilliance of *Las elegantes* lies in its ability to shift the focus from the author to the reader, creating a collective force that accumulates and circulates affect as an economy to maintain their *potencia* in generating new performances and archives departing from the book-*acción*. Affect becomes a weapon through which the collective expressions and sexual and gender dissident movements act as a war machine, an uncomfortable invasion.[89] *Las elegantes* is a small piece of a larger assemblage that validates the exhaustion and the artistic choices of contemporary women's cuir cultural production.

Considering emotions as analytical categories helps illuminate on how oppressive practices shape the literary canon and its history. To an uninformed reader who is unfamiliar with women's writing or cuir-feminist literary exercises, *Las elegantes* may appear to be just another weary anthology attempting to include more women's names in the canon, even going so far as to rescue mediocre writers solely because they are women, adhering to a gender quota. (Rumors spread that Felipe Garrido said that Tania Hinojosa's work lacked aesthetic quality and did not delve into humor with the same sagacity and "ojo crítico" (critical eye) as Juan José Arreola or Jorge Ibargüengoitia). However, to a more active reader—that is the same to say as less macho reader—the proposal of *Las elegantes* is filled with *potencia*. How should we respond to a literary tradition that continually erases the contributions and culture of cuir women? We must digest it and vomit a hoax to produce a different canon centered around emotions and cuir-feminists' communities. This is the cuir utopia of *Las elegantes* and the Emisarias. One question remains: is it truly important to invent new canons and imagine new generations of writers? This is a question that future Emisarias and elegant scholars will grapple with.

CODA

Acuerpar la lucha

Acuerpar es hacer del cuerpo, cuerpa, es juntas, poner
 el cuerpo-cuerpa para todas las demás

Acuerpar is making the body, a cuerpa, it is together,
 putting the body-cuerpa for all the others

DANIELA REA

Cristina Rivera Garza suggests that the writing process reaches its end when something previously unknown—yet intuited or quietly haunting—finally surfaces. But this revelation does not arrive as a neat solution or a moment of clarity; instead, it emerges as "un enigma con el puedo seguir viviendo" (an enigma with which I can keep living).[1] This book shows how women writers reimagine ways to push back against heteropatriarchal structures in the Mexican cultural sphere. Rather than solving gender disparities embedded in our cultural histories, these writers ignite non-normative projects, choosing to live on—despite exhaustion, tensions, and differences. When I started this project, I set out to understand what women writers have been doing over the past one hundred years to fight erasure and reclaim their place in the history of Mexican literature. I thought I was searching for a solution to the systemic silencing of their work. Instead, I discovered that the answer was not in finding a fix but in the emotions and affects these writers activate. Suddenly, the enigma became something I could live with—thanks to the practices of *acuerpamiento* (a type of bodily solidarity) these women writers embodied.

Acuerpar names the personal and collective action of our indignant bodies responding to the injustices experienced by others. It's a coming together that generates political energy to resist and act against patriarchal, colonial, racist, and capitalist oppressions. This practice brings both closeness and indignation, but it also revitalizes—a way to reclaim joy without losing the urgency of our outrage. The pieces studied in this book are held together by messy affects, one of which is the mix between *hartazgo* and the comforting joy of knowing we are not alone.[2] Throughout the book, the use of plural grammatical forms reflects the sense of communality created by the affects mobilized through the rise of transfeminist, antipatriarchal, antiracist, and decolonial movements. While these movements are not new, they represent an unprecedented collective force and have become the most active laboratory of public life in recent Latin American democracies. Their demands extend beyond legal equality, pointing to new ways of inhabiting public space with bodies grounded in difference. Of course, these movements are not the only ones pushing boundaries. So too are the fights against extractivism, the resistance of *pueblos originarios* (Indigenous peoples), the defense of migration rights, and the struggle for climate justice, to name just a few.

I believe the political urgency of our present demands that we take risks with the political subject of feminism and experiment with making cuir stick—not as an identity, but as an affect that disrupts the norm. At the same time, trans* studies remind us why some attachments to the norm might still be necessary. Afro-Latin American movements and the voices of *pueblos originarios* are rejecting feminism altogether, showing us—if we are willing to pay attention—how to build alliances across differences. Ecocriticism reminds us that we are not the only inhabitants of this planet. What unites these struggles and movements is that they are all under threat from the resurgence of hate speech, fascism, and neoconservatism. We may follow different paths and fight different battles, but we share a common desire: to change everything. And yet, this book changes nothing. So, I repeat to myself: Rivera Garza suggests that writing is not about achieving radical transformation or finding definitive answers. Instead, it might serve as a palliative—a way to sustain us and help us keep fighting.

Books take time. I began outlining this project in the midst of the #MeToo movement. By the time it erupted in 2017, Ni Una Menos had already been disrupting Latin America for two years. In Mexico, the Primavera Violeta had taken place on April 26, 2016. That day marked a shift—the feminist struggle grew from a movement led by a few individuals into a collective force, forging connections across the continent and addressing intersecting struggles, such as trans* and labor rights. By the time #MeToo made headlines, the accumulated rage and *hartazgo* across Latin America had reached a tipping point.

However, MeToo created a platform for sectors with more privilege—whether real or symbolic—to publicly denounce sexual harassment and abuses of power by men in Mexico's artistic and intellectual circles. This was not the first-time women writers and artists had organized to confront gender violence and disparities in the so-called lettered city, nor the first-time perpetrators were called out by name. But there was something different about #MeTooEscritores that shook the intellectual sphere to its core. What I remember most from those days were the shared feelings among friends and colleagues—rage, exhaustion, anxiety. Somewhere amid it all, I made the decision to write exclusively about women, whether as a political stance or simply out of feeling *harta*. I knew this project would not offer solutions, but exploring the circulation of affects in women's cuir literature felt like a hopeful path to follow through the chaos.

Books take a lot of time. In March 2020, Mexico witnessed its first national women's strike under the slogan: "Un día sin nosotras" (A day without us), led in part by the *colectiva* Brujas del Mar. Arussi Unda, the group's spokesperson, was recognized by *Time* as one of the most influential people of 2020: "Arussi is unstoppable with her pro-diversity feminism call for peace: just what Mexico needs right now."[3] However, Unda is also a prominent voice spreading hate speech against trans* people.[4] In March 2022, UNAM's *Centro de Investigaciones Interdisciplinarias en Ciencias y Humanidades* (CEIICH) hosted the panel "Aclaraciones necesarias sobre las categorías sexo y género" ("Necessary Clarifications on the Categories of Sex and Gender") featuring Marcela Lagarde, Amelia Valcárcel, Alda Facio, and Andrea Medina. Unsurprisingly, given the involvement of Valcárcel—one of the most visible figures in Spain's transphobic movement—the discussion revolved around the supposed *"borrado de mujeres"* (erasure of women) demonizing Judith Butler as a synecdoche of queer theory, and railing against the *"ideología de género"* (gender ideology). The panelists argued that questioning sex as a biological and legal category was part of a patriarchal agenda aimed at making women disappear. These two moments mark a turning point in the history of Mexican transfeminism. If the Primavera Violeta gave me hope that we could embody a body-territory grounded in the power of our differences—whether race, gender, sex, or class—the rise of transexclusionary discourses shattered that hope. And yet, one question still lingers: is there room for a chance to change?

In March of 2022, I attended a panel on performing authorship, where I presented parts of this book. Emily Hind served as the discussant, and the state of Florida was in full swing—pushing cruel immigration reform laws, banning critical theory and DEI curricula, and enacting extreme bans on gender-affirming care. During the discussion, Hind asked the panelists what we, as scholars, can do in light of the current political landscape. At the kind eyes of this brilliant scholar, all the panelists performed scholarship in a radical way akin to activism. I am not sure how the others felt about the question, though I do believe many engage in activism in different ways, both within and beyond the university. I don't remember if I provided an answer, but I do remember feeling uncomfortable. That discomfort came partly from my own idea of what an activist should look like—someone like Berta Cáceres, Alexandra R. DeRuiz, Yásnaya Aguilar Gil, or María Galindo. These activists expose their bodies and vulnerabilities in ways that I don't often see scholars of Latin American literature and cultural production doing (with perhaps a few exceptions), even those working in US institutions where academic freedom is under attack.

One important lesson I have learned from these activists is how to occupy public spaces. I admire how these women make their opponents and detractors uncomfortable, using that discomfort as a form of provocation, even though they know the price they may have to pay can be devastating—Berta Cáceres was murdered in 2016, after all. Statistically speaking, I will likely never have to pay with my life for making a few scholars uncomfortable with my ideas. I recognize that I am not occupying space in the same way Cáceres or María Galindo does. Yet, as a scholar, if there's anything I can do to fight the rise of fascism, it is to be a feminist killjoy whenever I find myself in a public space. While this may not change the larger landscape, it is a way for me to continue living, writing, and researching in response to Hind's unanswered question.

Uncomfortable scholarship and other forms of writing systematically document, record, and uncover the histories of those actively striving for change. This book exemplifies how heteropatriarchal structures effectively erase women's cuir culture. By recording the actions and reflections of their revolutionary thought, we make such erasure much harder to accomplish. Perhaps this is a positive task for scholars to undertake. Yet, I find myself feeling hopeless: to change everything, I must join others, take to the streets, and burn it all down. And yet, this too changes nothing. Still, perhaps the affective assemblage of the streets is something worth living for.

Books demand a hefty amount of time. During the editing stages of this manuscript, I finally fulfilled my promise to take to the streets for the Women's March on March 8, 2024—an unprecedented event that made history as

FIGURE 5.1. From left to right, the women in the group are Ave Barrera, Leslie Michelle Dennstedt, Cheyla Samuelson, Amanda Petersen, Sara Padilla, and Francesca Dennstedt. The group is taking to the streets, smiling and wearing bandannas, hats, and sunglasses, during the 2024 Women's March in Mexico City. Jacaranda trees bloom in the background, reaffirming the Primavera Violeta effect. From the author's personal archive.

the largest ever seen in Mexico City. (Has anyone noticed that each new women's march in Mexico City becomes unprecedented?) I was *acuerpada* by a group of women who, in one way or another, have been present throughout the writing of this book: the Mexican writer Ave Barrera, scholars Amanda Petersen and Cheyla Samuelson, Sara Padilla representing a new generation of Mexican writers, and my younger sister, Michelle. A lot of emotions were shared during the twelve miles we walked that day (sorry, Cheyla!). We all felt that we never thought we would live to see what was happening around us. The joy, the *hartazgo*, the sadness, the anger. . . . That day, we saw a past version of ourselves in the rage of the younger generations, and history seemed to repeat itself. Change still feels far away. But these new generations are living in a moment where it is very hard to erase the communal nature of our struggle—we are forever *acuerpadas*. This changes everything because we have never truly been alone; we have always had each other to sustain us and help us keep fighting. History repeats itself, but the *acuerpamiento* we experienced on the streets that day was a way of producing a present with the power to juxtapose temporalities in motion, reaffirming that we have never been alone.

For scholar Josefina Ludmer, this spiraling temporality allows us to move toward the future of the past and the past of the future.[5] The effects of the present momentum show how women have been using cuir ways of fighting, living, and building communities. In the context of writing and cultural production, this spiraling temporality positions *Cuir Dissidence* as a grain of sand that unearths not only the absences and erasures of women's cuir cultural production but also their connections, ways of living and writing, political engagements, and intimacies. After all, the canon is merely the result of the repetition of a list that seems indisputable only because the act of repetition is concealed. In contrast, a cuir canon—understood as the effect of a zone of collective contact—invites us to feel differently. And suddenly, the most basic data of literary history takes on a new meaning.

NOTES

INTRODUCTION

1. Joseph M. Pierce et al., "Introduction: *Cuir*/Queer Américas," *GLQ: A Journal of Gay and Lesbian Studies* 27, no. 3 (June 2021): 322.
2. Brad Epps, "Retos, riesgos, pautas y promesas de la teoría queer," *Revista Iberoamericana* 75, no. 225 (2008): 899; Bolívar Echeverría, "Queer, manierista bizarre, barroco," *Debate feminista* 16, no. 8 (1997): 9.
3. David Córdova García, "Teoría queer: Reflexiones sobre sexo, sexualidad e identidad. Hacia una politización de la sexualidad," in *Teoría Queer: Políticas bolleras, maricas, trans, mestizas*, ed. David Córdoba, Javier Sáez, and Paco Vidarte (Egales, 2005), 21.
4. Felipe Rivas San Martín, "Diga 'queer' con la lengua afuera: Sobre las confusiones del debate latinoamericano," *Caderno Espaço Femenino* 36, no. 1 (2023): 42.
5. Norma Mogrovejo, "Lo queer en América Latina. ¿Lucha identitaria, postidentitaria, asimilacionista o neocolonial?," in *Cartografías queer: Sexualidades y activismo LGBT en América Latina*, ed. Daniel Balderston and Arturo Matute Castro (Instituto Internacional de Literatura Iberoamericana / University of Pittsburgh, 2011), 233; Julieta Paredes, "The Neocolonial Queer," in *The Global Trajectories of Queerness: Re-thinking Same-Sex Politics in the Global South*, ed. Ashley Tellis and Sruti Bala (Brill Rodopi, 2015), 229.
6. Diego Falconí Trávez, Santiago Castellanos, and María Amelia Viteri, *Resentir lo queer en América Latina: Diálogos desde/con el Sur* (Egales, 2014), 10.
7. Alejandra Márquez, "Cuir-ing Queer. Speculations on Latin American Notions of Queerness," in *The Routledge Handbook of Queer Rhetoric*, ed. Jacqueline Rhodes and Jonathan Alexander (Routledge, 2022), 448.
8. Sayak Valencia, *Capitalismo gore* (Paidós, 2016), 192.

9. Pierce et al., "Introduction: *Cuir*/Queer Américas," 322.
10. Rivas San Martín, "Diga 'queer' con la lengua," 40.
11. Rivas San Martín, "Diga 'queer' con la lengua," 40.
12. José Esteban Muñoz, *Cruising Utopia: The Then and There of Queer Futurity* (New York University Press, 2009), 49; 64.
13. Muñoz, *Cruising Utopia*, 1.
14. Gabriela González Ortuño, "Teorías de la disidencia sexual: De contextos populares a usos elitistas: La teoría *queer* en América Latina frente a las y los pensadores de disidencia sexogenérica," *De raíz diversa* 3, no. 5 (2016): 181.
15. Carlos Monsiváis, "La noche popular: Paseos, riesgos, júbilos, necesidades orgánicas, tensiones, especies antiguas y recientes, descargas anímicas en forma de coreografías," *Debate Feminista* 18 (1998): 56.
16. Francesca Gargallo, "A propósito de lo queer en América Latina: ¿Existe, se expresa de algún modo el pensamiento queer en América Latina?" *Revista Blanco Móvil*, no. 112–113 (2009): 97.
17. Selma Rodal Linares, "Tatuar la ira sobre el cuerpo de la ciudad: Las pintas feministas como práctica estética," in *Cuerpos diseñados: Ensayos sobre el cuerpo imaginado latinoamericano*, ed. Ingrid Sánchez Téllez and Raúl Antonio Cera Ochoa (Fundación Universitaria San Mateo, 2021): 212.
18. "16A: Primero las mujeres, luego las paredes," *Restauradoras con Glitter*, accessed April 11, 2024, https://restauradorasconglitter.home.blog.
19. Marcela Suárez and Mirjana Mitrović, "Digital Violence as Affective Disciplining after Feminist Protests: The Case of #NotLikeThatLadies!," in *Sensing Collectives: Aesthetic and Political Practices Intertwined*, ed. Jan-Peter Voß, Nora Rigamonti, Marcela Suárez, and Jacob Watson (Columbia University Press, 2023): 266.
20. This violence is documented by Elizondo himself in *Autobiografía precoz* (Early autobiography) and, furthermore, it is one of those open secrets in Mexican literature. Emily Hind argues that this violence is part of performing authorship in Mexico that grants male writers, among other things, the necessary symbolic capital to be part of the canon. See more in Hind's *Dude Lit: Mexican Men Writing and Performing Competence, 1955–2012* (University of Arizona Press, 2019).
21. There is an ongoing debate regarding the translation of the word *feminicidio* into English as feminicide or femicide. I have chosen to maintain the Spanish original to avoid ambiguities. *Feminicidio* is a concept coined by Marcela Lagarde y de los Ríos, which she defines as follows: "La explicación del feminicidio se encuentra en el dominio de género: caracterizado tanto por la

supremacía masculina como por la opresión, discriminación, explotación y, sobre todo, exclusión social de niñas y mujeres.... Todo ello, legitimado por una percepción social desvalorizadora, hostil y degradante de las mujeres. La arbitrariedad e inequidad social se potencian con la impunidad social y judicial en torno a los delitos contra las mujeres." (The explanation for *feminicidio* lies within the domain of gender: characterized by both male supremacy and the oppression, discrimination, exploitation, and, above all, social exclusion of girls and women.... All of this is legitimized by a devaluing, hostile, and degrading social perception of women. Social arbitrariness and inequality are amplified by social and judicial impunity surrounding crimes against women.) Marcela Lagarde y de los Ríos, "¿A qué llamamos feminicidio?," in *Por la vida y la Libertad de las mujeres* (Camara de diputados. LIX Legislatura, 2005), 7. Lagarde y de los Ríos adopts the term *femicide* from Diana Russel, which refers to the cruel murder of a woman solely for being a woman. As Nuala Finnegan explains, the Spanish version provides a more comprehensive definition that includes "its systematic nature on the one hand and the involvement of the state on the other." In 2021, *feminicidio* was officially recognized as a crime in Mexico upon its incorporation into the Federal Penal Code. Nuala Finnegan, *Cultural Representations of Feminicidio at the US-Mexico Border* (Routledge, 2019), 3.

22. Ave Barrera. Interviewed by Emily Hind, "Ave Barrera al precipicio de la introducción al mundo anglófono," *A contra corriente: Una revista de estudios latinoamericanos* 19, no. 3 (2022): 334.
23. Rita Segato, *Contra-pedagogías de la crueldad* (Prometeo Editorial, 2018).
24. Dierdra Reber, *Coming to Our Senses: Affect and an Order of Things for Global Culture* (Columbia University Press, 2016), 9.
25. Eve Kosofsky Sedgwick, "Paranoid Reading and Reparative Reading, or, You're so Paranoid, You Probably Think This Essay Is About You," in *Touching Feeling: Affect, Pedagogy, Performativity* (Duke University Press, 2003), 126.
26. Heather Love, "Truth and Consequences: On Paranoid Reading and Reparative Reading," *Criticism* 52, no. 2 (2010): 239.
27. David Eng, "Colonial Object Relations," *Social Text* 34 no. 1 (2016); Audra Simpson, "Sovereignty, Sympathy, and Indigeneity," in *Ethnographies of US Empire*, ed. Carole McGranahan and John F. Collins (Duke University Press, 2018); and Reber, *Coming to Our Senses*.
28. Patricia Stuelke, *The Ruse of Repair: US Neoliberal Empire and the Turn from Critique* (Duke University Press, 2021), 29.
29. Stuelke, *The Ruse of Repair*, 16.

30. Eng, "Colonial Object Relations," 14.
31. Ignacio Sánchez Prado, "The Idea of the Mexican Women Writer: Gender, Worldliness, and Editorial Neoliberalization," in *Strategic Occidentalism: On Mexican Fiction, the Neoliberal Book Market, and the Question of World Literature* (Northwestern University Press, 2018), 140. As Nuala Finnegan explains in "Women Writers in the Land of 'Virile' Literature," in Mexico there is an apathy toward the category of "woman writer" because of its limitations and essentializing implications. Some authors that have complained about this approach are Ángeles Mastretta, Carmen Boullosa, Ana Clavel, and María Luisa Puga. Nuala Finnegan, "Women Writers in the Land of 'Virile' Literature," in *A History of Mexican Literature*, ed. Ignacio Sánchez Prado, Anna M. Nogar, and José Ramón Ruisánchez Serra (Cambridge University Press, 2016), 339.
32. Francesca Dennstedt and Laura J. Torres-Rodríguez "Introducción: Feminismos, luchas antipatriarcales y transformaciones materiales de la literatura mexicana contemporánea," *Revista de Estudios Hispánicos* 57, no. 7 (2023).
33. Facing similar issues in eighteenth-century studies, Laura Rosenthal raises similar questions: "Is there a way, then, to recover from recovery? Will our attention to women writers at some point transcend the category of 'women writers'? Should it?" Rosenthal suggests that contemporary scholarship is increasingly moving away from this category to explore a broader range of debates (commercial, civic, political, social, and aesthetic). For more, see Laura Rosenthal, "Introduction: Recovering from Recovery," *The Eighteenth Century* 50, no. 1 (2009): 2.
34. Adriana Pacheco Roldán, "El término 'boom femenino' es inadecuado e insuficiente," *Letras Libres*, May 31, 2023, https://letraslibres.com/literatura/adriana-pacheco-boom-femenino-escritoras-debate.
35. Muñoz, *Cruising Utopia*, 3.
36. Sara Ahmed, *Living a Feminist Life* (Duke University Press, 2017), 188.
37. Ignacio Sánchez Prado, "On Cosmopolitanism and the Love of Literature: Revisiting Harold Bloom Through His Final Books," *Los Angeles Review of Books*, March 2, 2021, https://lareviewofbooks.org/article/on-cosmopolitanism-and-the-love-of-literature-revisiting-harold-bloom-through-his-final-books.
38. Sánchez Prado, "On Cosmopolitanism."
39. Sara Ahmed, *The Cultural Politics of Emotion* (Edinburgh University Press, 2004), 8.
40. Ahmed, *The Cultural Politics of Emotion*, 8.
41. Ignacio Sánchez Prado, "Cultural Capital: Reflection from a Latin Americanist," *Genre* 56, no. 1 (2023): 54.

42. Sánchez Prado, "Cultural Capital," 63.
43. Hind, *Dude Lit*, 39.
44. Hind, *Dude Lit*, 39.
45. Wen Liu, "Sentir Abatido, regresivo y maquínico: Teoría queer y el giro afectivo," *Athenea Digital* 20, no. 2 (July 2020): 7, https://doi.org/10.5565/rev/athenea.2321.

CHAPTER 1

1. Brandon P. Bisbey, in *Between Camp and Cursi*, explains the prominence of *cursilería* in *cuir* Mexican literature, highlighting its use as a tool for addressing "social conflicts related to sexuality, gender, race, class, and modernity in a subversive manner." Similarly, Xiomara Verenice Cervantes-Gómez's article, "Paz's Pasivo: Thinking Mexicanness from the Bottom," analyzes Octavio Paz's *El laberinto de la soledad* through the lens of sexual positionality, proposing a queer framework described as "pasivo ethics." These examples illustrate how recent scholarship has engaged these themes in innovative and impactful ways. See more in Brandon P. Bisbey, *Between Camp and Cursi: Humor and Homosexuality in Contemporary Mexican Narrative* (SUNY Press, 2022), 8; and Xiomara Verenice Cervantes-Gómez, "Paz's Pasivo: Thinking Mexicanness from the Bottom," *Journal of Latin American Studies* 29, no. 3 (2020).
2. BDSM has replaced the formerly common SM, S/M, or S&M acronyms the stand for sadomasochism within the community because BDSM does not have the pathological associations and stands for a broader range of practices.
3. Robin Bauer, "Negotiating Critical Consent," in *Queer BDSM Intimacies: Critical Consent and Pushing Boundaries* (Palgrave Macmillan, 2014), 78.
4. Bauer, "Negotiating Critical Consent," 80.
5. Gayle Rubin, "Thinking Sex: Notes for a Radical Theory of the Politics of Sexuality," in *Theorizing Feminisms: A Reader*, ed. Elizabeth Hackett and Sally Haslanger (Oxford University Press, 2006), 530.
6. Leticia Sabsay, "Permeable Bodies: Vulnerability, Affective Powers, Hegemony," in *Vulnerability in Resistance*, ed. Judith Butler, Zeynep Gambetti, and Leticia Sabsay (Duke University Press, 2016), 278.
7. Judith Butler, "Bodily Vulnerability, Coalitions, and Street Politics," in *Differences in Common: Gender, Vulnerability and Community*, ed. Joana Sabadell-Nieto and Marta Segarra (Brill, 2014); Ewa Plonowska Zairek, "Feminist Reflections on Vulnerability: Disrespect, Obligation, Action." *SubStance* 42, no. 3 (2013): 68.
8. Maricela Guerrero et al., "#RopaSucia," *La tempestad*, March 8, 2017, https://www.latempestad.mx/ropasucia.

9. Guerrero et al., "#RopaSucia."
10. To see more about the project #RopaSucia, see Adriana Pacheco and Stephanie A. Malak, "#RopaSucia and *No me llamo mamacita*: Illocutionary Female Power Against Street Harassment, 'Locker Room Talk,' and 'Mansplaining,'" *Revista de Estudios Hispánicos* 53, no. 1 (2019).
11. Xitlalitl Rodríguez Mendoza, "BDSM: Te va a asustar pero te va gustar <3," *VICE*, November 12, 2015, https://www.vice.com/es/article/meterme-un-gancho-de-metal-por-el-culo-me-salvo-la-vida.
12. Rodríguez Mendoza, "BDSM: Te va a asustar."
13. I want to thank Rodríguez Mendoza who kindly enough shared with me an unpublished manuscript titled "Despido injustificado" (Unjust dismissal), which includes a section about her BDSM experience. All the fragments are from this manuscript and published with her permission.
14. Emily Hind, "Six Authors on the Conservative Side of the *Boom femenino*, 1985–2003: Boullosa, Esquivel, Loaeza, Mastretta, Nissán, Sefchovich," in *The Boom femenino in Mexico: Reading Contemporary Women's Writing*, ed. Nuala Finnegan and Jane Lavery (Cambridge Scholars Publishing, 201), 54.
15. Rodríguez Mendoza, interview by Francesca Dennstedt, November 9, 2021.
16. Rodríguez Mendoza, interview by Francesca Dennstedt, November 9, 2021.
17. Xitlalitl Rodríguez Mendoza, "Mi primer BDSM: La idea del amor romántico lastima a las mujeres," *VICE*, November 6, 2015, https://www.vice.com/es/article/mi-primera-experiencia-BDSM-la-idea-del-amor-romantico-lastima-a-las-mujeres.
18. Rodríguez Mendoza, "Mi primer BDSM."
19. Rodríguez Mendoza, "BDSM: Te va a asustar."
20. Brian L. Price, "A Portrait of the Mexican Artist as a Young Man: Salvador Elizondo's Dedalean Poetics," in *TransLatin Joyce: Global Transmissions in Ibero-American Literature*, ed. Brian L. Price, César A. Salgado, and John Pedro Schwarts (Palgrave Macmillan, 2014), 186; Begoña Alberti Soto, "Desviar la tradición: El arte de apropiación de la revista Mexicana S.nob," *Revista de Humanidades* 37 (2018): 17.
21. Scholars like Armando Pereira, Claudia Albarrán, and Juan Bruce-Novoa have identified the commonalities among "la generación de medio siglo." For a more detailed analysis, see Armando Pereira, "La generación del medio siglo: Un momento de transición de la cultura mexicana," in *Juan García Ponce y la generación de medio siglo* (Universidad Veracruzana, 1998); and Claudia Albarrán, "La generación de Inés Arredondo," *Casa del tiempo*, September 1998, https://www.uam.mx/difusion/revista/septiembre98/albarran.html.

22. To see more about how intellectuals defined themselves politically through literature at the time of the ideological collapse of the Mexican left, refer to *Una inquietude de amanecer: Literatura y política en México, 1962–1987* by Patricia Cabrera López (Plaza y Valdés, 2006). Although the analysis does not cover the "generación de medio siglo," it does help to contextualize the sudden fascination with eroticism as another response to the erosion of the ideological foundations of the period.
23. George Bataille, *Eroticism: Death and Sensuality*, trans. Mary Dalwood (Walker and Company, 1962), 65.
24. Tim Themi, "Bataille and the Erotics of the Real," *Parrhesia* 24 (2015): 312.
25. Bataille, *Eroticism*, 131.
26. Pierre Klossowski, *Sade My Neighbor* (Northwestern University Press, 1991).
27. Michel Foucault, "Sex, Power, and the Politics of Identity," in *Ethics: Subjectivity and Truth*, ed. Paul Rabinow, (The New Press, 1998), 165.
28. Amber Jamilla Musser, *Sensational Flesh: Race, Power, and Masochism* (New York University Press, 2014), 25.
29. Juan Carlos Ubilluz, *Sacred Eroticism: George Bataille and Pierre Klossowski in the Latin American Erotic Novel* (Bucknell University Press, 2006), 75.
30. Anna Katharina Schaffner, "Fetishism: George Bataille and Sexual-Textual Transgression," in *Modernism and Perversion: Sexual Deviance in Sexology and Literature, 1850–1930* (Palgrave Macmillan, 2012), 247.
31. George Bataille, *Inner Experience*, trans. Leslie Anne Boldt (SUNY Press, 1962), 135–36.
32. Gilles Deleuze, "Coldness and Cruelty," in *Masochism* (Zone Books, 1991), 37.
33. Musser, *Sensational Flesh*, 24; Elizabeth Freeman, *Time Binds: Queer Temporalities, Queer Histories* (Duke University Press, 2010), 119–20.
34. Ubilluz, *Sacred Eroticism*, 26.
35. Víctor Hugo Vásquez Rentería, "Inés Arredondo: 'Mariana,' 'Las mariposas nocturnas' y 'Sombra entre sombras': Los placeres de la pureza," in *Juan García Ponce y la generación de medio siglo* (Universidad Veracruzana, 1998), 334; 340.
36. Vásquez Rentería, "Inés Arredondo," 344.
37. Inés Arredondo, "Sombra entre sombras," in *Obras completas* (Siglo XXI Editores, 1988), 251.
38. Arredondo, "Sombra entre sombras," 250.
39. Arredondo, "Sombra entre sombras," 269.
40. Inés Arredondo, "Las mariposas nocturnas," in *Obras completas* (Siglo XXI Editores, 1988), 163.

41. Arredondo, "Las mariposas nocturnas," 164.
42. Lauren Berlant, *Cruel Optimism* (Duke University Press, 2011), 1.
43. Musser, *Sensational Flesh*, 5. In a similar line, Klossowski argues that in Sade the principal types of perversion are generally represented only by men: "However, monstrous, perverse, delirious a woman may be. She is never considered 'abnormal,' for it is written in the norms that by nature she lacks reflection, possesses no equilibrium or measure, and never represents anything but uncontrolled sensuous nature, more or less attenuated by a reflection prescribed by a man. Indeed, the more monstrous or mad she is the more fully a woman she is, according to the traditional representation, always colored by misogyny." Klossowski, *Sade My Neighbor*, 37.
44. Deleuze, "Coldness and Cruelty," 35–37.
45. Inés Arredondo, "Mariana," in *Obras completas* (Siglo XXI Editores, 1988), 99.
46. Arredondo, "Mariana," 99.
47. Arredondo, "Mariana," 103.
48. Klossowski, *Sade My Neighbor*.
49. Danielle Lindemann, *Dominatrix: Gender, Eroticism, and Control in the Dungeon* (University of Chicago Press, 2012), 10.
50. Arredondo, "Mariana," 103.
51. To see more about the BSDM panic, refer to Jane Gerhard, *Desiring Revolution: Second-Wave Feminism and the Rewriting of American Sexual Thought, 1920 to 1982* (Columbia University Press, 2001).
52. Deleuze, "Coldness and Cruelty," 23.
53. Rogelio Arenas Monreal, "La pareja y la mirada transgredida en 'Mariana,' de Inés Arredondo," in *Mujer y literatura mexicana y chicana: Culturas en contacto*, ed. Aralia López González et al. (El Colegio de Mexico, 2007), 187.
54. Arredondo, "Mariana," 101–2.
55. Freeman, *Time Binds*, 137.
56. Freeman, *Time Binds*, 137.
57. Giulia Ingarao, "El taller creativo en México de los cuarenta: Leonora Carrington y la Colonia Surrealista," in *México como punto de fuga real o imaginario: El exilio europeo en la víspera de la Segunda Guerra Mundial*, ed. Giovanni di Stefano and Michaela Peters (Meidenbauer, 2011), 29.
58. Claudia Albarrán, "La revista S.NOB: Laboratorio experimental de una generación," *Revuelta* 4 (2000): 63.
59. Jonathan P. Eburne, "Dante, Bruno, Vico S.Nob: The Wake in Mexico," *James Joyce Quarterly* 52, no. 2 (2015): 334.
60. Eburne, "Dante, Bruno, Vico S.Nob," 332.

61. Davis A. J. Murrieta Flores, "Bataillean Surrealism in Mexico: S.NOB Magazine (1962)," *Journal of Surrealism and the Americas* 11, no. 2 (2020): 144.
62. Elizabeth Anahí Cervantes González, "Índice y estudio preliminar de la revista S.NOB" (Undergraduate thesis, UNAM, 2010), 46.
63. Salvador Elizondo in Héctor de Mauleón, "Ocaso de un mundo lopezvelardino: Entrevista con Salvador Elizondo," *Confabulario* 21 (2004): 7.
64. An example is the case of Jorge Ibargüengoitia's "Señora: ¿Padece usted de volupsia?," a review of a fictional doctor's discovery and invention of a treatment for a mysterious illness called volupsia. This three-phase disease affects only women, staring with aphasia (loss of ability to understand or express speech, caused by brain damage), followed by ataxia (loss of muscle control), and ultimately leading to a prominent beard in the last and incurable phase. This one-paragraph review serves as a cautionary tale about the perceived dangers of women's liberation. The writer suggests that volupsia is a sexually transmitted disease whose irreversible consequence is masculinization.
65. Horna's collaborations in *S.Nob* have been identified by critics as projects that inaugurate a new, much more experimental facet of her work due to the creative freedom given by editors. After "Fetiches," Horna continues with this style in series such as *Historia de un vampiro* (1962), *Mujer y máscara* (1963), and *Una noche en el sanatorio de muñecas* (1963). Alicia Sánchez Mejorada, *Kati Horna y su manera cotidiana de captar la realidad* (Instituto Nacional de Bellas Artes y Literatura, 2004), 18.
66. Juana María Rodríguez, *Sexual Futures, Queer Gestures, and Other Latina Longings* (New York University, 2014), 4.
67. Susan Silas, "A Forgotten 20th-Century Photographer Who Folded Her Work into the Fabric of Life," *Hyperallergic*, November 23, 2016. https://hyperallergic.com/330722/a-forgotten-20th-century-photographer-who-folded-her-work-into-the-fabric-of-life. For more information on the collaborative aspect of Horna's photo, see Michel Otayek, "Photography, Mobility and Collaboration: Kati Horna in Mexico and Grete Stern in Argentina" (PhD diss., New York University, 2019).
68. Most of the photos are easily available via a Google search. Here is a link to the digital archive of the Hammer Museum, which includes a part of the "Oda a la necrofilia": https://hammer.ucla.edu/radical-women/art/art/untitled-horna-getty.
69. Murrieta Flores, "Bataillean Surrealism," 137.
70. When analyzing Freud's fetishism, Deleuze argues that the fetish is not a symbol "but as it were frozen, arrested, two-dimensional image, a photograph

to which one returns repeatedly to exorcise the dangerous consequences of movement." Deleuze, "Coldness and Cruelty," 31. Analyzing the photo, a genre that encompasses fetishism is outside of the scope of my research. However, the connection suggests that a more detailed analysis is possible.
71. Murrieta Flores, "Batailleann Surrealism," 138.
72. Fernbach, "Fetishism and the Future of Gender," 56.
73. Elva Peniche Montfort, "El cuerpo en la revista S.nob," in *Desafío a la estabilidad: Procesos artísticos en Mexico 1952–1967*, ed. Rita Eder (Turner, 2014), 236.
74. Peniche Montfort, "El cuerpo en la revista S.nob," 237.
75. Valerie Steele, *Fetish: Fashion, Sex, and Power* (Oxford University Press, 1996), 26.
76. In a different cultural context, Fernbach refers to this type of fetishism as "decadent." Unlike classical fetishism, decadent fetishism is not necessarily centered on the phallus. Instead, it is concerned with "the disavowal of cultural rather than corporeal lack.... The pleasures of decadent fetishism derive from creating and performing embodied subjectivities that result in anti-normative embodiments." Amanda Fernbach, *Fantasies of Fetishism: From Decadence to the Post-Human* (Rutgers University Press, 2002), 26–27. Central to Fernbach's argument are ideas of artifice, decadence, and the post-human, which align with the cultural changes of postmodernism that she addresses.
77. Otayek, *Photography, Mobility and Collaboration*, 260.
78. When reading Anne McClintock's book about British colonialism, *Imperial Leather*, I found the author's argument that "fetishes embody crises in social value" particularly riveting. McClintock's ideas about the fetish are compelling, as they help explain the relationship between non-normative sexual practices and the crisis of masculinity suggested throughout this chapter. Anne McClintock, *Imperial Leather: Race, Gender, and Sexuality in the Colonial Conquest* (Routledge, 1995), 184.
79. Xitlalitl Rodríguez Mendoza, "BDSM: Te va a sustar pero te va a gustar," *VICE*, November 12, 2015, https://www.vice.com/es/article/meterme-un-gancho-de-metal-por-el-culo-me-salvo-la-vida.

CHAPTER 2

1. I want to thank the invaluable support of Gabriela Martín (my academic spouse) for joining me on this and many other scavenger hunts. I am also very grateful to Michael K. Schuessler for sharing his knowledge and for mentioning the existence of this grave. Without his valuable references, this work would have not been possible.

2. There are differing opinions on whether to use gender pronouns that reflect an individual's self-presentation or historical gender norms. Jules Gill-Peterson advocates for the use of their pronouns, while scholars like Kim Gallon argue for adhering to the historical gender pronouns found in documents and newspapers of the relevant period. Documents chronicling the life of Balmori/Jurado predominantly use feminine pronouns for Conchita and masculine pronouns for Balmori, which aligns with the gendered nature of Spanish language. In English, I opt for gender-neutral pronouns when referring to Jurado/ Balmori to preserve their gender playfulness. This approach mirrors the use of both she and he pronouns in Spanish, reflecting the complexity of their gender expression. Julian Gill-Peterson, *Histories of the Transgender Child* (University of Minnesota Press, 2018); Kim Gallon, "'No Tears for Alden': Black Female Impersonators as 'Outsiders Within'" in the *Baltimore Afro-American*," *Journal of the History of Sexuality* 27, no. 3 (September 2018).

3. Diana Taylor highlights the challenge of translating the term *performance* into Latin American contexts, noting its instability. Diana Taylor, "Introducción: Performance, teoría y práctica," *Estudios avanzados de performance*, ed. Marcela Fuentes and Diana Taylor (Fondo de Cultura Económica, 2011), 7. In Mexico, the term *arte de acción* has gained widespread acceptance. Therefore, in this book, I use the term *acciones* to refer to Balmori's non-objectual art experiments. For further exploration of *arte de acción* in Mexico, readers can refer to Cristian Aravena et al., *Arte acción en México: Registros y residuos* (MUAC/UNAM, 2019). Specific details about the Balmoreadas can be found in Maris Bustamante, "Conditions, Roads, and Genealogies of Mexican Conceptualisms, 1921–1993," in *Arte no es vida: Actions by Artists of the Americas*, ed. Deborah Cullen (Museo del Barrio, 2008), and Dubravka Mindek and Miguel Molina Alarcón, "Migración ficticia identidades en las port-performances de Conchita Jurado (Ciudad de México, 1926–1931)" *Arte y políticas de identidad* 17 (January 2018): 123–38.

4. Julietta Singh, *No Archive Will Restore You* (Punctum Books, 2018), 23.

5. Singh, *No Archive Will Restore You*, 113.

6. I use *third sex* and *third gender* because in both the studied fiction and the literature about the period, these terms are used interchangeably. It serves as another good reminder that in Mexico, gender and sexuality are not independent categories, and therefore cuiridad is always imbricated between their folds.

7. Nelly Richard, *Abismos temporales: Feminismo, estéticas travestis y teoría queer* (Metales Pesados, 2018), 199.

8. Aníbal Quijano, "Colonialidad del poder eurocentrismo y América Latina," in *La colonialidad del saber: Eurocentrismo y ciencias sociales*. Perspectivas Latinoamericanas, ed. Edgardo Lander (Consejo Latinoamericano de Ciencias Sociales, 2000); María Lugones, "Heterosexualism and the Colonial /Modern Gender System," *Hypatia* 22, no. 1 (Winter 2007).
9. Esther Gabara, *Errant Modernism: The Ethos of Photography in Mexico and Brazil* (Duke University Press, 2008), 241; Múzquiz Blanco in Luis Cervantes Morales, *Memorias de Don Carlos Balmori: Escritas por su secretario particular* (Costa-Amic, 1969), 303.
10. Gabara, *Errant Modernism*, 242.
11. Felipe Rivas San Martín, "Travestismos," in *Perder la forma humana: Una imagen sísmica de los años ochenta en América Latina* (Museo Nacional Centro de Arte Reina Sofía, 2012), 255.
12. Gabriela Cano, "Ambientes bohemios: Diversidad sexual en la capital mexicana durante los fabulosos años veinte," *Mexican Studies / Estudios mexicanos* 36, no. 1. (2020): 172.
13. Cano, "Ambientes bohemios," 176.
14. López González de Orduña in Sara Ahmed, *La política cultural de las emociones*, trans. Cecilia Olivares Mansuy (UNAM/PUEG, 2015), 11; Mabel Moraña, "Postscríptum: El afecto en la caja de herramientas," in *El lenguaje de las emociones: Afecto y cultura en América Latina*, ed. Mabel Moraña and Ignacio M. Sánchez Prado (Editorial Iberoamericana / Vervuert, 2012), 317.
15. Cole Rizki, "Latin/x American Trans Studies: Toward a *Travesti*-Trans Analytic," in "Trans Studies en las Américas," ed. Claudia Sofía Garriga-López, Denilson Lopes, Cole Rizki, and Juana María Rodríguez, special issue of *TSQ: Transgender Studies Quarterly* 6 no. 2 (May 2019): 149; italics in original.
16. Cervantes Morales, *Memorias de Don Carlos*, 55.
17. Richard in Rivas San Martín, "Travestismos," 254.
18. Gabara, *Errant Modernism*, 247.
19. Cervantes Morales, *Memorias de Don Carlos*, 32.
20. In Latin American feminist discourses, *potencia* is a term that defines power as dynamic, a power based on our collective capacity. To see more about the uses of *potencia* in Spanish, see Liz Mason-Deese's "Translator's Foreword" in *Feminist International* by Verónica Gago.
21. Cristian Cabello, "Posmenopausia drag: *Las mujere*s y mi mamá, una reflectora disidente de la performatividad," in *Por un feminismo sin mujeres: Fragmentos del Segundo Circuito Disidencia Sexual* (Coordinadora Universitaria por la Disidencia Sexual, 2011), 126.
22. Cabello, "Posmenopausia drag," 128.

23. Ben Sifuentes-Jáuregui, *Transvestism, Masculinity, and Latin American Literature* (Palgrave, 2002), 7.
24. One of these characters was that of "la india" (the indian). Unfortunately, there is no information about this character nor about Jurado/Balmori's racial background. Therefore, an intersectional approach between race, ethnicity, and Jurado/Balmori's critique of gender normativity and the consumerism of the middle class is rendered impossible.
25. Cervantes Morales, *Memorias de Don Carlos*, 159.
26. Cervantes Morales, *Memorias de Don Carlos*, 168.
27. A more detailed analysis of the implications of this type of play and the idea of consent falls outside of the scope of this chapter. However, some of the ideas about consent in Chapter 1 could be extended to this case in a productive way.
28. Cervantes Morales, *Memorias de Don Carlos*, 229.
29. Cervantes Morales, *Memorias de Don Carlos*, 232.
30. Cervantes Morales, *Memorias de Don Carlos*, 232.
31. With short hair, loose and relatively short dresses (flappers), alethic bodies, and "modern" attitudes like smoking cigars, these women became the standing joke of various metropolis around the world during the twenties and thirties. Although the modern woman archetype does not represent a majority, it does symbolize a new type of woman who rebels against the imposed gender norms. Nerea Aresti Esteban, "La mujer moderna el tener sexo y la bohemia en los años veinte," *Dossiers Feministes* 10 (2007): 176. As pointed out by scholars like Joanne Hershfield and Anne Rubenstein, in the case of Mexico, the rebellion of "las pelonas"—a reference to their short hairstyle—was greeted with jokes and complaints that circulated widely in visual culture. Some of the jokes implied that these women had made themselves unattractive to men or sexually unavailable and therefore, were a threat that had to be stopped. Anne Rubenstein, "The War on 'Las pelonas': Modern Women and Their Enemies, Mexico City, 1924," in *Sex in Revolution: Gender, Politics, and Power in Modern Mexico*, ed. Jocelyn Alcott et al. (Duke University Press, 2006), 63.
32. Aresti Esteban, "La mujer moderna," 178.
33. Andrés Botas publishing house enjoyed great prestige, and releasing a first book under their label represented a consecrated launch for the authors, such as Mariano Azuela and José Vasconcelos. Vicente Leñero, *Asesinato: El doble crimen de los Flores Muñoz* (Seix Barral, 2020), 134. The irony lies in the fact that despite many women writers being published by Botas and winning literary prices, none of them are part of the literary canon: Julia Guzmán, Tina Vasconcelos de Berges, Concha de Villareal, and Corina Garza Ramos, among other forgotten names. Other literature examples from the same period of *Andréïda*

related to cuir history are *México marimacho* (Ediciones Botas, 1933) by Salvador Quevedo y Zubieta and the short story "Mi única amiga" included in *Confetti* (Ediciones Botas, 1935) by Tina Vasconcelos de Berges. While the first one delves into the "dangers" of female masculinities, the short story talks about the consequences of compulsory heterosexuality for two female friends.

34. Asunción Izquierdo Albiñana, *Andréïda (El tercer sexo)* (Ediciones Botas, 1938), 16.
35. Izquierdo Albiñana, *Andréïda*, 445.
36. Izquierdo Albiñana, *Andréïda*, 446.
37. To see more about what I mean by "coherent incoherence," read Francesca Dennstedt, "Aperitivo para digerir," introduction to *Cena de cenizas*, by Asunción Izquiero Albiñana (UNAM, 2022).
38. Sedgwick, "Paranoid Reading," 126.
39. Sedgwick, "Paranoid Reading," 130.
40. Robert McKee Irwin, *Mexican Masculinities* (University of Minnesota Press, 2003), 149.
41. McKee Irwin, *Mexican Masculinities*, 149.
42. Hind, *Feminism and the Mexican*, 43.
43. Emily Hind, "¿Carácter o personalidad? El pensamiento transicional de Asunción Izquierdo Albiñana: *Andréïda (El tercer sexo)* y *La selva encantada*," in *Luz rebelde: Mujeres y producción en el México posrevolucionario*, ed. Elissa Rashkin and Ester Hernández Palacios (Universidad Veracruzana, Dirección Editorial, 2019), 171.
44. Paul Fallon, "Melodrama and the Monster by Your Side in Asunción Izquierdo Albiñana's *Andréïda: El tercer sexo*," *Hispanic Review* 86, no. 4 (Autumn 2018): 483.
45. Manuel Pedro González, *Trayectoria de la novela en México* (Ediciones Botas, 1951), 348.
46. Emmanuel Carballo, "La última novela de una escritora enmascarada: *Los extraordinarios*," *México en la cultura* 650 (August 27, 1969): 9.
47. Vicente Leñero, *Asesinato*, 135.
48. Gonzales, *Trayectoria de la novela*, 348.
49. Hind, *Feminism and the Mexican*, 43. This statement proves hard to sustain since the author did belong to a generation of intellectual feminists. She was not only a member of the *Ateneo mexicano de mujeres* but a friend of some of the major feminists of her time, such as Anna Murià and the journalist Ana Cecilia Treviño, better known as Bambi. See more in Marcela del Río Reyes, "Ateneo mexicano de mujeres," *Revista Universo de el Búho* 6, no. 70 (2005–2006): 18–23, https://www.revistaelbuho.com.mx/magazine/070.html.

50. For more about her life, listen to the episode "Hablemos de . . . Asunción Izquierdo Albiñana" in *Hablemos Escritoras Podcast*; see the article "Ana Mairena más allá de la nota roja" by Diana Gutiérrez; or consult the aforementioned chronicle by Vicente Leñero.
51. Izquierdo Albiñana in Anna Bartra y Agustí / Bambi, "Correspondencia a propósito de Ana Mairena," *Plural* 10–12, no. 120 (1981): 7.
52. Asunción Izquierdo Albiñana published the following books: *La selva encantada* (The enchanted forest; Ediciones Botas, 1945) and *Taetzani* (Editorial Ideas, 1946) under the pseudonym Alba Sandoiz; *La ciudad sobre el lago* (The city on the lake; 1949) as Pablo María Fonsalba; *Los extraordinarios* (The extraordinary; Seix Barral, 1961) and *Cena de cenizas* (Dinner of ashes; Joaquin Mortiz, 1975) as Ana Mairena; two books of poetry titled *El cántaro a la puerta* (The pitcher at the door; 1952) and *Coplas a mi provincia* (Songs to my province; 1955); a poem in prose titled *Majakuagymoukeia* (1964), translated by Elinor Randall and published in *El corno emplumado*; a play named *El apostol regresa* (The apostle returns; B. Costa-Amic editor, 1958), and several short stories; she also kept a column in the newspaper *El día* until her death.
53. Izquierdo Albiñana in Bartra, "Correspondencia," 7.
54. Izquierdo Albiñana in Bartra, "Correspondencia," 7.
55. Murià in Bartra, "Correspondencia," 7.
56. Izquierdo Albiñana, *Andréïda*, 13.
57. Muñoz, *Cruising Utopia*, 7.
58. Fallon, "Melodrama and the Monster," 467.
59. Muñoz, *Cruising Utopia*, 12; Sedgwick, "Paranoid Reading," 130.
60. Julia Tuñón, "Nueve escritoras, una revista y un escenario: Cuando se junta la oportunidad con el talento," in *Nueve escritoras mexicanas nacidas en la primera mitad del siglo XX y una revista*, ed. Elena Urrutia (Instituto Nacional de las Mujeres; El colegio de México, 2006), 20.
61. Izquierdo Albiñana, *Andréïda*, 424–25.
62. Izquierdo Albiñana, *Andréïda*, 368–69.
63. Sedgwick, "Paranoid Reading," 131.
64. Izquierdo Albiñana, "Mi charla para ellas"; Esther Gabara briefly analysis Pisque Hadaly's column to suggest that she writes an advice column mixing frivolities with a critique of conservative gender stereotypes to mediate between popular culture and avant-garde literature, which relates to Hind's argument about Andréïda's character as one that negotiates between the figure of the intellectual and being a woman (Gabara, *Errant Modernism*, 157).
65. Izquierdo Albiñana, *Andréïda*, 67.
66. Sedgwick, "Paranoid Reading," 143.

67. Another example of Izquierdo Albiñana's perspective on gender, race, and class can be analyzed in her short story "La empalada" published in 1946 in the prestigious journal *El hijo pródigo*. This text tells the story of an indigenous woman who is unfaithful to the absent partner. When the partner returns, she accepts her cruel fate without putting up any kind of resistance—she is impaled by an "unmodern" culture indifferent to women's oppression, the narrator implies. In this story, gender seems to be the center to all oppressions.
68. Adrienne Rich, "Compulsory Heterosexuality and Lesbian Existence," *Signs* 5, no. 4 (Summer 1980): 648.
69. Izquierdo Albiñana, *Andréïda*, 44; 405.
70. Izquierdo Albiñana, *Andréïda*, 44.
71. Izquierdo Albiñana, *Andréïda*, 44.
72. Izquierdo Albiñana, *Andréïda*, 433.
73. María Jesús Fariña Busto, "El beso deseado de tu boca: Nombres y voces para una genealogía lesbiana (España y Portugal, primeras décadas del siglo veinte)," *Investigaciones feministas* 10, no. 1 (2019): 80.
74. Eve Kosofsky Sedgwick, *Epistemology of the Closet* (University of California Press, 1990), 53.
75. In *Plagio de palabras*, Elena Guiochins uses existentialism to question the sexual and gender identity of the characters. See more in Laura Lusardi, "'Who Knows What's Inside Our Heads?': La incertidumbre en *Plagio de palabras* de Elena Guiochins," *Hispanófila* 186 (June 2019): 35–47.
76. Appadurai, "Archive and Aspiration," in *Information Is Alive*, ed. Joke Brower and Arjen Mulder (V2_Publishing and NAI Publishers, 2003), 15–18.
77. Appadurai, "Archive and Aspiration," 24.
78. The archive is also an important concept for other of the bearded women. Mónica Mayer has not only built a physical archive in her private home but also uses the archive as a tool in her artistic pieces. As a case in point, in her piece *Archiva*, Mayer reunites seventy-six masterpieces of feminist art in Mexico. The artist frequently carries around a file to bring the public closer to the archive and counteract the invisibility of feminist art. See more about the uses of the archive in Mónica Mayer, *Intimidades . . . o no: Arte, vida y feminism*, ed. Julia Antivilo and Katnira Bello (Editorial Diecisiete, 2021). Also, the piece *Archiva* can be found online at "ARCHIVA: Obras maestras del arte feminista en México," Pinto mi Raya: De Archivos y Redes, September 3, 2014, https://www.pintomiraya.com/redes/archivo-ana-victoria-jimenez/item/158-archiva.html.

79. Roberto Cruz Arzabal, "Archivos potenciales: Domiciliación y colindancias en *Viriditas* de Cristina Rivera Garza," *Letras Femeninas* 42, no. 2 (Winter-Spring 2016–17): 43.
80. Lugones, "Heterosexualism," 191; 206.
81. María Galindo, *Feminismo bastardo* (Canal Press, Mantis, 2022), 155.
82. Galindo, *Feminismo bastardo*, 155.
83. Galindo, *Feminismo bastardo*, 121.
84. Valencia, "Welcome to Hairy Tales," January 22, 2009, *Sayak Valencia Triana* (blog) http://sayakvalencia.blogspot.com/2009/01/welcome-to-hairy-tales-presentado-en-la.html.
85. Lucas Platero, "Conocer nuestras genealogías," in *Transfeminismo o barbarie*, ed. Aingeru Mayor et al. (Kaótica libros, 2021), 43.
86. Fernández in Platero, "Conocer nuestras genealogías," 42.
87. Galindo, *Feminismo bastardo*, 113.

CHAPTER 3

1. Ahmed, *Living a Feminist Life*, 187.
2. Ahmed, "Affective Economies," *Social Text* 22, no. 2 (2004): 119.
3. Ellen B. Berry, *Women's Experimental Writing: Negative Aesthetics and Feminist Critique* (Bloomsbury, 2016), 5.
4. Berry, *Women's Experimental Writing*, 18.
5. Hind, *Dude Lit*.
6. Sarah E. L. Bowskill, *Gender, Nation and the Formation of the Twentieth-Century Mexican Literary Canon* (Routledge, 2011), 12–13.
7. María Elena Olivera Córdova, *Entre amoras: Lesbianismo en la narrativa mexicana* (UNAM, 2015), 168–69; Artemisa Téllez, "'A Chloe le gustaba Olivia': Implicaciones de una literatura que quisiera llamarse lésbica," in *Homofobia: Laberinto de la ignorancia*, ed. Julio Muñoz Rubio (UNAM, 2010), 179.
8. Artemisa Téllez, "'A Chloe le gustaba Olivia,'" 180.
9. Hind, *Feminism and the Mexican*, 2.
10. The examples are numerous. Gilda Salinas is perhaps a good case study since most of her books are self-published through her own publishing project called *Trópico de Escorpio* (Scorpio Tropic). For instance, *Las sombras del Safari* (Shadows of the safari; 1998) was initially published by Diana but soon went out of circulation until Salinas reprinted it under her own label. This book may serve as the primary testimony of spaces like the Safari, a bar where celebrities such as Chavela Vargas used to frequent. Another example is *Somos*

voces, a bookstore combined with an independent publishing house that frequently takes on the task of re-editing forgotten voices of sexual and gender dissidents. The distribution efforts of these types of cultural projects are very limited.

11. I refuse to give a summary of the case because I do not want to give more space to homophobia and misogyny. However, I do believe documenting these instances is an important job that, in this case, was done by Téllez. My reader has all the necessary tools to find her text and read it if they chose to do so. May the inconvenience be a reminder of the pain inflicted that gender and sexual dissident subjectivities must endure in the present literary scene.
12. Rosamaría Roffiel, "¿Existe o no la literatura gay?" *Fem* 11, no. 51 (1987): 40.
13. Rosamaría Roffiel, "¿Existe o no la literatura lésbica mexicana?" *Fem* 20, no. 155 (1996): 43.
14. *Buga* is a common term that nonheterosexual people use to describe heterosexual people.
15. Rosamaría Roffiel, *Amora* (Horas y Horas la Editorial, 1997), 11.
16. Jonathan Flatley suggests the term "affective maps" to support how aesthetic practices can represent the historization, emotional orientation and politization of one's affective experience. For Flatley, the affective map facilitates the mobility of affect while providing orientation. See more in Jonathan Flatley, *Affective Mapping: Melancholia and the Politics of Modernism* (Harvard University Press, 2008), 4, 7.
17. Claudia Schaefer, *Danger Zones: Homosexuality, National Identity, and Mexican Culture* (University of Arizona Press, 1996), 384.
18. Pablo Salvador Martínez, "Atracción fatal," *La jornada semanal* 19 (1989): 13.
19. Antonio Marquet, "La pasión según Roffiel," in *¡Que se quede el infinito sin estrellas!* (UAM, 2001), 229.
20. Trejo Fuentes in Olivera Córdova, *Entre amoras*, 130; Ignacio Trejo Fuentes, "Rosamaría Roffiel: *Amora*," *Tema y variaciones en literatura: Literatura gay* 17, no. 2 (2001): 187.
21. It's worth noting that more positive reviews were published by either feminist journals or spaces without a defined political view. To this point, Roffiel explains that "Paradójicamente los periódicos supuestamente más liberales y progresistas (*La Jornada* y *Uno más Uno*) le hicieron reseñas poco favorables. Algunos críticos trataron la novela como un 'mero panfleto feminista.' Por otro lado, la mayoría de los periódicos y revistas de la ciudad publicaron reseñas muy positivas" (Paradoxically, the supposedly more liberal and progressive newspapers (*La Jornada* and *Uno más Uno*) gave it unfavorable

reviews. Some critics treated the novel as a 'mere feminist pamphlet.' On the other hand, the majority of the city's newspapers and magazines published very positive reviews). Roffiel in Elena M. Martínez, Review of *Dos mujeres* by Sara Calderón Levi and *Amora* by Rosamaría Roffiel, *Letras Femeninas* 18, no. 1–2 (1992): 179. In the case of the more positive reviews mentioned here, it is interesting to note that one is published by *Letras femeninas*, one of the earliest academic journals devoted to gender-related issues in the context of Latin American literature and culture. The other one is published by *Fem*, the most important openly feminist magazine in Mexico during that time. See more about the history of *Fem* in *Fem: 10 años de periodismo feminista* (Planeta, 1998).
22. Berry, *Women's Experimental Writing*, 7.
23. Berry, *Women's Experimental Writing*, 2.
24. The list of these types of books keeps growing and gaining interest among readers and scholars. In the case of Mexico and beyond the work of Cristina Rivera Garza, the poetry of Sara Uribe is a good case of study. Other examples are *Chicas muertas* (*Death Girls*; 2014) by Selva Almada and *Huaco retrato* (*Undiscovered*; 2021) by Gabriela Wiener, showing that the surge of nonfiction is not limited to a specific geographical region. As I mentioned in Chapter 2, the influence of autotheory and Paul B. Preciado's writing is also relevant to this context.
25. Roffiel, *Amora*, 99; 165.
26. Roffiel, *Amora*, 111.
27. Juana María Rodríguez, "Queer Politics, Bisexual Erasure," *Lambda Nordica* 21 no. 1–2 (2016): 169.
28. Clare Hemmings, *Bisexual Spaces: A Geography of Sexuality and Gender* (Routledge, 2002), 3; 54; Rodríguez, "Queer Politics, Bisexual Erasure," 169.
29. Roffiel, interview with Francesca Dennstedt, Mexico City, May 13, 2019.
30. Ochs in Rodríguez, "Queer Politics, Bisexual Erasure," 170.
31. Ahmed, *Living a Feminist Life*, 188.
32. Marquet, "La pasión según Roffiel," 232.
33. Michael K. Schuessler and Miguel Capistrán, *México se escribe con J: Una historia de la cultura gay* (Planeta, 2010), 26.
34. Olivera Córdova, *Entre amoras*, 109.
35. Marquet, "La pasión según Roffiel," 232.
36. Roffiel in Téllez, "A Chloe le gustaba Olivia," 178.
37. Cañedo, "*Amora y Crema de vainilla*, momentos clave de la novela lésbica mexicana en 25 años," *Interdisciplinaria* 10, no. 27 (2020): 67.
38. Roffiel, *Amora*, 215.

39. Jack Halberstam, *The Queer Art of Failure* (Duke University Press, 2012).
40. Téllez, "'A Chloe le gustaba Olivia,'" 80.
41. Judith Butler, *Bodies That Matter: On the Discursive Limits of Sex* (Routledge, 1993), 128.
42. Cristina Rivera Garza, *Nadie me verá llorar* (Tusquets / Consejo Nacional para la Cultura y las Artes / Instituto Nacional de Bellas Artes, 1999), 145.
43. Sara Uribe, *Un montón de escritura para nada* (Dharma Books, 2019), 29.
44. Yolanda Segura, *Estancias que por ahora tienen luz y se abren hacia el paisaje* (Consejo para la Cultura y las Artes de Nuevo León, 2018), 48.
45. *Criseida* Santos Guevara, *La reinita pop no ha muerto* (Literal Publishing, 2013), 11.
46. Santos Guevara, *La reinita*, 75.
47. Santos Guevara, *La reinita*, 9.
48. Santos Guevara, *La reinita*, 9–10.
49. Santos Guevara in Alejandro Baillet, "Humor y amor lésbico," *La Jornada Hidalgo*, December 11, 2022, https://lajornadahidalgo.com/humor-y-amor-lesbico.
50. Santos Guevara, *La reinita*, 51.
51. Santos Guevara, *La reinita*, 80.
52. Santos Guevara in Alejandro Baillet, "Humor."
53. Berry, *Women's Experimental Writing*, 119.
54. Rita Felski, *Beyond Feminist Aesthetics: Feminist Literature and Social Change* (Harvard University Press, 1989), 11.
55. Santos Guevara, *La reinita*, 51.
56. Ahmed, "Affective Economies," 120.

CHAPTER 4

1. The edition used throughout this chapter corresponds to the Spanish version published in 2002 by Tusquets Editores. The English translation by Sarah Booker, published by Feminist Press in 2017, as well as the consequent rewriting of *La cresta de Ilión* in Spanish, resulting from the translation and published in 2018 by Random House, were not taken into consideration.
2. Cristina Rivera Garza, "Desapropiación para principiantes," *Literal Magazine*, May 31, 2017, https://literalmagazine.com/desapropiacion-para-principiantes.
3. Cristina Rivera Garza, *The Restless Dead: Necrowriting & Disappropriation*, trans. Robin Myers (Vanderbilt University Press, 2020), 53.
4. Cristina Rivera Garza in Anna María Iglesia, "Rivera Garza: 'El lenguaje del amor ha demostrado ser letal en muchos casos,'" *Letra global*, January 26, 2023,

https://cronicaglobal.elespanol.com/letraglobal/letras/20230126/rivera-garza-el-lenguaje-demostrado-letal-muchos/736676432_0.html.
5. Rivera Garza, *The Restless Dead*, 5.
6. Rivera Garza, *The Restless Dead*, 5.
7. To learn more about solidarity in difference in the aftermath of the Primavera violeta in México, please refer to Francesca Dennstedt, "Tactics of Feminist Disappropriation and Cultural Directions in Our Global Digital Era: A case for #NiUnaMenos in Times of #MeToo," in *Digital Performative Assemblies: Feminist Protest and Resistance*, edited by Shana MacDonald et al. (Lexington Books, 2022), 17–23.
8. Verónica Gago, *Feminist International: How to Change Everything*, trans. Liz Mason-Deese (Verso, 2020), 197. Another example of this form of thinking is the work of the Brazilian writer Vilma Piedade who coins the term "doloridade" as a response to "sororidade": "doloridad conlleva en su significado el dolor provocado en todas las Mujeres por el Machismo. Sin embargo, cuando se trata de Nosotras, Mujeres Prietas, hay un agravamiento de ese dolor. . . . La Sororidad parece no contemplar nuestra pretitud" (Doloridad [a neologism that combines the Spanish word for pain (*dolor*) with sorority] carries within its meaning the pain caused in all women by machismo. However, when it comes to us, Prieta women [women of color], that pain is intensified. . . . Sorority seems not to include our *pretitud* [racial identity]). (Piedade, *Doloridade*, 20).
9. Rivera Garza, *The Restless Dead*, 54. Here literature describes a historically determined and cultural significant form of writing, which has served as an organizing principle in the establishment of the Mexican canon since the nineteenth century until its declined in the late twentieth and early twenty-first centuries (Rivera Garza, *The Restless Dead*, 132). To see more about the revision of authorship in terms of disappropriation, refer to Francisco Estrada Medina, "Reimaginar la autoría: La desapropiación según Cristina Rivera Garza," *Letras femeninas* 42, no. 2 (2016/17): 27–34.
10. Harold Bloom, *The Western Canon: The Books and School of the Ages* (Harcourt Brace, 1994), 1.
11. John Guillory, *Cultural Capital: The Problem of Literary Canon Formation* (University of Chicago Press, 1993).
12. Sánchez Prado, "On Cosmopolitanism" and "Cultural Capital."
13. Ahmed, *The Cultural Politics of Emotion*, 11.
14. Ahmed, "Affective Economies."
15. Rivera Garza, *The Restless Dead*, 6; Rivera Garza, *The Restless Dead*, 113.
16. Muñoz, *Cruising Utopia*, 27.

17. Diana Taylor, *The Archive and the Repertoire: Performing Cultural Memory in the Americas* (Duke University Press, 2003). I use Taylor's concepts in the hopes for clarification. A more detailed analysis of the implications of the poetics of disappropriation for concepts like the archive (individual things) and repertoire (as embodied memory) is outside of the scope of this project.
18. Juan Bruce-Novoa, "Literatura de la desidentidad: Juan García Ponce y Cristina Rivera Garza," in *Cristina Rivera Garza: Ningún crítico cuenta esto...*, ed. Oswaldo Estrada (Ediciones Eón, 2008), Kindle; Osvaldo Zavala, "La tradición que retrocede: *La cresta de Ilión*, Amparo Dávila y la radicalización de la alteridad," in Estrada, ed., *Cristina Rivera Garza*; Oswaldo Estrada, "Against Representation: Women's Writing in Contemporary Mexico," *Hispanófila* 157 (2009): 64; Emily Hind, "El consumo textual y *La cresta de Ilión* de Cristina Rivera Garza," *Filología y lingüística* 31, no. 1 (2005): 36.
19. Berry, *Women's Experimental Writing*, 6.
20. The amount of work published on *La cresta de Ilión* is surprising, not to mention the extensive research on Rivera Garza herself. Two compilations, namely *Cristina Rivera Garza: Una escritura impropia* (Cristina Rivera Garza: An improper writing) and *Cristina Rivera Garza: Ningún crítico cuenta esto...* (Cristina Rivera Garza: No critic tells this...) provide a good introductory overview of her literature, catering to both specialized readers and a more mainstream audience.
21. After the publication of *La cresta de Ilión*, Amparo Dávila's work regained interest, leading to the formation of a community of writers, scholars, and readers who produced new significations of her work. Analyzing the broader impact of including Amparo Dávila's work as another piece of the affective canon is beyond the scope of this project. However, it's worth noting that her complete stories were republished in 2009 by Fondo de Cultura Económica, with a prologue written by Mariana Enríquez, which speaks of Dávila's influence beyond Mexico. Notably, there is now an entire school dedicated to "rewriting" "El huésped," with works such as Guadalupe Nettel's *El huésped* (*The Guest*; 2006) and Verónica Gerber Bicecci's *La compañia* (*The Company*; 2021), and Ave Barrera is currently working on a script based on this story. Additionally, Cristina Rivera Garza uses this short story as a pedagogical exercise in her creative writing classes (as mentioned in Leticia Rovecchio Antón, "Cristina Rivera Garza: 'En *La cresta de Ilión* la desesperación cultural va ligada con la violencia física,'" *PliegoSuelto: Revista de Literatura y Alrededores*, July 30, 2020, http://www.pliegosuelto.com/?p=29892). Translation efforts have also taken place, including the work done by Audrey Harris and Matthew Gleeson. Harris

has written an excellent short piece linking Dávila's work to the painter Remedios Varo, showcasing further possibilities of approaching the canon from an affective perspective. For more information, refer to Audrey Harris, "The Fern Cat," *The Paris Review*, February 21, 2017.
22. Roland Barthes, *S/Z*, trans. Richard Miller (Hill and Wang, 1974).
23. Marjorie Perloff has an excellent chapter on McCaffery's *Panopticon*. She touches various aspects of the experimental text that relate to *La cresta de Ilión*. See more in Marjorie Perloff, "'Voice Whisht Through Thither Flood': Steve McCaffery's *Panopticon* and *North of Intention*," in *Essays on Modernist and Postmodernist Lyric* (Northwestern University Press, 1990), 287.
24. Rivera Garza, *The Restless Dead*, 54.
25. Cheyla Samuelson, "Líneas de Fuga: The Character of Writing in the Novels of Cristina Rivera Garza" (PhD diss., University of California, Santa Barbara, 2011).
26. Marjorie Perloff, "'Voice Whisht Through Thither Flood,'" 287.
27. Samuelson, "Líneas de fuga."
28. To see more about the legacy of Amparo Dávila in Mexican writers, refer to Carmen Alemany, "El legado de Amparo Dávila en narradoras mexicanas actuales," *Brumal: Revista de investigación sobre lo Fantástico* 9, no. 1 (2021): 35–52. In this article, Alemany places the writing of Cecilia Eudave, Guadalupe Nettel, Daniela Tarazona, and Socorro Venegas as inheritors of Dávila's unusual atmospheres and fascination for the fantastic.
29. Verónica Saunero-Ward, "*La cresta de Ilión*: Lo fantástico posmoderno," *La palabra y el hombre* 137 (2006): 180; Zaca Guevara in Felipe Ríos Baeza, "Una novela hospitalaria: *La cresta de Ilión*, de Cristina Rivera-Garza," *Valenciana* 24 (2019): 105. For a detailed analysis of the intertextuality of *La cresta de Ilión* in relation to Dávila, see Gabriela Mercado, "Diálogo con Amparo Dávila y resolución de problemas de género en *La cresta de Ilión* de Cristina Rivera Garza," *Revista de Humanidades: Tecnológico de Monterrey* 22 (2007): 45–75.
30. Hind, "El consumo textual," 41.
31. Adriana Álvarez Rivera, "Ambiguedad y subversión fantástica en la narrativa de Amparo Dávila" (PhD diss., Universidad de Salamanca, 2016), 412.
32. Rivera Garza in Rovecchio Antón, "Cristina Rivera Garza."
33. Cristina Rivera Garza, *La cresta de Ilión* (Tusquets Editores, 2002), 17.
34. Ahmed, "Affective Economies," 66.
35. Ahmed, "Affective Economies," 66.
36. Ahmed, "Affective Economies," 66.
37. On September 13, 1847, six military cadets were killed in defense of Mexico City during one of the major battles of the Mexican-American war. Allegedly,

Escutia is the cadet who wrapped himself up in the Mexican flag and jumped from the roof to keep it from falling into enemy hands.
38. Rivera Garza, *La cresta de Ilión*, 19.
39. The term *cosexual* is used in the study of plants and their sex determination. Deborah Charlesworth explains the following: "In many sexually reproducing plant species (and some animals) all individuals are essentially alike in their gender condition. Many such 'sexually monomorphic' species are hermaphroditic. The term 'cosexual' (Lloyd, 1984) is used when individual plants have both sex functions, whether present within each flower (hermaphrodite), or in separate male and female flowers (monoecious)." Deborah Charlesworth, "Plant Sex Determination and Sex Chromosomes," *Heredity* 88 (2002): 94. In other words, a cosexual plant produces both pollen and ovules.
40. Ahmed, "Affective Economies," 67.
41. During the Xavier Villaurrutia award ceremony for *El invencible verano de Liliana* (2022), a book that reconstructs the feminicidio of Liliana, the sister of Rivera Garza, Felipe Garrido expressed regret over the book's limited discussion of Liliana's killer, Ángel González Ramos. No need to argue the insensitivity and the lack of a more substantial critical intervention from Garrido. It is sufficient to note that the critic was concerned about the disappearance of the *feminicida*, which in reality conceals the critic's fear of losing authority in the face of a *marea violeta y verde* (violet and green tide) that defies propriety—as the audience's screams soon made evident. For more information, refer to Alma Karla Sandoval, "Un verano invencible para todas: Sobre Felipe Garrido y Cristina Rivera Garza, un debate que no tendría razón de ser," *Revista Gafe: Literatura contemporánea y voces emergentes*, July 2022, https://gafe.info/un-verano-invencible-para-todas-sobre-felipe-garrido-y-cristina-rivera-garza-un-debate-que-no-tendria-razon-de-ser-por-alma-karla-sandoval/opinion/columnistas.
42. Rivera Garza, *La cresta de Ilión*, 39.
43. Rivera Garza, *La cresta de Ilión*, 39.
44. Rivera Garza, *La cresta de Ilión*, 143.
45. Sianne Ngai, *Ugly Feelings* (Harvard University Press, 2005): 213.
46. Ahmed, *The Cultural Politics of Emotion*, 64.
47. Adriana González Mateos, "La cresta de Ilión," *Debate Feminista* 27 (2003): 341.
48. González Mateos, "La cresta de Ilión," 341.
49. Christopher Domínguez Michael, "¿Quién teme a Amparo Dávila?" *Reforma*, May 3, 2003, http://www.reforma.com/elangel/articulo/291253/default.htm.
50. Lila McDowell Carsen analyses *La cresta de Ilión* in relation to US/Mexico border, suggesting that Rivera Garza creates a space where marginalized

bodies can freely navigate gender boundaries and national borders. For more information, refer to Lila McDowell, "'Te conozco de cuando eras árbol': Gender, Utopianism, and the Border in Cristina Rivera Garza's *La cresta de Ilión*," *Symposium: A Quarterly Journal in Modern Literatures* 64, no. 4 (2010): 229–42.

51. Rivera Garza in Rovecchio Antón, "Cristina Rivera Garza."
52. Domínguez Michael, "¿Quién teme a Amparo Dávila?"
53. Hind, "El consumo textual," 46.
54. Ríos Baeza, "Una novela *hospitalaria*," 108.
55. Hind, "El consumo textual," 40.
56. Gago, *Feminist International*, ix.
57. Gago, *Feminist International*, ix.
58. Gago, *Feminist International*, 3.
59. Rivera Garza, "Desapropiación para principiantes."
60. Gago, *Feminist International*, 3.
61. Rivera Garza, *La cresta de Ilión*, 34; Rich, "Compulsory Heterosexuality."
62. To see more about hospitality in *La cresta de Ilión*, refer to Ríos Baeza, "Una novela *hospitalaria*," where the author discusses the relationship between hospitality and the intertextuality of Rivera Garza.
63. Some of the scholars consulted for this chapter that address gender and/or sex are Gabriela Mercado, Stephen Silverstein, Jorge Ruffinelli, Oswaldo Estrada, Vinodh Venkatesh, Alejandra Márquez, and Encarnación Cruz Jiménez.
64. Cristina Rivera Garza, *Escrituras geológicas* (Iberoamericana Vervuert, 2022), 12.
65. Rivera Garza, *La cresta de Ilión*, 158.
66. Ríos Baeza, "Una novela *hospitalaria*," 106.
67. Rivera Garza, *La cresta de Ilión*, 68.
68. Rivera Garza, *La cresta de Ilión*, 68.
69. Didí Gutiérrez, *Las elegantes* (Paraíso perdido, 2021), 10; Baeza, "Dime que me quieres: El amor elegante," *Magno simposio exprés: Las elegantes 2021*, streamed live on YouTube by Editorial Paraíso Perdido, November 21, 2021, https://www.youtube.com/watch?v=OPJ8QoWCxsc, 1:36:10. All the information of "las elegantes" is taken from Gutiérrez's research included in the anthology unless otherwise specified.
70. Hind, *Dude Lit*, 34.
71. Finnegan, "Women Writers," 4. The same year that *Las bonitas* would be published, the best-seller *Arráncame la vida* (1985) by Ángeles Mastretta inaugurated what is known as the "boom femenino." See more in Nuala Finnegan and Jane E. Lavery, eds., *The Boom Femenino in Mexico: Reading Contemporary Women's Writing* (Cambridge Scholars Publishing, 2010).

72. Abigail Maritxu Aranda Márquez, "L@s novi@s de Las Elegantes," *Magno simposio exprés: Las elegantes 2021*, streamed live on YouTube by Editorial Paraíso Perdido, November 21, 2021, https://www.youtube.com/watch?v=OP-J8Q0WCxsc, 2:07:03.
73. Margitte Kristjansson, "Fashion's 'Forgotten Woman': How Fat Bodies Queer Fashion and Consumption," in *Queering Fat Embodiment*, ed. Cat Pausé et al. (Routledge, 2014), 131.
74. Aranda Márquez, "L@s novi@s de Las Elegantes," 2:05:12.
75. Gutiérrez, *Las elegantes*, 55–56.
76. The interview was published as part of a dossier that I coordinated for Tierra Adentro to commemorate Pride Month 2023. The interview can be accessed at Didí Gutiérrez, "Elegante se 'sale del clóset' editorial," Tierra Adentro, accessed April 13, 2024, https://tierraadentro.fondodeculturaeconomica.com/elegante-se-sale-del-closet-editorial.
77. According to Alexandra R. DeRuiz, "madrinas" in the seventies and eighties referred to "policías que andaban en carros sin placas y sin uniforme, tipo civiles, y que patrullaban las calles deteniendo a quienes creían sospechosos de algún crimen, incluyendo a personas de las disidencias sexuales" (Police officers driving unmarked cars and without uniforms, in civilian attire, who patrolled the streets detaining those they deemed suspicious of committing a crime, including individuals from sexual dissident communities). DeRuiz also highlights the troubling history of "El Torito" concerning trans* people: "fue ahí en donde muchas de mis hermanas y amigas vieron violado sus derechos humanos" (it was there that many of my sisters and friends saw their human rights violated). Alexandra R. DeRuiz, *Crucé la frontera en taconces: Crónicas de una TRANSgresora* (Egales Editorial, 2023), 166; 173.
78. Aranda Márquez, "L@s novi@s de Las Elegantes," 2:07:35.
79. Two other sources that bear witness to the violence during that period, particularly against trans*, travestis, and what we now recognize as other genderqueer identities, are the recently published memoir by trans activist Alexandra R. De Ruiz, titled *Crucé la frontera en tacones* (2023), and Susana Vargas's project, which unfortunately lacks critical perspectives while compiling the harmful images published by the tabloid newspaper *Alarma* during the time.
80. Pierre Bourdieu, *Distinction: A Social Critique of the Judgment of Taste* (Harvard University Press, 1984), 56; 190.
81. Deborah Lupton, *Food, the Body, and the Self* (Sage Publications, 1996), 95.
82. Kristjansson, "Fashion's 'Forgotten Woman,'" 133.
83. Rivera Garza, "Desapropiación para principiantes."

84. Didí Gutiérrez, "Recupera Didí Gutiérrez textos perdidos: Crea antología Las Elegantes," *Zócalo*, November 22, 2021, https://www.zocalo.com.mx/recupera-didi-gutierrez-textos-perdidos-crea-antologia-las-elegantes.
85. Alma Karla Sandoval and Denisse Buendía, *Vocabularia: Diccionaria feminista* (Ediciones Zetina, 2023), 59.
86. Huchín Sosa, "Oye, Perla Holguín, ¿sabes si estos libros de la 'elegante' Alí Boites estarán en el curso de policiaco en la UNAM? *Muerte en el Cerro de la Estrella* (1999), *Muerte en el Cerro del Tepozteco* (2002) y *Muerte en el Cerro de las Campanas* (2010)," Facebook, August 11, 2021.
87. Eduardo Huchín Sosa, "Diez escritoras de las que no habías oído hablar (ni siquiera en los artículos que se titulan de esa manera)," *Tediósfera: Un blog de Eduardo Huchín Sosa*, February 23, 2022, https://tediosfera.wordpress.com/2022/02/23/diez-escritoras-de-las-que-no-habias-oido-hablar-ni-siquiera-en-los-articulos-que-se-titulan-de-esa-manera.
88. Huchín Sosa, "Diez escritoras."
89. Gilles Deleuze and Felix Guattari, *A Thousand Plateaus: Capitalism and Schizophrenia*, trans Brian Massumi (University of Minnesota Press, 1987).

CODA

1. Epigraph. Daniela Rea Gómez, *Ya no somos las mismas y aquí sigue la Guerra* (Grijalbo, 2020), 125.
1. Rivera Garza in Rovecchio Antón, "Cristina Rivera Garza."
2. *Hartazgo* refers to a state of having had more than enough—often to the point of discomfort or annoyance—especially with food, drink, or an experience. It conveys a mix of excess, overindulgence, and satiety, but with an edge of being fed up or tired of something. While English has words like *glut*, *surfeit*, *overindulgence*, or *satiety*, none fully capture the layered emotional and physical sense that *hartazgo* carries in Spanish. It can refer both to literal fullness (e.g., from overeating) and figurative exhaustion (e.g., being fed up with someone or something).
3. Lydia Cacho, "The 100 Most Influential People of 2020: Arussi Unda," *Time*, September 22, 2020, https://time.com/collection/100-most-influential-people-2020/5888264/arussi-unda.
4. Jumko Ogata Aguilar, "Yo no quiero ser 'la chica-patrona,'" *Volcánicas*, August 31, 2021, https://volcanicas.com/yo-no-quiero-ser-la-chica-patrona.
5. Josefina Ludmer, *Aquí América Latina: Una especulación* (Eterna Cadencia, 2011), 24.

REFERENCES

Ahmed, Sara. *The Cultural Politics of Emotion*. Edinburgh University Press, 2004.
Ahmed, Sara. "Affective Economies." *Social Text* 22, no. 2 (2004): 117–39.
Ahmed, Sara. *La política cultural de las emociones*, translated by Cecilia Olivares Mansuy. UNAM/PUEG, 2015.
Ahmed, Sara. *Living a Feminist Life*. Duke University Press, 2017.
Alemany, Carmen. "El legado de Amparo Dávila en narradoras mexicanas actuales." *Brumal: Revista de Investigación sobre lo Fantástico* 9, no. 1 (2021): 33–52.
Albarrán, Claudia. "La generación de Inés Arredondo," *Casa del tiempo*, September 1998. https://www.uam.mx/difusion/revista/septiembre98/albarran.html.
Albarrán, Claudia. *Luna menguante: Vida y obra de Inés Arredondo*. Ediciones Casa Juan Pablos, 2000.
Albarrán, Claudia. "La revista S.NOB: Laboratorio experimental de una generación." *Revuelta* 4 (2006): 63–67.
Alberti Soto, Begoña. "Desviar la tradición: el arte de apropiación de la revista mexicana S.nob." *Revista de Humanidades* 37 (2018): 15–37.
Álvarez Rivera, Adriana. "Ambiguedad y subversión fantástica en la narrativa de Amparo Dávila." PhD diss., Universidad de Salamanca, 2016.
Appadurai, Arjun. "Archive and Aspiration." In *Information Is Alive*, edited by Joke Brower and Arjen Mulder, 12–25. V2_Publishing and NAI Publishers, 2003.
Aranda Márquez, Abigail Maritxu. "L@s novi@s de Las Elegantes." *Magno simposio exprés: Las elegantes 2021*. Streamed live on YouTube by Editorial Paraíso Perdido, November 21, 2021. https://www.youtube.com/watch?v=OPJ8QoWCxsc.
Aravena, Cristian, Sol Henaro, Alejandra Moreno, and Brian Smith. *Arte de acción en México: Registros y residuos*. MUAC and UNAM, 2019.

Arenas Monreal, Rogelio. "La pareja y la mirada transgredida en 'Mariana,' de Inés Arredondo." In *Mujer y literatura mexicana y chicana: Culturas en contacto*, edited by Aralia López González, Amelia Malagamba Ansótegui, and Elena Urrutia. El Colegio de Mexico, 1998.

Aresti Esteban, Nerea. "La mujer moderna, el tener sexo y la bohemia en los años veinte." *Dossiers Feministes* 10 (2007): 173–85.

Arredondo, Inés. "Mariana." In *Obras completas*. Siglo XXI editores, 1988.

Arredondo, Inés. "Las mariposas nocturnas." In *Obras completas*. Siglo XXI editores, 1988.

Arredondo, Inés. "Sombra entre sombras." In *Obras completas*. Siglo XXI editores, 1988.

Baeza, Laura. "Dime que me quieres: El amor elegante." *Magno simposio exprés: Las elegantes 2021*. Streamed live on YouTube by Editorial Paraíso Perdido, November 21, 2021. https://www.youtube.com/watch?v=OPJ8QoWCxsc.

Barrera, Ave. *Restauración*. Paraíso perdido, 2019.

Barrera, Ave. Interviewed by Emily Hind. "Ave Barrera al precipicio de la introducción al mundo anglófono." *A contra corriente: Una revista de estudios latinoamericanos* 19, no. 3 (2022): 327–44.

Barthes, Roland. *S/Z*, translated by Richard Miller. Hill and Wang, 1974.

Bartra, Anna y Agustí / Bambi. "Correspondencia a propósito de Ana Mairena." *Plural* 10–12, no. 120 (1981): 5–8.

Bataille, George. *Erotism: Death and Sensuality*, translated by Mary Dalwood. Walker and Company, 1962.

Bataille, George. *Inner Experience*, translated by Leslie Anne Boldt. SUNY Press, 1988.

Batiz, Huberto. "Los relatos de Inés Arredondo." *Unomásuno* 632 (1989): 1–3.

Bauer, Robin. "Negotiating Critical Consent." In *Queer BDSM Intimacies: Critical Consent and Pushing Boundaries*. Palgrave Macmillan, 2014.

Berlant, Lauren. *Cruel Optimism*. Duke University Press, 2011.

Berry, Ellen E. *Women's Experimental Writing: Negative Aesthetics and Feminist Critique*. Bloomsbury, 2016.

Bisbey, Brandon P. *Between Camp and Cursi: Humor and Homosexuality in Contemporary Mexican Narrative*. SUNY Press, 2022.

Bloom, Harold. *The Western Canon: The Books and School of the Ages*. Harcourt Brace, 1994.

Bowskill, Sarah E. L. *Gender, Nation and the Formation of the Twentieth-Century Mexican Literary Canon*. Routledge, 2011.

Bradu, Fabienne. "La escritura subterránea de Inés Arredondo." In *Señas particulares: Escritoras*. Fondo de cultura económica, 1987.

Bruce-Novoa, Juan. "Elena Poniatowska y la generación de medio siglo: Lilus, Jesusa, Angelina, Tina . . . y la errancia sin fin." *América sin nombre*, no. 11–12 (2008): 70–78.

Bruce-Novoa, Juan. "Literatura de la desidentidad: Juan García Ponce y Cristina Rivera Garza." In *Cristina Rivera Garza: Ningún crítico cuenta esto. . .*, edited by Oswaldo Estrada. Ediciones Eón, 2010. Kindle.

Bourdieu, Pierre. *Distinction: A Social Critique of the Judgment of Taste*. Harvard University Press. 1984.

Bustamante, Maris. "Conditions, Roads, and Genealogies of Mexican Conceptualisms, 1921–1993." In *Arte no es vida: Actions by Artists of the Americas*, edited by Deborah Cullen. Museo del Barrio, 2008.

Butler, Judith. "Imitation and Gender Insubordination." In *Inside/Out: Lesbian Theories, Gay Theories*, edited by Diana Fuss. Routledge, 1991.

Butler, Judith. *Bodies That Matter: On the Discursive Limits of Sex*. Routledge, 1993.

Butler, Judith. "Bodily Vulnerability, Coalitions, and Street Politics." In *Differences in Common: Gender, Vulnerability and Community*, edited by Joana Sabadell-Nieto and Marta Segarra. Brill, 2014. DOI: https://doi.org/10.1163/9789401210805.

Cabello, Cristian. "Posmenopausia *drag*: Las mujeres y mi mamá, una reflectora disidente de la performatividad." In *Por un feminismo sin mujeres: Fragmentos del Segundo Circuito Disidencia Sexual*. Coordinadora Universitaria por la Disidencia Sexual (CUDS), 2011.

Cabrera López, Patricia. *Una inquietud de amanecer: Literatura y política en México, 1962–1987*. Plaza y Valdés, 2006.

Cano, Gabriela. "Ambientes bohemios: Diversidad sexual en la capital mexicana durante los fabulosos años veinte." *Mexican Studies / Estudios mexicanos* 36, no. 1.2 (2020): 167–91.

Cañedo, César. "*Amora y Crema de vainilla*, momentos clave de la novela lésbica mexicana en 25 años." *Interdisciplinaria* 10, no. 27 (2020): 53–78.

Carballo, Emmanuel. "La última novela de una escritora enmascarada: *Los extraordinarios*." *México en la cultura* 650 (August 27, 1969).

Cartas, Frida. *Transporte a la infancia*. Almadia, 2023.

Cervantes-Gómez, Xiomara Verenice. "Paz's *Pasivo*: Thinking Mexicanness from the Bottom." *Journal of Latin American Studies* 29, no. 3 (2020): 333–47.

Cervantes González, Elizabeth Anahí. "Índice y estudio preliminar de la revista S.NOB." Undergraduate thesis, UNAM, 2010.

Cervantes Morales, Luis. *Memorias de Don Carlos Balmori: Escritas por su secretario particular*. Costa-Amic, 1969.

Charlesworth, Deborah. "Plant Sex Determination and Sex Chromosomes." *Heredity* 88 (2002): 94–101. https://doi.org/10.1038/sj.hdy.6800016.

Córdova García, David. "Teoría queer: Reflexiones sobre sexo, sexualidad e identidad. Hacia una politización de la sexualidad." In *Teoría Queer: Políticas bolleras, maricas, trans, mestizas*, edited by Davod Córdoba, Javier Sáez, and Paco Vidarte. Egales, 2005.

Cruz Arzabal, Roberto. "Archivos potenciales: Domiciliación y colindancias en *Viriditas* de Cristina Rivera Garza." *Letras Femeninas* 42, no. 2 (Winter–Spring 2016–17): 35–43.

Cruz Jiménez, Encarnación. "Juegos de género y polifonía en *Ningún reloj cuenta esto*." In *Cristina Rivera Garza: Ningún crítico cuenta esto. . .*, edited by Oswaldo Estrada. Ediciones Eón, 2010. Kindle.

Curiosidades históricas. Season 1, episode 1, "Carlos Balmori." Canal catorce, aired October 15, 2016, 24 min. https://canalcatorce.tv/?c=Programas&p=175&a=Det&t=196&ci=2845.

Deleuze, Gilles. "Coldness and Cruelty." In *Masochism*. Zone books, 1991.

Deleuze, Gilles, and Felix Guattari. *A Thousand Plateaus: Capitalism and Schizophrenia*, translated by Brian Massumi. University of Minnesota Press, 1987.

Delhumeau, Eduardo. *Don Carlos Balmori: Su extraordinaria vida y hazañas*. Omega, 1938.

Dennstedt, Francesca. "Aperitivo para digerir." Introduction to *Cena de cenizas*, by Asunción Izquierdo Albiñana. UNAM, 2022.

Dennstedt, Francesca. "Hablemos de . . . Asunción Izquierdo Albiñana." *Hablemos escritoras* (podcast), December 14, 2020. https://www.hablemosescritoras.com/posts/282.

Dennstedt, Francesca. "Tactics of Feminist Disappropriation and Cultural Directions in Our Global Digital Era: A Case for #NiUnaMenos in Times of #MeToo." In *Digital Performative Assemblies: Feminist Protest and Resistance*, edited by Shana MacDonald, Michelle MacArthur, and Brianna I. Wiens. Lexington Books, 2022.

Dennstedt, Francesca, and Laura J. Torres-Rodríguez. "Introducción: Feminismos, luchas antipatriarcales y transformaciones materiales de la literatura mexicana contemporánea." *Revista de Estudios Hispánicos* 57, no. 7 (2023): 125–42.

DeRuiz, Alexandra R. *Crucé la frontera en tacones: Crónicas de una TRANSgresora*. Egales editorial, 2023.

Domecq, Brianda. "La callada subversión." In *Sin imágenes falsas, sin falsos espejos: Narradoras mexicanas en el siglo XX*, edited by Aralia López González. El Colegio de México, 1995.

Domenella, Ana Rosa. "¿Cómo leemos y cómo leer a nuestras escritoras?" In *Estudios sobre las mujeres y las relaciones de género en México: Aportes desde diversas disciplinas*, edited by Elena Urrutia. El Colegio de México, 2002.

Duncan, Cynthia. "Eroticism and Sexual Transgression in *Dos Mujeres* and *Amora*: Shaping the Voice of Lesbian Fiction in Mexico." *Confluencia* 26, no. 2 (2011): 72–84.

Eburne, Jonathan P. "Dante, Bruno, Vico S.Nob: The Wake in Mexico." *James Joyce Quarterly* 52, no. 2 (2015): 329–49.

Echeverría, Bolívar. "Queer, manierista, bizarre, barroco." *Debate Feminista* 16, no. 8 (1997): 3–10.

Elizondo, Salvador. *Autobiografía precoz*. Editorial Aldus, 2000.

Eng, David. "Colonial Object Relations." *Social Text* 34, no. 1 (2016): 1–19.

Epps, Brad. "Retos, riesgos, pautas y promesas de la teoría queer." *Revista Iberoamericana* 75, no. 225 (2008): 897–920.

Estrada, Oswaldo. "Against Representation: Women's Writing in Contemporary Mexico." *Hispanófila* 157 (2009): 63–78.

Estrada Medina, Francisco. "Reimaginar la autoría: La desapropiación según Cristina Rivera Garza." *Letras femeninas* 42, no. 2 (2016/17): 27–34.

Falconí Trávez, Diego, Santiago Castellanos, and María Amelia Viteri, eds. *Resentir lo queer en América Latina: Diálogos desde/con el Sur*. Egales, 2014.

Fallon, Paul. "Melodrama and the Monster by Your Side in Asunción Izquierdo Albiñana's *Andréïda: El tercer sexo*." *Hispanic Review* 86, no. 4 (Autumn 2018): 463–85.

Fariña Busto, María Jesús. "El beso deseado de tu boca: Nombres y voces para una genealogía lesbiana (España y Portugal, primeras décadas del siglo veinte)." *Investigaciones feministas* 10, no. 1 (2019): 79–96.

Felski, Rita. *Beyond Feminist Aesthetics: Feminist Literature and Social Change*. Harvard University Press, 1989.

Fem: 10 años de periodismo feminista. Planeta, 1998.

Fernbach, Amanda. *Fantasies of Fetishism: From Decadence to the Post-Human*. Rutgers University Press, 2002.

Fernbach, Amanda. "Fetishism and the Future of Gender." In *Future Imaginings: Sexualities and Genders in the New Millennium*, edited by Delys Bird, Wendy Were, and Terri-Ann White. University of Western Australia Publishing, 2003.

Finnegan, Nuala, and Jane E. Lavery, eds. *The Boom femenino in Mexico: Reading Contemporary Women's Writing*. Cambridge Scholars Publishing, 2010.

Finnegan, Nuala. "Women Writers in the Land of "Virile" Literature." In *A History of Mexican Literature*, edited by Ignacio Sánchez Prado, Anna M. Nogar, and José Ramón Ruisánchez Serra. Cambridge University Press, 2016.

Finnegan, Nuala. *Cultural Representations of Feminicidio at the US-Mexico Border*. Routledge, 2019.

Flatley, Jonathan. *Affective Mapping: Melancholia and the Politics of Modernism.* Harvard University Press, 2008.

Freeman, Elizabeth. *Time Binds: Queer Temporalities, Queer Histories.* Duke University Press, 2010.

Frouman-Smith, Erica. "Women and the Problem of Domination in the Short Fiction of Inés Arredondo." *Letras femeninas* 23, no. 1.2 (1997): 163–170.

Foucault, Michel. "Sex, Power, and the Politics of Identity." In *Ethics: Subjectivity and Truth*, edited by Paul Rabinow and translated by Robert Hurley et al. New Press, 1998.

Gabara, Esther. *Errant Modernism: The Ethos of Photography in Mexico and Brazil.* Duke University Press, 2008.

Gago, Verónica. *Feminist International: How to Change Everything*, translated by Liz Mason-Deese. Verso, 2020.

Galindo, María. *Feminismo bastardo.* Canal Press, Mantis, 2022.

Gallon, Kim. "'No Tears for Alden': Black Female Impersonators as 'Outsiders Within' in the 'Baltimore Afro-American.'" *Journal of the History of Sexuality* 27, no. 3 (September 2018): 367–94.

Gargallo, Francesca. "A propósito de lo *queer* en América latina: ¿Existe, se expresa de algún modo el pensamiento queer en América latina?" *Revista Blanco Móvil*, no. 112–113 (2009): 94–98.

Gerhard, Jane. *Desiring Revolution: Second-Wave Feminism and the Rewriting of American Sexual Thought, 1920 to 1982.* Columbia University Press, 2001.

Gill-Peterson, Julian. *Histories of the Transgender Child.* University of Minnesota Press, 2018.

González, Manuel Pedro. *Trayectoria de la novela en México.* Ediciones Botas, 1951.

González Mateos, Adriana. "La cresta de Ilión." *Debate Feminista* 27 (2003): 341–44.

González Ortuño, Gabriela. "Teorías de la disidencia sexual: De contextos populares a usos elitistas. La teoría *queer* en América latina frente a las y los pensadores de disidencia sexogenérica." *De raíz diversa* 3, no. 5 (2016): 179–200.

Guillory, John. *Cultural Capital: The Problem of Literary Formation.* University of Chicago Press, 1993.

Gutiérrez, Diana (Didí). "Ana Mairena más allá de la nota roja." *Letras Libres*, November 1, 2018. https://letraslibres.com/revista/ana-mairena-mas-alla-de-la-nota-roja.

Gutiérrez, Didí. *Las elegantes.* Paraíso perdido, 2021.

Gutiérrez, Didí. "Elegante se 'sale del closet.'" *Tierra Adentro*, 2023. Accessed April 13, 2024. https://tierraadentro.fondodeculturaeconomica.com/elegante-se-sale-del-closet-editorial.

Gutiérrez de Velasco, Luz Elena. "Malamada-madre: Maternidad y renuncia en los cuentos de Inés Arredondo." In *Lo monstruoso es habitar en otro: Encuentros con Inés Arredondo*, edited by Luz Elena Zamudio. Universidad Autónoma Metropolitana and Juan Pablos Editor, 2005.

Halberstam, Jack. *The Queer Art of Failure*. Duke University Press, 2012.

Harris, Audrey. "The Fern Cat." *The Paris Review*, February 21, 2017. https://www.theparisreview.org/blog/2017/02/21/translating-amparo-davilas-moses-gaspar.

Hemmings, Clare. *Bisexual Space: A Geography of Sexuality and Gender*. Routledge, 2002.

Hemmings, Clare. "Invoking Affect: Cultural Theory and the Ontological Turn." *Cultural Studies* 19, no. 5 (2005): 548–67.

Hershfield, Joanne. *Imagining la Chica Moderna: Women, Nation, and Visual Culture in Mexico, 1917–1936*. Duke University Press, 2008.

Hind, Emily. "El consumo textual y *La cresta de Ilión* de Cristina Rivera Garza." *Filología y Lingüística* 31, no. 1 (2005): 35–50.

Hind, Emily. *Feminism and the Mexican Woman Intellectual from Sor Juana to Poniatowska: Boob Lit*. Palgrave Macmillan, 2010.

Hind, Emily. "Six Authors on the Conservative Side of the *Boom Femenino*, 1985–2003: Boullosa, Esquivel, Loaeza, Mastretta, Nissán, Sefchovich." In *The Boom femenino in Mexico: Reading Contemporary Women's Writing*, edited by Nuala Finnegan and Jane Lavery. Cambridge Scholars Publishing, 2010.

Hind, Emily. "¿Carácter o personalidad? El pensamiento transicional de Asunción Izquierdo Albiñana: *Andréïda (el tercer sexo)* y *La selva encantada*." In *Luz rebelde: Mujeres y producción en el México posrevolucionario*, edited by Elissa Rashkin and Ester Hernández Palacios. Universidad Veracruzana, 2019.

Hind, Emily. *Dude Lit: Mexican Men Writing and Performing Competence, 1955–2012*. University of Arizona Press, 2019.

Huchín Sosa, Eduardo. "¡Qué elegancia, la nicromancia!: Una lectura espiritista de Las Elegantes." *Magno simposio exprés: Las elegantes 2021*. Streamed live on YouTube by Editorial Paraíso Perdido, November 21, 2021.

Ingarao, Giulia. "El taller creativo en México de los cuarenta: Leonora Carrington y la Colonia Surrealista." In *México como punto de fuga real o imaginario: El exilio europeo en la víspera de la Segunda Guerra Mundial*, edited by Giovanni di Stefano and Michaela Peters. Meidenbauer, 2011.

Izquierdo Albiñana, Asunción. *Andréïda (El tercer sexo)*. Ediciones Botas, 1938.

Klossowski, Pierre. *Sade My Neighbor*. Northwestern University Press, 1991.

Kristjansson, Margitte. "Fashion's 'Forgotten Woman': How Fat Bodies Queer Fashion and Consumption." In *Queering Fat Embodiment*, edited by Cat Pausé, Jackie Wykes, Samantha Murray. Routledge, 2014.

Lagarde y de los Ríos, Marcela. "¿A qué llamamos feminicidio?" In *Por la vida y la libertad de las mujeres*. Camara de diputados. LIX Legislatura, 2005. https://catedraunescodh.unam.mx/catedra/mujereS/Menu_superior/Feminicidio/2_Info_nac/12.pdf.

Leñero, Vicente. *Asesinato: El doble crimen de los Flores Muñoz*. Seix barral, 2020.

Lindemann, Danielle J. *Dominatrix: Gender, Eroticism, and Control in the Dungeon*. University of Chicago Press, 2012.

Liu, Wen. "Sentir abatido, regresivo y maquínico: Teoría queer y el giro afectivo," *Athenea Digital* 20, no. 2 (July 2020): e-2321. https://doi.org/10.5565/rev/athenea.2321.

López González, Aralia, ed. *Mujer y literatura mexicana y chicana: Culturas en contacto 2*. El Colegio de México, 1990.

Love, Heather. "Truth and Consequences: On Paranoid Reading and Reparative Reading." *Criticism* 52, no. 2 (2010): 235–41.

Ludmer, Josefina. *Aquí América Latina: Una especulación*. Eterna Cadencia, 2011.

Lugones, María. "Heterosexualism and the Colonial/Modern Gender System." *Hypatia* 22, no. 1 (Winter 2007): 186–209.

Lupton, Deborah. *Food, the Body, and the Self*. Sage Publications, 1996.

Lusardi, Laura. "'Who Knows What's Inside Our Heads?': La incertidumbre en *Plagio de palabras* de Elena Guiochins." *Hispanófila* 186 (June 2019): 35–47.

Mahieux, Viviane. "The Chronicler as Streetwalker: Salvador Novo and the Performance of Genre." *Hispanic Review* 76, no. 2 (2018): 155–77. http://www.jstor.org/stable/27668835.

Marquet, Antonio. "La pasión según Roffiel." In *¡Que se quede el infinito sin estrellas!* UAM, 2001.

Márquez, Alejandra. "Intermitencias de género y sexualidad en la crónica mexicana contemporánea." *Chasqui: Revista de literatura latinoamericana* 46, no. 2 (2017): 48–60.

Márquez, Alejandra. "Traces of Lesbianism in Cristina Rivera Garza's *La cresta de Ilión* (2002) and Valeria Luiselli's *Los ingrávidos* (2011)." *IMEX: México Interdisciplinario* 7, no. 13 (2018): 60–72.

Márquez, Alejandra. "Cuir-ing *Queer*: Speculations on Latin American Notions of Queerness." In *The Routledge Handbook of Queer Rhetoric*, edited by Jacqueline Rhodes and Jonathan Alexander. Routledge, 2022.

Martínez, Elena M. Review of *Dos mujeres* by Sara Calderón Levi and *Amora* by Rosamaría Roffiel. *Letras Femeninas* 18, no. 1–2 (1992): 175–79.

Martínez, Pablo Salvador. "Atracción fatal." *La jornada semanal* 19 (1989): 13.

Martínez-Zalce, Graciela. *Una poética de lo subterráneo: La narrativa de Inés Arredondo*. Fondo de cultura económica, 1996.

Martínez-Zalce, Graciela. "Presentir la verdad o inventar la utopía." In *Lo monstruoso es habitar en otro: Encuentros con Inés Arredondo*, edited by Luz Elena Zamudio. Universidad Autónoma Metropolitana and Juan Pablos Editor, 2005.

Mauleón, Héctor de. "Ocaso de un mundo lopezvelardino: Entrevista con Salvador Elizondo." *Confabulario* 21(2004): 7.

Mayer, Mónica. *Intimidades . . . o no: Arte, vida y feminism*, edited by Julia Antivilo and Katnira Bello. Editorial Diecisiete, 2021.

McClintock, Anne. *Imperial Leather: Race, Gender, and Sexuality in the Colonial Conquest*. Routledge, 1995.

McDowell Carlsen, Lila. "'Te conozco de cuando era árbol': Gender, Utopianism, and the Border in Cristina Rivera Garza's *La cresta de Ilión*." *Symposium: A Quarterly Journal in Modern Literatures* 64, no. 4 (2010): 229–42.

McKee Irwin, Robert. *Mexican Masculinities*. University of Minnesota Press, 2003.

Medina, Cuauhtémoc, and Susana Vargas. *¿Qué pasa? ¿Ya nadie quiere ser hombre? Más "mujercitos"! Festines secretos de invertidos*. Editorial RM, 2014.

Mercado, Gabriela. "Diálogo con Amparo Dávila y resolución de problemas de género en *La cresta de Ilión* de Cristina Rivera Garza." *Revista de Humanidades: Tecnológico de Monterrey* 22 (2007): 45–75.

Mindek, Dubravka, and Miguel Molina Alarcón. "Migración ficticia e identidades en las proto-performances de Conchita Jurado (Ciudad de México, 1926–1931)." *Arte y políticas de identidad* 17 (January 2018): 123–38.

Mogrovejo, Norma. "Lo queer en América Latina: ¿Lucha identitaria, post-identitaria, asimilacionista o neocolonial?" In *Cartografías queer: Sexualidades y activismo LGBT en América Latina*, edited by Daniel Balderston and Arturo Matute Castro. Instituto Internacional de Literatura Iberoamericana / University of Pittsburgh, 2011.

Monreal, Rogelio Arenas. "La pareja y la mirada transgredida en 'Mariana,' de Inés Arredondo." In *Mujer y literatura mexicana y chicana: Culturas en contacto 1*, edited by Aralia López González. El Colegio de México, 1988.

Monsiváis, Carlos. "De la Santa doctrina al espíritu público (Sobre las funciones de la crónica en México)." *Nueva revista de filología hispánicas* 35, no. 2 (1987): 753–71.

Monsiváis, Carlos. "La noche popular: Paseos, riesgos, júbilos, necesidades orgánicas, tensiones, especies antiguas y recientes, descargas anímicas en forma de coreografías." *Debate Feminista* 18 (1998): 55–73.

Moraña, Mabel. "Postscríptum: El afecto en la caja de herramientas." In *El lenguaje de las emociones: Afecto y cultura en América Latina*, edited by Mabel Moraña and Ignacio M. Sánchez Prado. Editorial Iberoamericana / Vervuert, 2012.

Muñoz, José Esteban. *Cruising Utopia: The Then and There of Queer Futurity.* New York University Press, 2009.

Murrieta Flores, Davis A. J. "Bataillean Surrealism in Mexico: *S.NOB* Magazine (1962)." *Journal of Surrealism and the Americas* 11, no. 2 (2020): 120–51.

Musser, Amber Jamilla. *Sensational Flesh: Race, Power, and Masochism.* New York University Press, 2014.

Ngai, Sianne. *Ugly Feelings.* Harvard University Press, 2005.

Olivera Córdova, María Elena. *Entre amoras: Lesbianismo en la narrativa mexicana.* UNAM, 2015.

Otayek, Michel. "Photography, Mobility and Collaboration: Kati Horna in Mexico and Grete Stern in Argentina." PhD diss., New York University, 2019.

Pacheco Roldán, Adriana, and Stephanie A. Malak. "#RopaSucia and *No me llamo mamacita*: Illocutionary Female Power Against Street Harassment, 'Locker Room Talk,' and 'Mansplaining.'" *Revista de Estudios Hispánicos* 53, no. 1 (2019): 235–59. doi:10.1353/rvs.2019.0007.

Palma, Alejandro, Cécile Quintana, Alejandro Ramírez Lámbarry, Alicia V. Ramírez Olivares, and Felipe Ríos Baeza. *Cristina Rivera Garza: Una escritura impropia.* Ediciones de Educación y Cultura, 2015.

Paredes, Julieta. "The Neocolonial Queer." *The Global Trajectories of Queerness: Rethinking Same-Sex Politics in the Global South,* edited by Ashley Tellis and Sruti Bala. Brill Rodopi, 2015.

Peniche Montfort, Elva. "El cuerpo en la revista S.nob." In *Desafío a la estabilidad: Procesos artísticos en México 1952–1967,* edited by Rita Eder. Turner, 2014.

Pereira, Armando. "La generación del medio siglo: Un momento de transición de la cultura Mexicana." In *Juan García Ponce y la generación de medio siglo.* Universidad veracruzana, 1998.

Perloff, Marjorie. "'Voice Whisht Through Thither Flood': Steve McCaffery's *Panopticon* and *North of Intention.*" In *Essays on Modernist and Postmodernist Lyric.* Northwestern University Press, 1990.

Pettersson, Aline. "El erotismo y lo perverso." In *Lo monstruoso es habitar en otro: Encuentros con Inés Arredondo,* edited by Luz Elena Zamudio. Universidad Autónoma Metropolitina and Juan Pablos Editor, 2005.

Pierce, Joseph M., María Amelia Viteri, Diego Falconí Trávez, Salvador Vidal-Ortiz, and Lourdes Martínez-Echazábal. "Introduction: *Cuir*/Queer Américas: Translation, Decoloniality, and the Incommensurable." *GLQ* 27, no. 3 (June 2021): 321–27.

Piedade, Vilma. *Doloridad/Dororidad,* translated by Lucía Tennina and Rafaela Vasconcellos. Mandacaru Editorial, 2021.

Platero, Lucas. "Conocer nuestras genealogías." In *Transfeminismo o barbarie*, edited by Aingeru Mayor, Aitzole Araneta, Alicia Ramos, et al. Kaótica Libros, 2021.

Plonowska Ziarek, Ewa. "Feminist Reflections on Vulnerability: Disrespect, Obligation, Action." *SubStance* 42, no. 3 (2013): 67–84. https://www.jstor.org/stable/24540725

Preciado, Paul B. *Testo Yonqui*. Editorial Anagrama, 2020.

Price, Brian L. "A Portrait of the Mexican Artist as a Young Man: Salvador Elizondo's Dedalean Poetics." In *TransLatin Joyce: Global Transmissions in Ibero-American Literature*, edited by Brian L. Price, César A. Salgado, and John Pedro Schwartz. Palgrave Macmillan, 2014.

Quevedo y Zubieta, Salvador. *México marimacho*. Ediciones Botas, 1933.

Quijano, Aníbal. "Colonialidad del poder, eurocentrismo y América Latina." In *La colonialidad del saber: Eurocentrismo y ciencias sociales. Perspectivas Latinoamericanas*, edited by Edgardo Lander. Consejo Latinoamericano de Ciencias Sociales, 2000.

Rea Goméz, Daniela, ed. *Ya no somos las mismas y aquí sigue la guerra*. Grijalbo, 2020.

Reber, Dierdra. *Coming to Our Senses: Affect and an Order of Things for Global Culture*. Columbia University Press, 2016.

Rich, Adrienne. "Compulsory Heterosexuality and Lesbian Existence." *Signs* 5, no. 4 (Summer 1980): 631–60.

Richard, Nelly. *Abismos temporales: Feminismo, estéticas travestis y teoría queer*. Metales Pesados, 2018.

Río Reyes, Marcela del. "Ateneo mexicano de mujeres." *Revista Universo de el búho* 6, no. 70 (2005–2006): 18–23. https://www.revistaelbuho.com.mx/magazine/070.html.

Ríos Baeza, Felipe A. "Una novela *hospitalaria*: *La cresta de Ilión*, de Cristina Rivera-Garza." *Valenciana*, no. 24 (2019): 95–177.

Rivas San Martín, Felipe. "Travestismos." In *Perder la forma humana: Una imagen sísmica de los años ochenta en América Latina*. Museo Nacional Centro de Arte Reina Sofía, 2012.

Rivas San Martín, Felipe. "Diga 'queer' con la lengua afuera: Sobre las confusiones del debate latinoamericano." *Caderno Espaço Femenino* 36, no. 1 (2023): 36–54.

Rivera Garza, Cristina. *Nadie me verá llorar*. Tusquets / Consejo Nacional para la Cultura y las Artes / Instituto Nacional de Bellas Artes, 1999.

Rivera Garza, Cristina. *La cresta de Ilión*. Mexico: Tusquets Editores, 2002.

Rivera Garza, Cristina. "Escrituras colindantes." *No hay tal lugar: U-tópicos contemporáneos.* (blog), July 10, 2004. https://cristinariveragarza.blogspot.com/2004/07/#108947489616105760.

Rivera Garza, Cristina. "La inquietante (e internacional) semana de las mujeres barbudas." *Tentación* 8 (Summer 2005): 18–25.

Rivera Garza, Cristina. *Los Muertos indóciles: Necroescrituras y desapropiación.* Tusquets Editores, 2013.

Rivera Garza, Cristina. *The Restless Dead: Necrowriting & Disappropriation*, translated by Robin Myers. Vanderbilt University Press, 2020.

Rivera Garza, Cristina. *Escrituras geológicas.* Iberoamericana Vervuert, 2022.

Rizki, Cole. "Latin/x American Trans Studies: Toward a *Travesti*-Trans Analytic." in "Trans Studies en las Américas," edited by Claudia Sofía Garriga-López, Denilson Lopes, Cole Rizki, and Juana María Rodríguez. Special issue, *TSQ: Transgender Studies Quarterly* 6 no. 2 (May 2019): 156–64.

Rodal Linares, Selma. "Tatuar la ira sobre el cuerpo de la ciudad: Las pintas feministas como práctica estética." In *Cuerpos diseñados: Ensayos sobre el cuerpo imaginado latinoamericano*, edited by Ingrid Sánchez Téllez and Raúl Antonio Cera Ochoa. Fundación universitaria San Mateo, 2021.

Rodríguez, Juana María. *Sexual Futures, Queer Gestures, and Other Latina Longings.* New York University Press, 2014.

Rodríguez, Juana María. "Queer Politics, Bisexual Erasure." *Lambda nordica* 21, no. 1–2 (2016):169–82.

Roffiel, Rosamaría. "¿Existe o no la literatura gay?" *Fem* 11, no. 51 (1987): 40–41.

Roffiel, Rosamaría. *Amora.* Horas y Horas la Editorial, 1997.

Roffiel, Rosamaría. "¿Existe o no la literatura lésbica mexicana?" *Fem* 20, no. 155 (1996): 43–44.

Roffiel, Rosamaría. "Entrevista con Rosamaría Roffiel." Interview by Elena M. Martínez. *Confluencia*, no. 8/9 (1993): 179–80.

Romano Hurtado, Berenice. "Los límites borroneados del cuerpo: Inés Arredondo." In *Los monstruoso es habitar al otro*, edited by Luis Elena Zamudio. UAM, 2005.

Rosenthal, Laura J. "Introduction: Recovering from Recovery." *The Eighteenth Century* 50, no. 1 (2009): 1–11.

Rubenstein, Anne. "The War on 'Las pelonas': Modern Women and Their Enemies, Mexico City, 1924." In *Sex in Revolution: Gender, Politics, and Power in Modern Mexico*, edited by Jocelyn Alcott, Mary Kay Vaughan, and Gabriela Cano. Duke University Press, 2006.

Rubin, Gayle. "Thinking Sex: Notes for a Radical Theory of the Politics of Sexuality." In *Theorizing Feminisms: A Reader*, edited by Elizabeth Hackett and Sally Haslanger. Oxford University Press, 2006.

Ruffinelli, Jorge. "Ni a tontas ni a locas: La narrativa de Cristina Rivera Garza." *Nuevo Texto Crítico* 21, no. 41(2008): 33-41.
Ruiz, Bladimir. "Las fronteras sexuales de la identidad: Lesbianismo y feminismo en 'Amora' de Rosamaría Roffiel." *Letras Femeninas* 30, no. 2 (2004): 143-66.
Sabsay, Leticia. "Permeable Bodies: Vulnerability, Affective Powers, Hegemony." In *Vulnerability in Resistance*, edited by Judith Butler, Zeynep Gambetti, and Leticia Sabsay. Duke University Press, 2016.
Samuelson, Cheyla. "Líneas de Fuga: The Character of Writing in the Novels of Cristina Rivera Garza." PhD diss., University of California, Santa Barbara, 2011.
Sánchez-Mejorada, Alicia. *Kati Horna y su manera cotidiana de captar la realidad.* Instituto Nacional de Bellas Artes y Literatura, 2004.
Sánchez Prado, Ignacio. "La destrucción de la escritura viril y el ingreso de la mujer en el discurso literario: *El libro vacío* y *Los recuerdos del porvenir*." *Revista de crítica literaria latinoamericana* 32, no. 63/64 (2006): 149-67.
Sánchez Prado, Ignacio. "The Idea of the Mexican Woman Writer: Gender, Worldliness, and Editorial Neoliberalization." In *Strategic Occidentalism: On Mexican Fiction, the Neoliberal Book Market, and the Question of World Literature*. Northwestern University Press, 2018.
Sánchez Prado, Ignacio. "Cultural Capital: Reflections from a Latin Americanist." *Genre* 56, no. 1 (2023): 49-67. doi: https://doi.org/10.1215/00166928-10346808.
Sandoval, Alma Karla, and Denisse Buendía. *Vocabularia: Diccionaria feminista.* Ediciones Zetina, 2023.
Santos Guevara, Criseida. *La reinita pop no ha muerto*. Literal Publishing, 2013.
Saunero-Ward, Verónica. "*La cresta de Ilión*: Lo fantástico posmoderno." *La palabra y el hombre* 137 (2006): 173-83. https://cdigital.uv.mx/handle/123456789/203.
Schaefer, Claudia. *Danger Zones: Homosexuality, National Identity, and Mexican Culture.* University of Arizona Press, 1996.
Schaefer, Claudia. "Roffiel, RosaMaría (México; 1945)." In *Latin American Writers on Gay and Lesbian Themes: A Bio-Critical Sourcebook*, edited by David William Foster and Emmanuel S. Nelson. Greenwood Press, 1994.
Schaffner, Anna Katharina. "Fetishism: George Bataille and Sexual-Textual Transgression." In *Modernism and Perversion: Sexual Deviance in Sexology and Literature, 1850-1930*. Palgrave Macmillan, 2012.
Schuessler, Michael K., and Miguel Capistrán, eds. *México se escribe con J: Una historia de la cultura gay*. Planeta, 2010.

Sedgwick, Eve Kosofsky. *Epistemology of the Closet.* University of California Press, 1990.
Sedgwick, Eve Kosofsky. "Paranoid Reading and Reparative Reading, or, You're so Paranoid, You Probably Think This Essay is About You." In *Touching Feeling: Affect, Pedagogy, Performativity.* Duke University Press, 2003.
Sedgwick, Eve Kosofsky. "Melanie Klein and the Difference Affect Makes." *South Atlantic Quarterly* 106, no. 3 (2007): 625–42.
Segato, Rita. *Contra-pedagogías de la crueldad.* Prometeo Editorial, 2018.
Segato, Rita. "Pedagogías de la crueldad: El mandato de la masculinidad (fragmentos)." *Revista de la universidad de México*, November 2019. https://www.revistadelauniversidad.mx/articles/9517d5d3-4f92-4790-ad46-81064bf00a62/pedagogias-de-la-crueldad.
Segura, Yolanda. *Estancias que por ahora tienen luz y se abren hacia el paisaje.* Consejo para la Cultura y las Artes de Nuevo León, 2018.
Sifuentes-Jáuregui, Ben. *Transvestism, Masculinity, and Latin American Literature.* Palgrave, 2002.
Silverstein, Stephen. "Deleuzo-Guattarian Becoming in Cristina Rivera Garza's "La cresta de Ilión." *Letras femeninas* 41, no. 2 (2015): 116–32.
Simpson, Audra. "Sovereignty, Sympathy, and Indigeneity." In *Ethnographies of US Empire*, edited by Carole McGranahan and John F. Collins. Duke University Press, 2018.
Singh, Julietta. *No Archive Will Restore You.* Punctum Books, 2018.
Sitbon, Clara. "The Literary Hoax: The Art of Authorial Forgery." In *Deception: An Interdisciplinary Exploration*, edited by Emma Williams and Iman Sheeha. Inter-Disciplinary Press, 2015.
Steele, Valerie. *Fetish: Fashion, Sex and Power.* Oxford University Press, 1996.
Stuelke, Patricia. *The Ruse of Repair: US Neoliberal Empire and the Turn from Critique.* Duke University Press, 2021.
Suárez, Marcela, and Mirjana Mitrović. "Digital Violence as Affective Disciplining after Feminist Protests: The Case of #NotLikeThatLadies!" In *Sensing Collectives: Aesthetic and Political Practices Intertwined*, edited by Jan-Peter Voß, Nora Rigamonti, Marcela Suárez, and Jacob Watson. Columbia University Press, 2023.
Taylor, Diana. *The Archive and the Repertoire: Performing Cultural Memory in the Americas.* Duke University Press, 2003.
Taylor, Diana. "Introducción: Performance, teoría y práctica." In *Estudios avanzados de performance*, edited by Marcela Fuentes and Diana Taylor. Fondo de Cultura Económica, 2011.

Téllez, Artemisa. "'A Chloe le gustaba Olivia': Implicaciones de una literatura que quisiera llamarse lésbica." In *Homofobia: Laberinto de la ignorancia*, edited by Julio Muñoz Rubio. UNAM, 2010.

Teresa Ochoa, Adriana de. "Entre el calígrafo y el poeta maldito: *Ethos* y autofiguración en *Farabeuf* y la autobiografía de Salvador Elizondo." In *Salvador Elizondo: Ida y vuelta. Estudios críticos*, edited by Claudia L. Gutiérrez Piña and Elba Sánchez Rolón. Universidad de Guanajuato, 2016.

Themi, Tim. "Bataille and the Erotics of the Real." *Parrhesia* 24 (2015): 312–35.

Trejo Fuentes, Ignacio. "Rosamaría Roffiel: *Amora.*" *Tema y variaciones en literatura: Literatura gay* 17, no. 2 (2001): 179–87.

Tuñón, Julia. "Nueve escritoras, una revista y un escenario: Cuando se junta la oportunidad con el talento." In *Nueve escritoras mexicanas nacidas en la primera mitad del siglo XX y una revista*, edited by Elena Urrutia. Instituto Nacional de las Mujeres; El colegio de México, 2006.

Ubilluz, Juan Carlos. *Sacred Eroticism: George Bataille and Pierre Klossowski in the Latin American Erotic Novel*. Bucknell University Press, 2006.

Uribe, Sara. *Un montón de escritura para nada*. Dharma Books, 2019.

Valencia, Sayak. *Capitalismo gore*. Paidós, 2016.

Vasconcelos de Berges, Tina. *Confetti*. Ediciones Botas, 1935.

Vásquez Rentería, Víctor Hugo. "Inés Arredondo: 'Mariana,' 'Las mariposas norturnas' y 'Sombra entre sombras': Los placeres de la pureza." In *Juan García Ponce y la generación de medio siglo*. Universidad Veracruzana, 1998.

Venkatesh, Vinodh. "Transgreciones de la masculinidad: Ciudad y género en *Nadie me verá llorar*." In *Cristina Rivera Garza: Ningún crítico cuenta esto . . .*, edited by Oswaldo Estrada. Ediciones Eón, 2010. Kindle.

Villiers de L'Isle-Adam. *Tomorrow's Eve*, translated by Robert Martin Adams. University of Illinois Press, 1982.

Zaca Guevara, María Reyna. "Los cuentos de Amparo Dávila y *La Cresta de Ilión* de Cristina Rivera Garza: Un diálogo intertextual." Masters thesis, Benemérita Universidad Autónoma de Puebla, 2005.

Zamudio, Luz Elena. "Reconstrucción de la imagen de Malintzin a través de la palabra." In *Lo monstruoso es habitar en otro: Encuentros con Inés Arredondo*, edited by Luz Elena Zamudio. Universidad Autónoma Metropolitina and Juan Pablos Editor, 2005.

Zavala Oswaldo. "La tradición que *retrocede*: *La cresta de Ilión*, Amparo Dávila y la radicalización de la alteridad." In *Cristina Rivera Garza: Ningún crítico cuenta esto . . .*, edited by Oswaldo Estrada. Ediciones Eón, 2010. Kindle.

INDEX

Page numbers in *italic* refer to figures.

A toda máquina, 34
Abramo, Paula, 29
academia, 6
acciones, 19, 66–72, 74–75, 79, 93, 95, 165
   arte de acción, 142, 165, 183
activism, 6, 13, 72, 83, 85, 91, 110, 152
acuerpar, 149
aesthetics, 19, 98, 114, 172
   baroque, 24
   cuir, 15, 84, 116
   experimental, 114
   and literature, 29, 36, 38, 40, 42
   negative, 98–12, 114–15, 117, 125, 171
   travesti, 66, 7, 73
affect
   in canon formation, 16–17, 25, 33, 91, 99
   in cuir dissidence, 8–9, 18, 7, 150
   as economy, 21, 123–24, 126, 147
   as method, 3, 12–13, 20, 98–99
   in restorative criticism, 56
   See also Ahmed, Sara

agency
   in Balmori/Jurado, 70, 80
   in BDSM, 34–35, 38
   in Arredondo, 38, 42, 44, 45, 47, 51
   in Izquierdo Albiñana, 87–88
   women's, 25, 27, 56
Aguilar Gil, Yásnaya, 152
Ahmed, Sara, 16, 98, 124, 129, 131. *See also* affect
AIDS, 12, 28, 111
Alatriste, Gustavo, 54–55
Albarrán, Claudia, 41, 54, 160n21
Almadía, 70
Alonso, Odette, 101
Álvarez Rivera, Adriana, 127
Amezcua, Vizania, 93
Amo, Luz de, 55, 58
Amor que se atreve a decir su nombre (Muñoz, Gutiérrez), 101
Amora (Roffíel), 20, 98–100, 102, 104–11, 114, 117, 172n21
Ampuero, María Fernanda, 14
Andréïda (El tercer sexo) (Izquierdo Albiñana) 68, 81, 83–91, 167n33

[199]

anxiety
    as emotion, 125–26, 129–13, 135, 151
    in reader/viewer, 27, 94, 117, 122
    as social, 80, 83
Aparicio, Mario, 91
Appadurai, Arjun, 93
Árboles petrificados (Dávila), 127
archive(s)
    as cuir, 7, 20, 67, 70
    as embodied, 64, 67
    gender dissidence, 19, 95, 68, 93–95
    physical archives, 25, 92, 125, 138, 140, 144, 147.
    production of, 15 93
    See also Taylor, Diana
Arenas Montreal, Rogelio, 52
Arredondo, Inés, 13, 19, 23, 25, 27, 36, 38–52, 56
assemblage, 56, 98–99, 111, 123, 142–43, 147, 152
authorship, 1, 18, 99, 124, 142, 151, 156n20, 175n9
autobiography, 20, 106, 116, 146n20

Baeza, Laura, 144
Balmoreadas, 64, 69–71, 73, 75, 77–78, 80, 93–94, 165n3
Balmori, Carlos, 64, *65*, 66–80, 93–95, 165n2. *See also* Jurado, Concepción
Barrera, Ave, 10, 12, 141, *153*
Barrera, Jazmina, 15, 30
Barthes, Roland, 126
Bataille, George, 37–41, 47, 50, 53, 54
Batis, Huberto, 36, 40–41
BDSM
    as pleasure, 26, 55, 63
    as experience, 25, 38, 62, 159n2
    in Mexican literature, 27, 100, 127
    in Rodríguez Mendoza, 19, 25, 28–35, 160n13
    in Arredondo, 39, 42, 46, 53, 60
becoming, 67, 75–76, 88, 117, 134
Berkins, Lohana, 72
Berlant, Lauren, 45
Bermúdez, María Elvira, 141, 147
Berry, Ellen E., 99–100, 105, 117
bisexuality, 20, 89, 106–8, 110, 113
Bloom, Harold, 16, 124
bloque negro, El, 6
Blum, Liliana, 27
body-territory, 151
borderlands, 119
Botas, Ediciones, 70, 81, 84, 167n33
Bourdieu, Pierre, 124, 140
Bowskill, Sara E. L., 99, 144
Bradu, Fabienne, 41
Bruce-Novoa, Juan, 125, 160n21
Brujas del mar, colectiva, 151
Bustamante, Maris, 71
Butler, Judith, 9, 49, 112, 151

Caballero Prado, Amaranta, 68, 91
cabaña, La (García Ponce), 38
Cabello, Cristian, 75–76
Cáceres, Berta, 152
Calderón, Felipe, 115
Campobello, Nellie, 13
Cano, Gabriela, 71, 93
Cañedo, César, 107
canon
    and affect, 2, 3, 16–17, 104, 140, 176n21
    cuir and, 20, 67, 100, 103, 112, 120, 154
    as deceiving mechanism, 2, 21–22
    erasure within, 1, 41, 97, 99, 137, 141, 144, 167n33

canon (*continued*)
   formations of, 25, 98–99, 123–24, 147, 156n20, 175n9
   overwriting of, 10, 15, 18, 91, 114, 142
   snap and, 108, 111, 119
capitalism, 13, 77, 116
Carballo, Emmanuel, 84
Cárdenas, Nancy, 97
Cardona, Ishtar, 93
Carrington, Leonora, 19, 23, 27, 54–62
Cartas, Frida, 101
Casa Refugio Citlatépetl, 91
Casas vacías (Navarro), 30
Castellanos, Rosario, 13, 35, 58
Castellanos, Santiago, 5
castration, 46, 50, 56–58, 110, 129–30
Castro, Abril, 91
censorship, 2, 15, 54, 90, 98, 100, 109
Cerda, Dahlia de la, 1
Cervantes Morales, Luis, 69–70, 73, 78
Chimal, Alberto, 27
choking, 27, 42, 46
class, 1, 73–80, 88, 140, 151, 159n1, 167n24, 170n67
Clavel, Ana, 92, 158n31
Colina, José de la, 54
collective memory, 10, 93
coloniality of power, 68, 93
communal writing, 21, 142
communality, 123–25, 135–36, 150
complicity, 23, 27, 51, 53, 56–58, 62–63, 116, 133
compulsory heterosexuality, 77, 103, 105, 133, 168n33
condesa sangrienta, La (Pizarnik), 23
Congelada de la Uva, La, 27
consent, 26, 42, 45, 47, 50, 167n27
Contemporáneos, Los, 71

Córdoba García, David, 5
corporality, 72–74, 95, 138
Cortázar, Julio, 40, 138
Crema de vainilla (Téllez)27, 100
cresta de Ilión, La (Rivera Garza), 20–21, 112–13, 121–35, 144, 147, 174n1, 176n20, 176n21
crónicas, 25, 27–30, 32–33, 35, 53, 62–63
Crucé la frontera en tacones (DeRuiz), 101, 180n77, 180n179
cruel optimism, 45, 132
Cruz, Sor Juana Inés de la, 101
Cruz Arzabal, Roberto, 93
cuiridad, 6–8, 15–16, 27–28, 67, 99, 111–19, 134, 165n6
Cultural Capital (Guillory), 124
cultural histories, 3, 13, 98, 119, 149
cultural production, 2, 15–20, 91, 144, 147, 152, 154
cultural sphere, 2–3, 29, 149
cultural studies, 6, 13
Curiosidades históricas, 71
cursilería, 25, 159n1

dance of the 41, 71
Dávila, Amparo, 13, 21, 121–22, 126–36, 147, 177n28
De amores marginales (Muñoz), 101
death drive, 56–57, 60, 62
Deleuze, Gilles, 51–52, 163n70
Delhumeau, Eduardo, 69–70, 73
DeRuiz, Alexandra R., 101, 152, 180n77
disgust, 12, 23, 27, 94, 139
desire
   and affect, 123, 150
   and archive, 65, 67–68
   erotic, 5–6, 9, 41–47, 55, 61–62, 72–80, 88–89, 139

desire (*continued*)
  and gender, 81–83, 87, 90, 128–31
  and sexuality, 97, 10, 108–9
disappropriation, 122–24, 131, 133, 136–37, 141–42, 146, 175n9, 176n17
disidentification, 95, 108, 117
Domecq, Brianda, 41
Domenella, Ana Rosa, 42
Domínguez Michael, Christopher, 132
Don Carlos Balmori, su extraordinaria vida y hazañas (Delhumeau), 70
Dos mujeres (Levi Calderón), 100
drag, 49, 60, 72, 75–76
drug war, 115
dude lit, 99, 131, 136, 142
Dueñas, Guadalupe, 13, 21, 136, 141, 143, 147
Durazo Moreno, Arturo "El negro," 140

Eburne, Jonathan P., 54
Echeverría, Bolívar, 4
edgeplay, 26, 42, 46
editopatriarcado, 4
elegantes, Las (Gutiérrez), 20–21, 121–25, 135–47
Elizondo, Salvador, 10, 17, 36–37, 40, 54–55, 59, 156n20
emotional map, 104
emotions
  and cuir, 8, 125, 147
  and reading, 10, 21, 107, 111, 125, 149
  as sites of knowledge, 30, 124, 147
  as uneasy, 12, 61, 96–98, 103–04, 114–17, 122, 126–27, 153
Enciclopedia de México, 70
Encuentro de Escritoras Mexicanas, 102
Enríquez, Mariana, 14, 176n21

Epistemology of the Closet (Sedgwick), 90
Epps, Brad, 4
erasure
  of bisexuality, 108, 110
  canonical, 2–3, 10, 15, 19, 18
  of women writers, 2, 15, 18–21, 98, 100–101, 144, 149, 152
eroticism
  and aesthetics, 19, 36
  and BDSM, 8, 28, 39, 51
  and literature, 19, 39–49, 53, 79, 161n22
  as restorative criticism, 19, 25, 27, 53, 56
  as transgression, 36–38, 54–57, 59–60
errancia sin fin, La (García Ponce), 40
esclavos, Los (Chimal), 27
escrituras geológicas, 106, 134
espejos, Los (Arredondo), 40
Esquivel, Laura, 109
establishment literary, 23, 9, 16, 20, 36, 112, 126, 175n9
Estancias que por ahora tienen luz y se abren hacia el paisaje (Segura), 113
Estrada, Oswaldo, 125
ethics, 3, 13, 23, 69, 80, 111–15, 122–23, 142
Excélsior, 70
experimental forms of writing, 54, 98–99, 105–09, 111–14, 117, 125–26, 132, 136

Fabre, Luis Felipe, 24
Facio, Alda, 151
Faesler, Carla, 93
Faesler, Juliana, 93
failure
  and affect, 69, 99
  in *Amora*, 100, 102, 104, 108–11

failure (*continued*)
　in cuir literature, 20, 112, 114–15, 119
　and gender, 76, 87, 144
Falconí Trávez, Diego, 5
Fallon, Paul, 83, 85
Farabeuf (Elizondo), 10, 12, 38, 40
Fariña Busto, María Jesús, 89
fatness, 138–39
fear
　and affect, 122, 126, 128–31
　of castration, 56–57
　and gender, 81, 84, 86, 90, 94, 178n41
　and sex, 26, 33
　and violence, 43, 48, 100
Felski, Rita, 117
Fem, 102, 105
feminicidio, 12, 115, 156n2, 178n41
feminism
　and aesthetics, 99, 105
　and cuir, 6, 95, 150, 151
　and lesbianism, 105
　and neoliberalism, 88
　and *pueblos originarios*, 150
Feminismo bastardo (Galindo), 94
Feminist International (Gago), 132, 166n20
feminist killjoy, 16, 98, 102–4, 108, 112, 116, 152
Fernback, Amanda, 58
Ferrer, Hilda, 144
fetish, 27, 43, 53, 57–58, 60, 163n70, 164n78
fetishism
　definition of, 57–60
　and gender, 55–57
　as kink, 27
Figura de paja (García Ponce), 40, 102
Foucault, Michel, 38, 47
Fountain-Stokes, Lawrence La, 72

Franco, Jean, 13
Freeman, Elizabeth, 53
Freud, Sigmund, 130, 163n70
Frouman-Smith, Erica, 41
Fuentes, Diana, 144
futurity, 7 , 111

Gabara, Esther, 71, 74, 169n64
Gago, Verónica, 72, 123, 132–33, 166n20, 175n8
Galindo, María, 94–95, 152
Gamboa, Federico, 122
García Márquez, Gabriel, 109, 138
García Ponce, Juan, 36–38, 40, 54, 102, 160n21
García Riera, Emilio, 54
Gargallo, Francesca, 9, 92
Garrido, Felipe, 130, 147, 178n41
Garro, Elena, 13, 35
Gatopardo, 146
gay desire, 101
gaze, the
　in Arredondo, 44, 48–41, 53
　in Horna, 59, 62
　and masculinity, 37, 53, 56
gender-based violence, 84–86, 88
gender ideology, 151
"generación de la insolencia," 36, 38, 50, 54, 56
gestures, 7, 27, 53, 56, 59
Gil, Eve, 93
ginealogía, 89
Glorieta a las Mujeres que Luchan, *11*
González, Manuel Pedro, 84
González Mateos, Adriana, 92–93, 131
González Ortuño, Gabriela, 8
Guerrero, Maricela, 29
Guillory, John, 124
Guiochins, Elena, 92, 170n75

Gutiérrez, Didí, 21, 121–22, 137–41, 143–44, *145*
Gutiérrez, León Guillermo, 101
Gutiérrez de Velasco, Luz Elena, 41

Halberstam, Jack, 11
hartazgo (weariness), 18, 150, 151, 153, 181n2
heteropatriarchy, 32, 104, 107
Hind, Emily, 17, 32, 83–84, 100, 125–27, 132–36, 144, 151–52
hoax, 21, 141–44, 147
homophobia, 83, 111, 172n11
Horna, Kati, 19, 27, 55–59, 61–62, 163n65
Huchín Sosa, Eduardo, 144, 146
humor, 93, 116, 144, *145*, 147

Ibargüengoitia, Jorge, 36, 54–55, 147, 164n64
indeterminacy, 7, 111, 116–17, 125
Infinita (Krauze), 97
Inmaculada o los placeres de la inocencia (García Ponce), 38
Inner Experience (Bataille), 39, 54
inquietante [e internacional] semana de las mujeres barbudas, La, 68, 91, 93–94
intersectionality, 88, 167n24
intimacies, 19, 25–26, 62, 154
Izquierdo Albiñana, Asunción, 68, 83–91, 95, 141, 147, 169n52

Jornadas Culturales Gay, 102
jouissance, 19, 37–39, 41, 43, 53
joy, 63, 70, 77, 104, 150, 153
Jurado, Concepción, 64–80, 93–95, 163n2, 167n24. *See also* Balmori, Carlos

kink, 26, 28, 31
Kinsey test, 114
Klossowski, Pierre, 37, 39, 49, 53, 162n43
Krauze, Ethel, 97
Kristjansson, Margitte, 138, 141

laberinto de la soledad, El (Paz), 17, 159n1
Lagarde, Marcela, 151, 156n21
Lamborghini, Osvaldo, 23
Laverde Austin, Paula, 140, 144
Lechedevirgen Trimegisto, 27, 72
Leñero, Vicente, 84, 167n33, 169n50
Lerma, Víctor, 93
lesbian continuum, 88–89
lesbian literature, 20, 97–98, 100–2, 109–12, 115–20
lesbianism, 20, 89, 102, 105, 107–12, 116
Letras femeninas, 105, 172n21
lettered city, 2–6, 8, 18–19, 25–33, 63, 91, 133, 151
Levi Calderón, Sara, 100
Lewis, Vek, 72
LGBTQ+ movements, 8, 95
Lindemann, Danielle J., 49
Linea nigra (Barrera), 30
L'Isle-Adam, Auguste Villiers, 81
literary critique, 15, 19–20, 96–97, 111, 119
Living a Feminist Life (Ahmed), 16, 98
Lomelí, Luis Felipe, 93
López González, Aralia, 41
Lucero, 55
Lucrecias (Damián, Navarro, Ángel, Eme Vázquez, and Arévalo), 138
Ludmer, Josefina, 154

Magic Wand, 28, 31, 63
Malheiros, Clarissa, 93

Marín, Guadalupe, 141
marrana negra de la literatura, La
	(Velázquez), 27
Marquet, Antonio, 104, 107, 110
Martínez, Elena M., 105, 173n21
Martínez-Zalce, Graciela, 41
masculinity
	and eroticism, 44, 56, 59, 61, 164n78
	and gender violence, 12, 135
	and literary sphere, 55, 99
	as performance, 73, 135
mask, 56–57, 59–61, 95
masochism
	as BDSM, 25, 38, 46–47, 50, 53
	as restorative criticism, 38–39, 49, 51
Mason-Deese, Liz, 132
Mayer, Mónica, 92, 170n78
McCaffery, Steven, 126
McKee Irwin, Robert, 83
Medina, Andrea, 151
Melchor, Fernanda, 14
Melo, Juan Vicente, 36, 54
Memorias de Don Carlos Balmori
	(Cervantes Morales), 70
memory preservation, 13
messy
	in literature, 19, 23–25, 33, 35, 39, 48
	and pleasure, 9, 27, 62, 63
	as relationalities, 18, 87, 123, 138, 150
MeToo
	MeTooEscritoresMexicanos, 29
	as movement, 150–51, 175n7
Mexican Revolution, 36, 65
México se escribe con J (Schuessler and Miguel Capistrán), 118–19
Miguel Lanz Duret literary award, 36
modern woman, 59, 80–81, 85, 87, 167n31

modernity, 7, 36
Mogrovejo, Norma, 5
Monsiváis, Carlos, 9, 25, 28
montón de escritura para nada, Un
	(Uribe), 113
Monumento Hipsográfico, *13*
Moscona, Myriam, 92
muerte me da, La (Rivera Garza), 93
muertos indóciles, Los (Rivera Garza), 141
Muñoz, José Esteban, 7, 56, 85
Muñoz, Mario, 101
Murrieta Flores, David A. J., 54, 57
Museo del Chopo, 24, 102
Musser, Amber, 47, 162n43

Nadie me verá llorar (Rivera Garza), 112
Navarro, Brenda, 14, 30
necrophilia, 27, 53, 55, 59–62
negative aesthetics, 98–100, 111–12, 114–15, 117, 125
negotiation, 3, 25–27, 47
Nettel, Guadalupe, 1, 177n28
Ni una menos, 150
normativity, 72, 167n24
Novo, Salvador, 28
nuevo boom femenino, 14

objects of feeling, 17, 123
Ochoa, Marcia, 72
Ojeda, Mónica, 14
Olivera Córdoba, María Elena, 99
overwriting the canon, 10, 15, 20

Palou, Pedro Ángel, 93
Pandora (Blum), 27
Panteón Civil de Dolores, 64, 66
Paraíso perdido, 137, 145, 146
paranoid writing, 82–83, 85, 88, 90–91

Paredes, Julieta, 5
patriarchy, 37, 39, 44, 47, 53–59, 68, 92, 149–51
Paz, Octavio, 17, 25, 137, 159n1
pedagogies of cruelty, 12, 28–30, 35, 105, 144
Peniche Montfort, Elva, 58
performance
    as art, 27, 94, 123, 142, 165n3
    as authorship, 17, 138, 140, 142, 146
    as gender, 68, 71, 73, 142
Peri Rossi, Cristina, 92
perversion, 24, 39, 49, 51, 61, 162n43
Petersen, Amanda, 153
Pettersson, Aline, 41
Picture of Dorian Gray, The (Wilde), 90
pintas (feminist graffiti), 10, *11*, 18
Pitol, Sergio, 36
Pizarnik, Alejandra, 23
Plagio de palabras (Guiochins), 92, 170n75
Platero, Lucas, 95
play
    in BDSM, 25–26, 38, 42, 127, 167n27
    breath, 46
    impact, 46
    rope, 32–33
Playboy, 55, 59
pleasure
    as affect, 3–4, 12, 37
    erotic, 25, 33, 37–38, 46–48, 55–56, 59
    female, 19, 27, 33, 42, 46, 51–53, 60–61, 79
    in reading, 23, 32, 63, 134
Poniatowska, Kitzia, 55, 58
positionality
    and dissidence, 6, 159n1
    as political, 72, 94–95, 107
    troubled, 72, 107–8
    and women, 8, 40, 45, 94, 106–7
post-menopause, 75
postporno, 27
potencia, 75, 125, 132–35, 143, 147, 166n20
Povinelli, Elizabeth, 134
pranks, 64, 69–70, 77–78
Preciado, Paul B., 72, 173n24
pride, 71, 180n76
Primavera Violeta, 29, 123, 150–51, *153*, 175n7
prizes, 14, 84
public sphere, 30, 34–35, 74, 143
puerquitos, 69, 74–75, 79

Queer Art of Failure, The (Halberstam), 111
queer theory, 5–6, 8, 94, 112, 151

race, 1, 26, 80, 151, 159n1, 167n24, 170n67
Rayuela (Cortázar), 40
Rea, Daniela, 138, 149
recovery work, 13–15, 21, 126, 136, 141–42
reinita pop no ha muerto, La (Santos Guevara), 20, 98–99, 101, 11, 114
relationality, 6, 24, 62, 105, 110, 115
reparative criticism, 13, 123, 124
repertoire, 125
Restauración (Barrera), 10, 12, 38
Restauradoras con Glitter, 10, 12, 15
restoration
    Barreras' fiction as, 10, 12–13, 15, 38
    and canon, 10
    as feminist critique, 10, 12, 13, 67, 90
    as methodology, 10, 13, 15, 19, 27, 91, 123

restoration (*continued*)
  pintas as, 10, 13
restorative criticism
  and affect, 56, 67, 88, 91
  as form of critique, 2, 15, 59, 69, 91, 94, 122, 141
  and pleasure, 27, 39, 47, 51
Revista de literatura mexicana, 36
Richard, Nelly, 72–73
Río subterráneo (Arredondo), 39
Ríos Baeza, Felipe A., 132, 135, 179n62
Rivas San Martín, Felipe, 5
Rivera Garza, Cristina, 1, 14, 91, 112, 122, 131–32, 136, 173n24, 178n41
Rivero, Laura Sofía, 144
Rizki, Cole, 72
Rodríguez, Juana María, 56
Rodríguez Mendoza, Xitlalitl, 19, 25–35, 53, 56, 62–63
Roffiel, Rosa María, 20, 98, 100–110, 117–19, 172n21
Rojas, Paulina, 101
Romano Hurtado, Berenice, 41
RopaSucia, 28–29, 32, 33
Rubin, Gayle, 24, 26
rupture, 16, 37, 38, 50, 59, 98

sadomasochism, 9, 24, 31, 38, 40, 46–51, 59, 159n2
Salazar, Teresa, 54
Salvador Martínez, Pablo, 104
Samuelson, Cheyla, 126, *153*
Sánchez Prado, Ignacio, 16–17, 124, 158n31
Santa (Gamboa), 112
Santos Guevara, Criseida, 20, 98, 100, 114–19
Schaefer-Rodríguez, Claudia, 104, 107

Sedgwick, Eve Kosofsky, 12, 83, 86
Segato, Rita, 12
Segovia, Tomás, 36, 40, 54
Segura, Yolanda, 113–14
señal, La (Arredondo), 39–40
sex toys, 9, 27–28, 31, 63
sexism, 14, 29
sexual liberation movement, 36
Sharpe, Christina, 134
shibari, 32–33
Sifuentes-Jáuregui, Ben, 72, 76
Singh, Julieta, 67
síntesis rara de un siglo loco, La (Téllez-Pon), 101
Sitbon, Clara, 143
S/M dynamics, 24, 27, 38, 49, 53, 159n2
S.Nob Magazine, 36, 53, 55–57, 163n65
sodomía en la Nueva España, La (Fabre), 24
solidarity in difference, 123, 175n7
Sosa Villada, Camila, 72
Stuelke, Patricia, 13
Suárez, Amelia, 93
subaltern politics, 7
subjectivity, 37–38, 42–43, 45, 47–48, 53, 56, 61
sublime, 16–17

Taller de Teoría y Crítica Diana Morán, 1, 13, 41
Taylor, Diana, 125, 165n3, 176n17
Televisa, 34
Téllez, Artemisa, 99–101, 107
Téllez-Pon, Sergio, 101
temporality, 7, 85, 108, 124, 129, 134, 154
Teología y pornografía (García Ponce), 38, 40

third gender, 19, 68, 80–81, 86, 89–90, 165n6
Tierra Adentro, 144, 180n76
Torres-Rodríguez, Laura, 14
toxic masculinity, 135
trans, 72, 97, 100–101, 140, 150, 151, 180n77, 180n79
transexclusionary social movements, 9, 68, 93, 95, 151. *See also* transphobia
transfeminism, 6, 67, 151
transphobia, 20, 95. *See also* transexclusionary social movements
Transporte a la infancia (Cartas), 101
travesti
  in aesthetics, 66, 71, 73–75
  as positionality, 72, 76–77, 88, 95
  trava, 72
travestismo, 72–73, 75–77, 79
Trejo Fuentes, Ignacio, 104
Treviño, Ana Cecilia, 51, 168n49
Trías, Fernanda, 14–15

Unda, Arussi, 151
unintelligibility, 99–100, 112–13
United States, 12–13, 51, 85, 88, 138, 152
Universal, El, 36
Universal Gráfico, El, 70
Universidad Autónoma de Querétaro, 6
Uribe, Sara, 113, 138, 173n24
utopia, 85, 88, 100, 134

Valcárcel, Amelia, 151
Valdés, Carlos, 36
Valencia, Sayak, 68, 91, 94
vampiro de la colonia Roma, El (Zapata), 25, 103
Vásquez Rentería, Víctor Hugo, 40–41

Vega, Patricia, 93
Velázquez, Carlos, 27
Venegas, Socorro, 141, 177n28
Venegas, Yvonne, 91
Versas y diversas (Rojas and Alonso), 100
Vice, 28, 30, 32
Vicens, Josefina, 13, 35
Vindictas Collection, 141, 146
Viriditas (Rivera Garza), 93
visibility, 9, 14, 32, 36, 101
Viteri, María Amelia, 5
voyeurism, 27, 37, 52–53, 55, 127
vulnerability
  and eroticism, 19, 30, 38, 41, 47–49, 53, 57, 66
  and gender performance, 76
  and Mexican woman writer, 28–29, 31–34, 53

Wayar, Marlene, 72
Western Canon, The (Bloom), 124
Wilde, Oscar, 90
women writers
  canon and, 1–2, 13, 42, 112, 123, 141–42, 167n33
  communality, 135, 144
  critique of category, 14, 97
  in cuir dissidence, 2, 9, 16, 20, 25, 98, 123, 149–51
  and perversion, 26–28, 33–34
  in twentieth and twenty-first centuries, 13, 15, 18, 53, 143
  visibility of, 13, 29, 30, 33–36, 101, 122, 135, 141–42
  See also vulnerability
Women's Experimental Writing (Berry), 99
Women's march, 96, 152–53
writerly text, 126

yeguas del apocalipsis, Las, 72

Zamudio Rodríguez, Luz Elena, 41
Zavala, Oswaldo, 125
Zsurmuk, Mónica, 93

www.ingramcontent.com/pod-product-compliance
Lightning Source LLC
Chambersburg PA
CBHW030652230426
43665CB00011B/1059